BEYOND TRACKING

Finding Success in Inclusive Schools

Edited by Harbison Pool
and Jane A. Page

Published by
Phi Delta Kappa Educational Foundation
Bloomington, Indiana

Cover Illustration by Jim Hummel
Cover design by Victoria Voelker

Library of Congress Catalog card Number 94-68703
ISBN 0-87367-470-7
Copyright © 1995 by Harbison Pool and Jane A. Page
Bloomington, Indiana

TABLE OF CONTENTS

SECTION III
Strategies that Help Meet All Students' Needs

SECTION IV
Untracking in the Real World

INTRODUCTION

The evils of tracking are well-documented. Tracking promotes "dumbed-down," skill-drill, ditto-driven, application-deficient curricula. It contributes to the destruction of student dreams and the production of low student self-esteem. Even when it is not intended, whole-class stratified groupings promote elitism, de facto racism, and classism. These placements can start as early as six weeks into kindergarten; and even though placements supposedly are flexible, they generally are permanent. Once a buzzard, always a buzzard! Furthermore, tracking often results in dull, unimaginative, uninspired teaching, particularly (though by no means solely) where low-track students are concerned (see, for example, Oakes 1985).

Many school districts in this country still practice whole-grade, between-class ability grouping, at least at some levels. In recent years, this practice, known as "tracking" in the United States and "streaming" in Great Britain, again has been scrutinized by researchers. But the debate is not just a scholarly one. Advocates for minorities and exceptional children have questioned both the wisdom and fairness of tracking. For many people, a tracked class is inherently undemocratic and inappropriate in a country that values equality and opportunity for all.

But tough questions remain: Does untracking make sense for all students, at all levels, or in all subjects? Will gifted and precocious students be sacrificed at the altar of socially and politically correct heterogeneity? What happens when tracked classes are untracked? Can veteran teachers who are accustomed to working with groups with a comparatively narrow range of abilities succeed with mixed-ability classes? What about inexperienced teachers? Can we expect their students to profit from inclusive student placements?

A big part of the answer to each of these questions lies in the recognition that tracked classes cannot be replaced with the same old curricula taught in the same old ways to more diverse groups of students. One size does not fit all. Meeting different individual needs is not accomplished with an undifferentiated, teach-to-the-middle curriculum. The inadequacies of a teacher-centered class that emphasizes rote memory and separate subjects become very conspicuous in untracked schools.

1

Conventional instructional approaches will not be replaced, but they must be supplemented with other strategies. Team teaching and cooperative learning contribute to the success of untracking efforts. Role-playing, hands-on activities, simulations, debates, improvisations, circle meetings, and apprenticeships should be at least as common as the traditional grammar lesson or the standard biology lecture. Bigelow calls for "an anti-tracking pedagogy" that offers "a new covenant, one that promises students an education rooted in their lives, with much greater initiative and participation" (1993, p. 19).

Teachers must comprehend why they are being asked to untrack. It is critical for teachers to understand that untracking will strengthen curricula and instruction for all students. Parents, teachers, and board members must realize that children will not be condemned to a watered-down curriculum, but that individualized assignments will enrich learning for all of them.

Increasing numbers of schools are beginning to "untrack." In some instances, this is an intentional, voluntary act, the result of an informed and positive decision. In other cases, the reorganization has been forced by a vocal segment of the citizenry or by a court order. More often than not, the change is undertaken in a piecemeal fashion. Whatever their reason for trying to untrack, and however limited their effort may be, educators in such a transition can benefit from research, practical ideas, and reports from those already involved in untracking.

Recognizing this fact, Phi Delta Kappa sponsored Leadership Skill Institutes on the theme, "Beyond Tracking," at eight locations across the United States in the fall of 1992. We had the opportunity to coordinate the institute held in Savannah, Georgia. Our involvement with Phi Delta Kappa in this enterprise was prompted, in part, by the problems encountered by school systems in our area that were struggling with untracking and related decisions.

The Leadership Skill Institute in Savannah served as the catalyst for *Beyond Tracking: Finding Success in Inclusive Schools*. However, this book is by no means a compilation of proceedings. Most of the chapters were written specifically for this book. These authors are professionals who are active in the areas they address. They include distinguished researchers, some of whom presented at the institute, and other individuals in the field.

The book is divided into four sections. Jomills Braddock from the University of Miami and Bob Slavin from Johns Hopkins University provide the foundation for the question posed by Section I, "Should Tracking Be Abolished?" Their chapter, "Why Ability Grouping Must

2

End: Achieving Excellence and Equity in American Education," is followed by others that add background information on the history and nature of the tracking/untracking controversy. We conclude this section with Paul George's exploration into how teachers and principals might best cope with the less-than-ideal circumstances in which many find themselves, as he asks, "Is It Possible to Live with Tracking and Ability Grouping?"

The second section, "Striving for Inclusiveness in Schools and Classrooms," asks educators to re-examine the roadblocks presented by their schools and to strive for the goal of inclusiveness. Jeannie Oakes from UCLA anchors this section with her chapter, "More Than Meets the Eye: Links Between Tracking and the Culture of Schools."

Section III, "Strategies that Help Meet All Students' Needs," presents approaches for putting sensible theories into practice in actual classrooms. The first two chapters in this section, by Sally Reis of the University of Connecticut and Thomas Erb of the University of Kansas and his associates, describe methods developed for gifted students that can improve education for all students in an untracked school. The chapter by Paul George from the University of Florida, "Untracking Your Middle School: Nine Tentative Steps Toward Long-Term Success," identifies specific guidelines that teachers, supervisors, and principals will find particularly helpful. Other chapters present methods to stimulate optimal outcomes for all learners. The strategy for moving beyond tracking that, in recent years, has become arguably the most studied and most widely acclaimed is discussed by Bob Slavin in his "Synthesis of Research on Cooperative Learning."

Anne Wheelock, an independent education writer associated with the Massachusetts Advocacy Center, opens Section IV. She draws from her extensive research on successful untracked schools. Additional examples of changes in specific classrooms, schools, systems, and states are described in the remaining chapters of that section.

We appreciate the generous support and encouragement from officials at Phi Delta Kappa throughout this undertaking. Four individuals deserve personal acknowledgment: Howard Hill, director of Chapter Programs; Derek L. Burleson, editor of Special Publications until his retirement at the end of June 1993; Donovan R. Walling, who assumed the editorship on Derek's retirement; and David M. Ruetschlin, staff associate. Howard worked with us every step of the way to develop a well-attended and highly rated Leadership Skill Institute. He also contributed a chapter, which appears in Section II. Derek helped us to plan the book, and Donovan and David have carried the project to fruition.

We are indebted to our many colleagues at Georgia Southern University and Armstrong State College and fellow members of the GSU and Savannah Chapters of Phi Delta Kappa, who assisted us in countless ways. We recognize the contribution of graduate assistants, Becky Godown, Karen Chester, Jim Dothard, Mark Copley, June Taylor, and Catherine Deever. We are grateful to Donna Colson and her staff in the GSU College of Education Word Processing Center and to Kim Degrange, secretary of the Department of Educational Foundations and Curriculum, for their invaluable work with the manuscript. Finally, we extend special thanks to Ron Davison, chair of the Department of Educational Leadership, Technology, and Research, and Fred Page, Coordinator of Laboratory Experiences, for their patience and understanding as they worked with us in this venture.

References

Bigelow, B. "Getting Off the Track." *Rethinking Schools* 7, no. 4 (1993): 1, 18-20.

Oakes, J. *Keeping Track: How Schools Structure Inequality*. New Haven, Conn.: Yale University Press, 1985.

SECTION I

Should Tracking
Be Abolished?

WHY ABILITY GROUPING MUST END: ACHIEVING EXCELLENCE AND EQUITY IN AMERICAN EDUCATION*

BY JOMILLS HENRY BRADDOCK, II
AND ROBERT E. SLAVIN

"The only thing that matters in my life is school, and there they think I'm dumb and always will be. I'm starting to think they're right. Hell, I know they put all the black kids together in one group if they can, but that doesn't make any difference either. I'm still dumb. Even if I look around and know that I'm the smartest in my group, all that means is that I'm the smartest of the dumbest.

"Upper tracks? Man, when do you think I see those kids? I never see them. Why should I? Some of them don't even go to class in the same building with me. If I ever walked into one of their rooms, they'd throw me out before the teacher even came in. They'd say I'd only be holding them back from their learning" (Cottle 1974, p. 24)

The quotation above is an excerpt of a conversation with Ollie Taylor, an 11-year-old African-American boy in Boston who recently had been assigned to the low track in his school. In this conversation, Ollie illustrates many of the problems and dilemmas of ability grouping, especially in integrated schools. First, and most obvious, Ollie re-

*This chapter is adapted from a paper presented at the conference of the Common Destiny Alliance in September 1992 in Washington, D.C. Used by permission of the Common Destiny Alliance, Vanderbilt University, Nashville.

minds us of the shame of being assigned to the low track. At age 11, Ollie has a great deal of information about his capabilities relative to other students. Yet assignment to the low track puts a stamp on him that is altogether different from anything that he learned about himself in heterogeneous classes.

Second, Ollie reflects the belief that the low track is designed especially for black students, that race is one factor in assignment to tracks.

Third, Ollie sees the profound division between students in high and low tracks, describing a feeling that students and teachers alike would "throw him out" if he dared to trespass on their area of the school.

Effects of Ability Grouping

Ollie Taylor's experiences are far from atypical. They are not unique to African-American students or to other minority students. A recent longitudinal study (Braddock and Slavin 1992) shows the pervasive negative effects of ability grouping for all students. This is our analysis of data from the National Longitudinal Study (NELS:88), which provides unusually rich information on ability grouping practices and student outcomes in a nationally representative sample of schools and students. We looked at eighth-graders who attended schools in which ability grouping was or was not used, and we then examined many outcomes for these students in the tenth grade, statistically controlling for prior grades and test scores, gender, ethnicity, socioeconomic status, school size, and other variables. We compared high, average, and low achievers separately in the tracked schools to their counterparts in the untracked schools.

The results were striking. Students in the low track performed significantly less well than did similar low achievers in untracked schools on composite and core-subject achievement tests (reading, mathematics, science, and social studies). Yet there was no consistent corresponding benefit of ability grouping for high or average achievers. Put another way, Ollie Taylor's pain was no one's gain.

Test scores were not the only indicators of the negative effects of tracking. Low-track eighth-graders were much more likely to end up in non-college-preparatory programs in tenth grade than were untracked low achievers. This effect suggests that being in the low track in eighth grade slams the gate on any possibility that a student can take the courses leading to college. The gate remained open for equally low-achieving eighth-graders who had the good fortune to attend untracked schools.

Like Ollie Taylor, low-track students in our study had lower self-esteem than did untracked low achievers, and they had markedly less positive perceptions of intergroup relations in their schools. Again, these negative impacts were not offset by any positive effects on any outcomes for high or average achievers.

The NELS:88 data we analyzed provide the largest, best controlled, multi-year study of ability grouping ever conducted. However, the effects of ability grouping have been studied for 70 years, and the outcomes of scores of studies have been similar to what we found. The following sections review research on the main outcomes of ability grouping.

Opportunities to Learn

Students cannot learn what they have not been taught. One of the clearest outcomes of ability grouping at all instructional levels is that students in low-ability groups are exposed to substantially less material and to lower-quality instruction than are students in middle- or high-ability groups (Oakes, Gamoran, and Page 1992). The pace of instruction is slower in low reading groups (Barr and Dreeben 1983; Gamoran 1986) and in low-track classes in middle and high schools (Page and Valli 1990). Further, students in low-ability groups are likely to be exposed to more low-level basic skills than are students in middle and high groups (Oakes 1985; Powell, Farrar, and Cohen 1985). Even more to the point, low achievers in tracked settings are exposed to far less context and to lower-level content than are similarly low-achieving students in mixed-ability classes (Oakes 1990).

In fact, Oakes (1985) found that the level and pace of instruction provided to heterogeneous middle school classes was like that given to the top track in tracked schools. The presence of low achievers in heterogeneous classes does not cause teachers to slow down or "dumb down" their curriculum; instead, it appears to allow low achievers to benefit from the same richer and more fast-paced curriculum traditionally offered to the top track. This is not to say that instruction in top-track classes is optimal for high achievers, or for anyone else.

Ability Grouping and Achievement

In the long history of research and debate on the effects of grouping, the arguments for and against have remained essentially the same (Slavin 1990b). Proponents of ability grouping have claimed that grouping is necessary to individualize instruction for students and to accommodate their diverse needs. In particular, they have been concerned about the possibility that including low achievers in heteroge-

9

neous classes would slow down the progress of high achievers and have claimed that high achievers benefit from the challenge and example of other high achievers. In contrast, opponents of ability grouping have been concerned about the negative effects of the practice on low achievers, in particular denying them access to high-quality instruction, and have opposed the practice on principle as undermining social goals of equity in our society. There is an interesting lack of parallelism in these arguments. The pro-grouping argument is primarily concerned with effectiveness, while the anti-grouping argument is primarily concerned with equity and democratic values. Consequently, the burden of proof in terms of effectiveness must be on those who would track.

Clearly, ability grouping fails to meet this burden of proof. Reviews of research on ability grouping in elementary schools (Slavin 1987) and in secondary schools (Slavin 1990b) have failed to find any positive effects of between-class ability grouping for any subgroup of students. These reviews consider studies done in many types of schools over many years. Many of the studies used either random assignment to ability-grouped or nongrouped classes or case-matching procedures to ensure that the grouped and ungrouped classes were identical in prior performance. Not only were average achievement levels no better in ability-grouped classes, but hardly any individual studies found educationally meaningful positive effects. Trivial differences on achievement measures (less than 10% of a standard deviation) have been found for high, average, and low achievers. Reviewers of studies comparing ability-grouped and nongrouped classes agree that there are no overall positive effects of ability grouping on achievement (see, for example, Esposito 1973; Gamoran 1986; Kulik and Kulik 1982, 1984a).

There is some disagreement about differential effects for high and low achievers. Some studies, such as our recent re-analysis of the NELS:88 data (Braddock and Slavin 1992) and a similar recent longitudinal study by Hoffer (1991) found significant negative effects of ability grouping for low achievers, with no corresponding advantage for high achievers. Others, such as Fuligni, Eccles, and Barber (1990), found small positive effects of ability grouping for high achievers and negative effects for low achievers. Most studies comparing ability-grouped and ungrouped students find no difference in achievement (Slavin 1987, 1990b).

The only exception in the research concerns the effects of programs for the gifted. There is general agreement that acceleration programs are effective. For example, gifted seventh-graders who take Algebra I (usually given to students in ninth grade) perform far better on algebra tests and only a little worse on Math 7 tests than equally bright students who take Math 7 (Fox 1979; Kulik and Kulik 1984*b*). However, there is little reliable evidence to favor the far more common enrichment programs often provided to gifted students (Slavin 1990*a*, 1991). Research in this area often appears to favor enrichment programs because it fails to control adequately for student ability levels, but well-controlled randomized studies are few and fail to support separate programs for the gifted (see, for example, Mikkelson 1962).

Whatever the effects of programs for the gifted, it is important to keep in mind that such programs serve only 3% to 5% of students. No serious reviewer suggests that there are educationally important positive effects of comprehensive ability-grouping plans for a broader range of high achievers (for example, the top 33% of students). Even if there were evidence in favor of enrichment programs for the gifted, there still would be no evidence whatsoever to deny that such enrichment programs might be effective for all students, not just gifted ones.

Ability Grouping and Segregation

One of the most consistent impacts of ability grouping is to create classes that have disproportionate numbers of students from certain races or social classes. As Ollie Taylor put it, "I know they put all the black kids together in one group if they can." In high schools, black and Hispanic students are greatly over-represented in the vocational track and under-represented in academic programs (Braddock 1989). These groups also are over-represented among the low tracks in junior high and middle school (Jones, Erickson, and Crowell 1972) and in low reading groups in elementary school (Heller 1985). Further, the U.S. Office of Civil Rights has estimated that more than half of U.S. elementary schools have at least one "racially identifiable" classroom in the highest or lowest grade. A racially identifiable classroom is one in which the proportion of students of a given race is substantially different from that in the school as a whole. This is considered an indication of discriminatory ability grouping (Wenning 1992). Leaving aside race and ethnicity, students from low socioeconomic circumstances also are greatly over-represented in the low tracks (Alexander, Cook, and McDill 1978; Heyns 1974).

Ability Grouping and Intergroup Relations

Before our 1992 study, relatively little was known about the direct effect of ability grouping on attitudes among students of different ethnic groups. One earlier study compared inter-ethnic attitudes in ability-grouped and heterogeneous sixth grades in New Mexico schools containing Hispanic and non-Hispanic students. Intergroup attitudes were consistently higher in the heterogeneous classes (Sarthory 1967). However, the effects of between-class ability grouping are more profound than this. By separating students into classes that are composed predominantly of one or another ethnic group, ability grouping limits the number of positive relationships that might develop across ethnic lines. Without such positive relationships, the development of broader interracial understanding and tolerance is unlikely (Allport 1954). Our evidence from the NELS:88 data suggests that ability grouping has major consequences for both students' perceptions of race relations in their schools and their reports of "racist remarks."

Other studies show that student friendship patterns are closely linked to academic-track placements. In high school, students choose friends from within their own track (Alexander and McDill 1976; Rosenbaum 1976). Even in the early elementary grades, students' opportunities for interaction with students of different abilities and races are affected by the teacher's grouping practices in the classroom (Epstein 1985).

Ability Grouping, Self-Esteem, and Feelings of Inferiority

The most poignant aspect of the previously excerpted conversation with Ollie Taylor was the degree to which placement in the low track made him feel inferior and worthless. A considerable body of research shows that Ollie's feelings are not unique. We found students in the low track to have significantly lower self-esteem than low achievers in mixed-ability classes; there were no differences for middle and high achievers. Earlier studies also have found that, in comparison to others, students in low tracks are low in academic self-esteem — even when controlling for their actual achievement — and report feelings of inferiority, shame, and anger (Oakes 1982; Ogletree 1968; Persell 1977; Rosenbaum 1976; Sarthory 1967; Schafer and Olexa 1971). In addition, our study found that tracked low achievers had more feelings that their fate was out of their hands (external locus of control) than did untracked low achievers (Braddock and Slavin 1992).

The experience of being in the low track has many effects beyond low self-esteem and feelings of inferiority. Controlling for their achievement and other factors, students in the low track are more likely to be delinquent than are other students (Wiatrowski et al. 1982) and are less likely to complete their education (Rosenbaum 1976).

Alternatives to Ability Grouping

Arguments in favor of ability grouping depend entirely on the assertion that grouping is necessary to meet the unique needs of children of different performance levels, especially those of high achievers. Yet evidence from dozens of studies over a 60-year period has consistently failed to find any benefits of between-class ability grouping for students at any performance level. Given the segregative impact of ability grouping, the negative effects of grouping on such outcomes as self-esteem, delinquency, and dropout rates, and the anti-egalitarian nature of the practice, there is little reason to maintain the between-class ability-grouping practices so prevalent in American schools.

While it is easy in concept to say that ability grouping should be reduced or eliminated, it is much more difficult to bring about in practice. An old Russian proverb is appropriate: "It's easy to make an aquarium into fish soup, but hard to make fish soup back into an aquarium." American schools have been ability grouping for decades and know few alternatives to the practice. Strong political pressures, especially from parents of high achievers, inhibit change. Teachers need to learn about, witness, and experiment with new practical methods for teaching heterogeneous classes; and parents, teachers, and students themselves need to be satisfied that a change from homogeneous to heterogeneous grouping will meet the needs of all students, including high achievers.

A few general principles of untracking seem to be worth stating at the outset. First, untracking must be seen as a part of an overall improvement in instructional practices and curriculum for all students. Untracking must never be, or appear to be, taking from high achievers to give to low achievers. Instead, it must be seen as bringing into the school methods and materials that are better for all students.

Second, the expectations for student performance in untracked schools must be similar to those formerly characteristic of the top track. As noted earlier, Jeannie Oakes' (1985) observational research in homogeneous and heterogeneous middle school classes found that the pace and quality of instruction in the untracked classes was like that in the high tracks. Schools that undertake untracking need to make certain that this is the case and, indeed, is perceived to be the case. For example, some schools that have successfully untracked have put their former gifted teachers in charge of helping teachers make all classes "gifted" classes, in the sense that all classes can experience activities typical of enrichment programs for the gifted (see Wheelock 1992).

One alternative to ability grouping often proposed (for example, Oakes 1985) is the use of cooperative learning. Research on cooperative learning at all grade levels consistently finds positive effects when these methods incorporate two major elements: group goals and individual accountability (Slavin 1990*a*). That is, the cooperating groups must be rewarded or recognized based on the sum or average of individual learning performances. Cooperative-learning methods also have made consistently positive impacts on intergroup relations (Slavin 1985) and on such outcomes as self-esteem, acceptance of mainstreamed academically handicapped students, and ability to work cooperatively (Slavin 1990*a*).

One category of cooperative-learning methods may be particularly useful in schools that are moving toward heterogeneous class assignment. These are Cooperative Integrated Reading and Composition (Stevens et al. 1987) and Team-Assisted Individualization — Mathematics (Slavin and Karweit 1985; Slavin, Madden, and Leavey 1984). Both methods are designed to accommodate a wide range of student performance levels in one classroom, using both homogeneous and heterogeneous within-class grouping. These programs have been successfully researched in grades three to six but often are used up to the eighth-grade level. Cohen's (1986) Complex Instruction and Sharan and Sharan's (1992) Group Investigation also are effective cooperative-learning programs designed for use in heterogeneous classes.

In addition to cooperative learning, many other strategies are known to be effective for students in general and are likely to be particularly appropriate for teaching heterogeneous classes. One is the use of active-teaching strategies (Brophy and Good 1986). A much broader range of students can benefit from engaging, active, well-organized lessons than can learn from worksheets and textbooks. Another such strategy is an emphasis on "constructivist" teaching, in which students begin with large, "authentic" problems and work together to discover how to solve them and, along the way, learn the more basic skills underlying the solutions (Brown, Collins, and Duguid 1989). Particularly well-researched problems using this approach are writing-process models (Hillocks 1984) and new mathematics approaches (Carpenter et al. 1989). The use of "scaffolding," as in Reciprocal Teaching, can provide all learners with increased responsibility for their own learning and thereby make success available to a broader range of students (Palincsar 1986).

Extending learning time for low achievers can be an effective means of helping them keep up with a demanding curriculum. Extra time embedded in the school day for preteaching or remedial work closely linked to the students' regular classroom work can help low achievers succeed in heterogeneous, high-expectations classes (MacIver 1992).

Effective assistance for low achievers is extremely important in untracking efforts, not only for the benefit of the low achievers but also to keep teachers from feeling as though they must slow down the curriculum. If untracking is to be effective for everyone, schools must maintain a fast-paced, high-expectations curriculum for all students; and targeted assistance to low achievers must be part of this plan. Targeted assistance can be provided by peer tutors, volunteer tutors, special-education or Chapter I teachers, or even computers.

None of the instructional methods that have promise for teaching heterogeneous classes can be put in place immediately. All require top-quality staff development over an extended period. In addition, it is important to involve teachers in making decisions about staff development and how the school will change to increase its effectiveness for all students. It is also important to see that teachers are able to make individual choices about whether to use particular teaching methods or curriculum materials. Untracking is fundamentally a school-level decision. Teachers and others should participate in making the decision; but once it is made, it will apply to the whole school or, at least, to whole grades within a school. However, it does not make sense to require that all teachers use specific methods.

Finally, it is important to begin untracking where it is easiest to do so — in the early grades. In a district with tracked elementary grades, untracking in the elementary grades should probably be taken on before the middle grades. In districts with heterogeneously grouped elementary schools, middle schools — not high schools — should be the focus of untracking efforts. The reasons for this should be obvious. First, it is important to move from success to success. A major push to untrack high schools may well fail on political or practical bases and thereby undermine the broader policy. Changes in grouping policies are easier to carry out in the elementary and early middle school grades. Also, it is difficult (though certainly not impossible) to untrack tenth-graders who already have years of experience in tracked settings. Schools need to make a long-term commitment to the eventual reduction or elimination of tracking. But to do so across the board — or in high schools before successfully changing the elementary or middle schools — invites turmoil and failure.

Why Tracking Must End

Tracking is ineffective. It is harmful to many students. It inhibits development of interracial respect, understanding, and friendship. It undermines democratic values and contributes to a stratified society. There are effective and practical alternatives. Tracking must end.

Academic tracking is an anachronism. There may have been a time when curriculum tracking in schools actually coincided with the needs of the society and the economy. That is, a designated number of academically proficient students were needed to pursue further education and careers that depended on that education, while a number of nonacademically oriented students were needed to enter the workforce directly and perform jobs that required less education.

That situation has changed dramatically. Corporate leaders and educators recently have focused increased attention on the level and type of skills American youth bring to the workforce and the content and quality of their high-school courses and programs of study. If schools are to meet the requirements of our economy for a more highly skilled future work force, public schools must provide more equitable access to learning opportunities that cultivate reasoning, inference, and critical thinking. Writing off a substantial proportion of our students never made sense from a social standpoint, and it rapidly is becoming suicidal from an economic standpoint.

The effects of curriculum tracking and ability grouping on students' learning opportunities are especially negative for students of color, who are over-represented among the low groups. African-American and Hispanic students constitute our largest — and fastest growing — student population, and the future well-being of the country depends on their access to a high-quality education.

The nation's changing demographics require attention to issues of social cohesion in an increasingly pluralistic society. As the American population becomes more racially and culturally diverse, issues of intergroup tolerance and understanding take on greater significance for our national well-being. The adverse effects of tracking on students' social skills and affective outcomes related to racial intolerance suggest the need for change.

References

Alexander, K.L.; Cook, M.A.; and McDill, E.L. "Curriculum Tracking and Educational Stratification." *American Sociological Review* 43, no. 1 (1978): 47-66.

Alexander, K.L., and McDill, E.L. "Selection and Allocation Within Schools: Some Causes and Consequences of Curriculum Placement." *American Sociological Review* 41, no. 6 (1976): 963-80.

Allport G. *The Nature of Prejudice.* Cambridge, Mass.: Addison-Wesley, 1954.

Barr, R., and Dreeben, R. *How Schools Work.* Chicago: University of Chicago Press, 1983.

Braddock, J.H., II. *Tracking of Black, Hispanic, Asian, Native American, and White Students: National Patterns and Trends.* Baltimore: Johns Hopkins University, Center for Research on Effective Schooling for Disadvantaged Students, 1989.

Braddock, J.H., II, and Slavin, R.E. *Life in the Slow Lane: A Longitudinal Study of Effects of Ability Grouping on Student Achievement, Attitudes, and Perceptions.* Baltimore: Johns Hopkins University, Center for Research on Effective Schooling for Disadvantaged Students, 1992.

Brophy, J.E., and Good, T.L. "Teacher Behavior and Student Achievement." In *Handbook of Research on Teaching, 3rd ed.*, edited by M.C. Wittrock. New York: Macmillan, 1986.

Brown, J.S.; Collins, A.; and Duguid, P. "Situated Cognition and the Culture of Learning." *Educational Researcher* 18, no. 1 (1989): 32-42.

Carpenter, T.P.; Fennema, E.; Peterson, P.L.; Chiang, C.P.; and Loef, M. "Using Knowledge of Children's Mathematics Thinking in Classroom Teaching: An Experimental Study." *American Educational Research Journal* 26, no. 4 (1989): 499-531.

Cohen, E.G. *Designing Groupwork: Strategies for the Heterogeneous Classroom.* New York: Teachers College Press, 1986.

Cottle, T.L. "What Tracking Did to Ollie Taylor." *Social Policy* 5, no. 2 (1974): 21-24.

Epstein, J. "After the Bus Arrives: Desegregation in Desegregated Schools." *Journal of Social Issues* 41, no. 3 (1985): 23-43.

Esposito, D. "Homogeneous and Heterogeneous Ability Grouping: Principal Findings and Implications for Evaluating and Designing More Effective Educational Environments." *Review of Educational Research* 43, no. 2 (1973): 163-79.

Fox, L.H. "Programs for the Gifted and Talented: An Overview." In *The Gifted and Talented: Their Education and Development*, edited by A.H. Passow. Chicago: University of Chicago Press, 1979.

Fuligni, A.J.; Eccles, J.S.; and Barber, B.L. "The Long-Term Effects of Seventh-Grade Ability Grouping in Mathematics." Paper presented at the annual meeting of the American Educational Research Association, Boston, April 1990.

Gamoran, A. "Instructional and Institutional Effects of Ability Grouping." *Sociology of Education* 59, no. 4 (1986): 185-98.

Heller, E.J. "Pupil Race and Elementary School Ability Grouping: Are Teachers Biased Against Black Children?" *American Educational Research Journal* 22, no. 4 (1985): 465-83.

17

Heyns, B. "Social Selection and Stratification Within Schools." *American Journal of Sociology* 79, no. 6 (1974): 1434-51.

Hillocks, G., Jr. "What Works in Teaching Composition: A Meta-Analysis of Experimental Treatment Studies." *American Journal of Education* 93, no. 1 (1984): 133-70.

Hoffer, T.B. "The Effects of Ability Grouping in Middle School Science and Mathematics on Students' Achievement." Paper presented at the annual meeting of the American Educational Research Association, Chicago, April 1991.

Jones, J.D.; Erickson, E.L.; and Crowell, R. "Increasing the Gap Between Whites and Blacks: Tracking as a Contributory Source." *Education and Urban Society* 4, no. 3 (1972): 339-49.

Kulik, C.-L.C., and Kulik, J.A. "Effects of Ability Grouping on Secondary School Students: A Meta-Analysis of Evaluation Findings." *American Educational Research Journal* 19, no. 3 (1982): 415-28.

Kulik, C.-L.C., and Kulik, J.A. "Effects of Ability Grouping on Elementary School Pupils: A Meta-Analysis." Paper presented at the annual meeting of the American Psychological Association, Toronto, August 1984. a

Kulik, C.-L.C., and Kulik, J.A. "Effects of Accelerated Instruction on Students." *Review of Educational Research* 54, no. 3 (1984): 409-25. b

MacIver, D. *Motivating Disadvantaged Early Adolescents to Reach New Heights: Effective Evaluation, Reward, and Recognition Structure.* Baltimore: Johns Hopkins University, Center for Research on Effective Schooling for Disadvantaged Students, 1992.

Mikkelson, J.E. "An Experimental Study of Selective Grouping and Acceleration in Junior High School Mathematics." Doctoral dissertation, University of Minnesota, 1962. *Dissertation Abstracts* 23, 4226-4227.

Oakes, J. "The Reproduction of Inequity: The Content of Secondary School Tracking." *Urban Review* 14, no. 2 (1982): 107-20.

Oakes, J. *Keeping Track: How Schools Structure Inequality.* New Haven, Conn.: Yale University Press, 1985.

Oakes, J. *Multiplying Inequalities: The Effects of Race, Social Class, and Tracking on Opportunities to Learn Mathematics and Science.* Santa Monica, Calif.: Rand Corporation, 1990.

Oakes, J.; Gamoran, A.; and Page, R. "Curriculum Differentiation: Opportunities, Outcomes, and Meanings." In *Handbook of Research on Curriculum: A Project of the American Educational Research Association*, edited by P.W. Jackson. New York: Macmillan, 1992.

Ogletree, E.L. "Research Verifies Ill Effects of Ability Grouping." *Phi Delta Kappan* 50, no. 4 (1968): 223.

Page, R., and Valli, L., ed. *Curriculum Differentiation: Interpretive Studies in U.S. Secondary Schools.* Albany: State University of New York Press, 1990.

Palincsar, A.S. "The Role of Dialogue in Providing Scaffolded Instruction." *Educational Psychologist* 21, nos. 1-2 (1986): 73-98.

Persell, C.H. *Education and Inequality: A Theoretical and Empirical Synthesis*. New York: Free Press, 1977.

Powell, A.G.; Farrar, E.; and Cohen, D.K. *The Shopping Mall High School: Winners and Losers in the Educational Marketplace*. Boston: Houghton Mifflin, 1985.

Rosenbaum, J.E. *Making Inequality: The Hidden Curriculum of High School Tracking*. New York: John Wiley and Sons, 1976.

Sarthory, J.A. "The Effects of Ability Grouping in Multi-Cultural School Situations." Doctoral dissertation, University of New Mexico, 1967. Dissertation Abstracts, 29, 451A. University Microfilms No. 68-11, 664.

Schafer, W., and Olexa, C. *Tracking and Opportunity: The Locking-Out Process and Beyond*. Scranton, Pa.: Chandler, 1971.

Sharan, Y., and Sharan, S. *Group Investigation: Expanding Cooperative Learning*. New York: Teachers College Press, 1992.

Slavin, R.E. "Cooperative Learning: Applying Contact Theory in Desegregated Schools." *Journal of Social Issues* 41, no. 3 (1985): 45-62.

Slavin, R.E. "Ability Grouping and Student Achievement in Elementary Schools: A Best-Evidence Synthesis." *Review of Educational Research* 57, no. 3 (1987): 293-336.

Slavin, R.E. "Ability Grouping, Cooperative Learning, and the Gifted." *Journal for the Education of the Gifted* 14, no. 1 (1990): 3-8. a

Slavin, R.E. "Achievement Effects of Ability Grouping in Secondary Schools: A Best-Evidence Synthesis." *Review of Educational Research* 60, no. 3 (1990): 471-99. b

Slavin, R.E. "Are Cooperative Learning and Untracking Harmful to the Gifted?" *Educational Leadership* 48, no. 6 (1991): 68-71.

Slavin, R.E., and Karweit, N.L. "Effects of Whole-Class, Ability Grouped, and Individualized Instruction on Mathematics Achievement." *American Educational Research Journal* 22, no. 3 (1985): 351-67.

Slavin, R.E.; Madden, N.A.; and Leavey, M. "Effects of Team-Assisted Individualization on the Mathematics Achievement of Academically Handicapped and Non-Handicapped Students." *Journal of Educational Psychology* 76, no. 5 (1984): 813-19.

Stevens, R.J.; Madden, N.A.; Slavin, R.E.; and Farnish, A.M. "Cooperative Integrated Reading and Composition: Two Field Experiments." *Reading Research Quarterly* 22, no. 4 (1987): 433-54.

Wenning, R.J. "The Characteristics of Discriminatory Ability Grouping and Evidence of Its Extent." Paper presented at the annual meeting of the American Educational Research Association, San Francisco, April 1992.

Wheelock, A. *Crossing the Tracks: How "Untracking" Can Save America's Schools*. New York: New Press, 1992.

Wiatrowski, M.; Hansell, S.; Massey, C.R.; and Wilson, D.L. "Curriculum Tracking and Delinquency." *American Sociological Review* 47, no. 1 (1982): 151-60.

UNDERSTANDING OURSELVES: THE ANCESTRY OF TRACKING

BY KATHLEEN CRUIKSHANK

There has been a continual contradiction in our history between an autocratic or systematizing impulse in schools and a democratic impulse that focuses on the development of the individual. These two impulses have coexisted throughout our education history. The democratic impulse often is expressed in the purported purposes of schooling, the autocratic impulse in the means by which we have sought to achieve those purposes. As a result, these contradictory impulses have undermined our achievement of education goals.

This fundamental contradiction can be found in the early history of U.S. public schools. The earliest schools in the country, those of the New England colonies, were designed to teach literacy so that the learner might achieve salvation through study of the Bible. Because the idea of salvation allowed for neither individual interpretation nor any variation in the curriculum, the means of teaching were strictly catechetical — that is, rote memorization of responses to questions asked by the teacher.

After the American Revolution, the notion of universal schooling gained support as a way of training children to sustain the new republic. Despite this democratic ideal, the methods of teaching appear not to have changed from those used in the Colonial schools. During the mid-19th century, some of the more perceptive teachers in the country began to grapple with this contradiction. How is it possible, they asked, to produce students capable of independent thought and moral judgment if their schooling is done by rote memorization? Thus well over a hundred years ago, teachers were posing a question that still confronts us today.

While these early schools may have been autocratic in their pedagogy and in the way they regarded children, they may have been less so than are modern schools. That is, those schools may have allowed for more individuality in learning than we do in today's graded schools.

Today we operate on an assumption of sameness that precedes any judgments about individual children. When we divide people by tracking or grouping, we make the assumption that the individuals in a group are essentially the same and can be treated without individual distinctions. Otherwise, there would be no reason to label them. We may deny this assumption of sameness, but it does affect our thinking. One example of this assumption of sameness occurs when schools automatically group students in age-graded schools.

The practice of grading students by age and achievement was not adopted until well after public schooling had become established in this country. Early schools usually consisted of one school teacher and several students of various ages and achievement levels. Teachers organized their time into many brief recitation periods to hear from small groups of students who were working at similar levels. While these groups could be considered "achievement groups," there was no assumption that all students should be working at the same level and were somehow defective for not doing so. Students merely were members of small groups who were working their way through what was to be learned. More often than not, there were striking combinations of different ages in those groups; older boys whose farm responsibilities held them back from regular school attendance shared recitation time with younger children. One moved from book to book when one was ready to do so.

Over the course of the 19th century, the tension between autocratic and democratic impulses pervaded education. Industrialization and urbanization brought changes in the organizational patterns of schools. The first and perhaps most radical response to this problem was imported from Great Britain: the monitorial school. In monitorial schools, one teacher "taught" several hundred students by organizing the school into battalions of younger students taught by older students. The best monitorial schools experimented with what is now known as peer tutoring and cooperative learning; but they frequently were portrayed as militaristic (Kaestle 1973). Monitorial schools came to be seen as merely a management strategy for organizing large numbers of students, and they eventually were rejected as mechanistic and impersonal.

The more familiar way of dealing with masses of children was the graded school — that is, a school with classes grouped by achievement level. The graded school enjoyed a generally favorable reputation, although it imposes a sameness that is at least as stifling as the regimentation of the monitorial school. The monitorial schools faded out of existence within a few decades of their introduction, but the graded school persisted for well over a century and became a standard for organizing schools.

The reason that graded schools lasted and monitorial schools did not may be their timing. The monitorial school was introduced in the United States before industrialization was fully developed and the factory had become the popular model of organization and progress. By the time the graded schools were introduced to respond to increasing urbanization, industrialization was beginning to dominate the U.S. economy. The factories provided a rich metaphor for potential application to schools, and the organization of city schools and factories grew hand-in-hand.

As city schools developed into large school systems, a class of education "managers" emerged. Superintendents were expected to create the same kinds of miracles in schools that industrial managers had created in factories, and so superintendents adapted the means of industry to do so. Thus standardization, specification at all stages of the process of schooling, and "task analysis" as a means of determining curriculum became the tools of these new school "managers." The graded school fit perfectly into that scheme.

At the same time, the graded school was a very desirable setting for teachers, since they no longer were required to meet the needs of a diverse group of children. Instead of being taught individually, the whole group could be taught the same thing at the same time. This was more "efficient," and "efficiency" was seen as the wave of the future.

However, setting up graded classrooms was only the first step. Grouping students implied group expectations, not just individual expectations. Further, those expectations had to be coordinated among a number of grades, which came to be determined by age. Thus the pace of individual development was compared to other children's development. We now take these practices for granted, but they represent a standardization of the learning experience that assumes that children of a given age are alike in their readiness and their ability to deal with the material presented to them. To the extent that such expectations ignore individuality, they also are dehumanizing.

Another factor that reinforced the dehumanizing tendency of schools was the separation of teaching from administration, with distinctly more power and prestige being accorded to administrators. Massive numbers of young women became teachers during the middle to late 19th century. However, because of cultural beliefs about the role of women, the nature of teaching had to be redefined in order to justify this female presence in the public arena. Women filled the need for labor in the schools; but the intellectual component of their teaching was determined by men, either through textbooks or through direct instruction and supervision.

This particular historical factor is important to a discussion of tracking, not because of the gender distinction but because of the implications that such a distinction had for the distribution of decision-making power within schools. It came to be assumed by most people that to teach meant to comply with the judgment of others.

The industrialization of schooling was reinforced by massive immigration, beginning in the early 19th century. Education leaders, most of whom were English Protestants, suddenly were confronted with immigrants who, the educators believed, could not be assumed to share the values on which the schools had been built. These leaders saw themselves as the pillars of a democratic society and struggled to bring a good education to every child in the country. However, they had two visions of education, one for native-born children and one for the "foreign" children. These men assumed that there were fundamental differences among children based on ethnicity or skin color or religion or regional background. It was not a diversity to be embraced as enriching our common culture, but a concern to be dealt with; and it provided the context for education reform. The tension between autocratic and democratic impulses expressed in their work defined the inequitable social vision within which the systematization of schools occurred.

Finally, the 19th century also saw the application of the "scientific" approach to human behavior. That approach had led to astounding industrial development, and it was believed that it also would make possible ever greater mastery of the human environment. Among these "social sciences" was psychology, which was established in universities, first within departments of philosophy or in conjunction with departments of pedagogy, in the last decade of the 19th century (O'Donnell 1985).

Psychology added quantification to the values that dominated U.S. schooling in the 20th century when it imported Binet's intelligence test from France. The development of the myth of mental measurement, however inherently faulty, made possible the illusion that one human being could judge the potential of another's mind. This laid the foundation for tracking. Mass IQ testing and the beginnings of overt tracking practices inexorably separated "our" children from the children of the "others."

All these forces worked toward a systematization of schooling that was at odds with teachers' increasing emphasis on the welfare of the individual child as the central focus for decisions about schools. The tension between systematization and pedagogical wisdom underlies discussions of tracking. But this tension does not indicate a polarization of interests between teachers and administrators.

Not all administrators were committed to the increased bureaucratization of schools. In fact, the two most remarkable 19th century revolutions in teaching were pioneered by city superintendents who had been handed total control of their school systems and had created what they described as a machine that functioned like clockwork. Both men realized that they had destroyed the life of learning and set out to reform pedagogical practice. E.A. Sheldon, in Oswego, New York, introduced the "object method," which constituted the first break from rote memorization of books, brought the world into the classroom and took the children into the world, and revolutionized teacher education. Francis W. Parker, in Quincy, Massachusetts, tried to liberate both his teachers and his students to pursue learning with passion and joy. In the process, he brought to national attention the struggle between autocratic and democratic impulses for control of the classroom. His efforts laid the groundwork for, among other things, the whole language movement and interdisciplinary instruction.

The examples of these two superintendents demonstrate that it is inaccurate to personify the tension in U.S. education history as the opposition of teachers and administrators, although the evolution of their distinct roles is part of that tension. Rather, we must recognize the elements of that tension in decisions made in both classrooms and administrative offices. Our preoccupation with *how* schooling will be delivered obscures our failure to confront the question of *what* we are trying to accomplish.

There are interesting parallels between our current school reforms and the reforms of the 19th century. School reform in both periods was characterized by severe criticism of the schools; assumptions that business and industry, because of their material success, should provide the models for schooling; and comparisons of the United States to foreign powers on the basis of economic competition. (In the late 19th and early 20th centuries, Germany was perceived as our primary economic rival.) The values of materialism, competition, and reform — or change controlled from the top — were applied to education during both reform periods.

By the early 20th century, the problems of classrooms were seen as "business problems" — that is, "in what manner the working unit of the school plant may be made to return the largest dividend upon the material investment of time, energy, and money" (Callahan 1962). Of particular importance was the application of "scientific management" to the schools. Scientific management, developed to increase the efficiency of industrial processes, involved breaking a given task into its most minute components, deciding how each component could be done most efficiently, and then training people to do the jobs in precisely that way. Extensive quantitative research was done to establish the desired processes. The role of the workers was strict obedience to management; all decisions regarding how their work was to be done were left to their supervisors.

By the 1920s, procedures had been developed for analyzing the activities of life and setting detailed objectives for schooling that would prepare students for those activities. As an example of this approach, Franklin Bobbitt, a professor of educational administration at the University of Chicago, took one of the seven education goals established by a national study group and broke it down into 38 abilities. He further subdivided each of those abilities into habits, knowledge, dispositions, attitudes, etc., thus potentially creating some 13,000 objectives for the seven goals (Bobbitt 1920).

Traits of secretaries, homemakers, and others were ascertained by job analysis, and recommendations for schooling were made accordingly (Charters 1924, 1926). Educators using scientific management would predetermine the product to be graduated from schools, decide which students would be the raw material to make into that product, and then itemize in detail the processes by which the students would become the product. This method became the dominant model for schooling in the early part of this century.

Note the underlying assumptions of this model. First, the student has no autonomy; he or she will be trained on the basis of someone else's assessment of talent, in accordance with someone else's interpretation of what the student's role in society should be. Many of the educators who advocated this approach argued that scientific management addressed the individual differences of students. Yet, the definition of those differences comes not from the individuals, but from someone else's categorization of them. In fact, scientific management has much in common with our current practice of tracking.

In 1916, John Dewey wrote:

> How one person's abilities compare in quantity with those of another is none of the teacher's business. It is irrelevant to his work. What is required is that every individual shall have opportunities to employ his own powers in activities that have meaning. (p. 172)

We need to look more closely at the ideas of Dewey and others like him, who staunchly maintained that the integrity of the child's mind must remain foremost. The curriculum of the school that Dewey led for eight years at the University of Chicago, even as the flood of scientific management swirled around him, was one of academic integrity built on the child's natural interests in the fundamental activities of human survival, both in his or her immediate environment and historically. Out of those interests, teachers worked collaboratively with each other and with the children to pursue projects and research that would provide a solid academic foundation for their later studies. The teachers were creators, researchers, and students; they were the center of the enterprise and its driving force. And the needs of their classrooms *as they perceived them* determined the direction of organization and study.

We must look to the past to understand our contemporary model of organization and control in school systems and how that model restricts the choices available to teachers to teach as they know they should. Ability or achievement grouping has its origins in the rapid increase in the school population and the need to produce workers for an industrializing economy. The graded school was introduced in order to teach a large number of students more efficiently. It was based on the assumption that children of the same age somehow possess the same potential for learning. That assumption made possible whole-group instruction, which implied that if children are being instructed as a group, the size of the group is irrelevant.

Ability or achievement grouping was one remedy to the problem of teaching with limited resources. But that problem clearly requires other remedies, remedies more consistent with our democratic values. Education must be built on those democratic values: respect for the dignity of every individual and for the potential of every child. That respect requires that our teaching provide the most creative and imaginative environments of which we are capable, that we continue to study and create, and that we never set limits on what our children can achieve. Every child should have the opportunity for unrestricted growth. That is the future we should seek beyond tracking.

References

Bobbitt, F. "The Objectives of Secondary Education." *School Review* 28, no. 10 (1920): 738-49.

Callahan, R.E. *Education and the Cult of Efficiency: A Study of the Social Forces that Have Shaped the Administration of Public Schools.* Chicago: University of Chicago Press, 1962.

Charters, W.W. "Functional Analysis as the Basis for Curriculum Construction." *Journal of Educational Research* 10, no. 3 (1924): 214-21.

Charters, W.W. "The Traits of Homemakers." *Journal of Home Economics* 18, no. 12 (1926): 673-85.

Dewey, J. *Democracy and Education: An Introduction to the Philosophy of Education.* New York: Macmillan, 1916.

Kaestle, C.F., ed. *Joseph Lancaster and the Monitorial School Movement: A Documentary History.* New York: Teachers College Press, 1973.

O'Donnell, J.M. *The Origins of Behaviorism: American Psychology, 1870-1920.* New York: New York University Press, 1985.

3

CONDITIONS THAT ENHANCE THE REINTEGRATION OF SCHOOLS

BY ANNE WHEELOCK

Few schools, even those grounded in the deepest commitments to democratic schooling, have untracked completely. Cultural norms, political realities, and a variety of legal constraints may slow or inhibit reform. Some of the constraints are budgetary or contractual. Others are political or regulatory, as is the case when state regulations mandate special or separate classes for "gifted" or "nongifted" students.

Dismantling tracking in schools is far more complex than simply regrouping students or substituting one curriculum or instructional strategy for another. As Jeannie Oakes (1992) has suggested, untracking requires changes not only in teaching and learning but also in political relationships and in the school culture.

Whatever the pace of change or the particular conditions of a given school or community, certain conditions facilitate untracking. These include school-based leadership with teacher and parent support for change; ample time for staff development; a multi-year plan for change; a phase-in process by grade, team, or department; and a hospitable policy context.

School-Based Leadership with Teacher and Parent Support for Change

The process of untracking requires an effective partnership of the principal and teachers who are willing to reach out for the support of

29

parents. This partnership determines the pace and scope of untracking. While it is not necessary for all teachers in a building to support alternatives, the enthusiasm of at least some teachers is essential.

Principals in untracking schools understand that their own leadership responsibility is pivotal during a period of change. As Janet Altersitz of Desert Sky Middle School in Glendale, Arizona, warns:

> Little will happen without the principal's interest, active participation, and leadership. It will be the principal's enthusiasm and modeling that will gain the attention and respect of faculty members. Soliciting appropriate funds, reviewing test data, and keeping various publics informed are key duties for the principal.*

Leadership for untracking requires taking responsibility for articulating the school's mission to various constituencies and communicating research-based knowledge to teachers, parents, and school-board members, all the while understanding the alternative perspectives of different stakeholders. For example, Sue Galletti, principal of Washington's Lake Stevens Middle School, remarks:

> I have become increasingly convinced that understanding the context within which arguments are presented (by thoroughly understanding both points of view) is more important for creating a change than being able to articulate only one point of view.

Principals in untracking schools also must be instructional leaders familiar with learning theory and innovative strategies for mixed-level groups. They must be available to help teachers develop professional skills and expertise. Principals of untracking schools themselves cite the need for "vision and courage" and "persistence, patience, and willingness to risk." "One must be both an idealist and a pragmatist to make untracking work," says Margaret Bray of Ferndale Middle School in High Point, North Carolina.

Many principals exercise leadership by establishing organizational conditions that enhance the likelihood for teacher success in heterogeneous classrooms. Christine Rath, principal of Concord High School in Concord, New Hampshire, underscores the value of common planning time to ensure that teachers communicate with one another about successful strategies. Principals also make scheduling arrangements that foster professional conversations and facilitate teacher decision making.

---

*In this essay, quotations and examples of heterogeneously grouped schools that are not otherwise identified first appeared in my book, *Crossing the Tracks* (1992).

Supportive school leadership must be combined with teacher commitment to introduce change. Margaret Bray, principal of Ferndale Middle School in High Point, North Carolina, notes: "At least several convinced teachers and some teachers trained as 'in-house experts' on workable techniques are the most important resources a school needs to sustain an untracking effort." Jake Burks, associate superintendent of Harford County Public Schools in Bel Air, Maryland, adds that involving teachers requires a school climate that both encourages taking risks and stimulates dissatisfaction with the status quo. He advises:

> You need a lot of teacher collegiality and support to make this work. It's especially important to establish a climate that allows teachers to take risks. Teachers in our school were totally safe in trying different things. We also spent a lot of time on study and inquiry. Meaningful change won't occur until the people involved experience dissonance between what we know from research and what we're doing that might be the opposite.

Teachers themselves recognize that their commitment and willingness to experiment and their involvement in planning for change are crucial to success. Teachers from the Graham and Parks School in Cambridge, Massachusetts, note:

> Untracking alone does not solve anything. It's what happens with kids after mixed-ability grouping occurs that matters. This must be put into teachers' hands — by empowering them, having them critically examine the current program, investigate other schools through visits or reading, and then develop their own ways.

Among the first challenges teachers and principals face is how to engage parents as powerful allies in the process of untracking. As many teachers have learned, parents can be either allies or opponents of change. Parents of children who have been placed in "special" programs are especially sensitive to changes in grouping. Parents of children with disabilities often are wary of changes that they fear will overwhelm their children or result in less attention to individual learning needs. Likewise, parents of children labeled "gifted" may fear that changes will result in fewer challenges for their children or undermine their children's chances to excel.

In many schools, adopting alternatives to tracking has required educating parents about relevant research and alternative approaches to curriculum and instruction. Schools must persuade parents that untracking strengthens the mainstream of the school so that all students will master complex material and no children will lose ground. Principals and teachers in these schools are called on to demonstrate that students have more to gain from learning together in the mainstream than from learning apart in separate, labeled programs. Moreover, once untracking begins, schools must sustain parents' support.

In many communities where educators seek to implement heterogeneous grouping as a means of realizing a broader school vision, the most vocal parents in opposition to change are often those who expect their children to enter selective programs for "gifted and talented" students. These parents may be both politically powerful in the community and sophisticated in countering arguments in favor of heterogeneous grouping. They may reconsider their opposition to change when they understand that inclusive schooling can offer all students an education that is sometimes reserved only for students labeled "gifted."

Sue Galletti, principal of Lake Stevens Middle School, tells this story of her experience as principal of Islander Middle School, Mercer Island, Washington:

> Our school was in a district where test scores were significantly higher than [those of] other districts in the state. Our parents were all college-educated, and they were very committed to sorting kids into gifted programs. When our school made the commitment to more inclusive programs, some of our parents were sophisticated enough to counter all our arguments with their own about why certain children needed to be separated into gifted classrooms. At the time, we had about 10% of our students in gifted classes, and we used a variety of measures to put them there. . . . We required students to have an IQ score of 130, and we used this marker plus achievement scores on subtests to arrive at a total score for identifying "gifted" students.
>
> We had lots of parent meetings, but this did not work effectively to convince parents to abandon the program. Finally, we called in a group of 30 parents who were most vocal against eliminating separate gifted programs. We met in the library, and we gave them the sixth-grade test data that we used to select students for the gifted classes for 250 real live kids. Their task was to identify 26 students for the gifted program. The parents quickly realized that 55 of these students had an IQ of 130 or above. One student had an IQ of 150 but would not qualify because of his achievement scores, and another had an IQ of 129 but qualified once achievement scores were included. When the parents realized that they couldn't make decisions, they began to ask to expand the gifted program. I explained that, even with an expanded program, I knew

how some of the students would rank, and that many of the parents in the room had children who would not quality.

At that point, the whole tenor in the room changed; and I saw lots of nonverbal reaction. We then began one hour of serious conversation, and those parents walked out of that meeting understanding that what they needed was a "gifted" program for 100% of the kids. At the time, that meant a "humanities" program with integrated instruction, cooperative learning, and a focus on thinking skills. The parents decided they would go to the school board with this idea, and I thought the community was going to massacre us. But they didn't. They lauded us and the proposal as the only way to go! We still identified "top" kids by IQ, but it was used purely to make sure that we spread those students around into different working groups. And the parents are very happy with what we have done.

Other principals use a variety of approaches to win support for untracking from skeptical parents. Some offer parents opportunities to participate in professional development programs to learn about teaching and learning in heterogeneous classes. Others invite parents to meet with teachers before the grouping changes are implemented, sometimes in large forums, sometimes in one-to-one meetings, and sometimes in neighborhood "coffees" in the homes of PTO or school-board members. These meetings benefit all parents when they focus on the expectations for learning that will apply to all students.

Still others work hard to demonstrate that all children will gain from changes and that no one will lose learning opportunities available in tracked settings. For example, at Jericho Middle School in Jericho, New York, principal Anna Hunderfund assured parents concerned about the elimination of the school's pull-out "gifted-and-talented" program that nothing would be taken away from their children. She explained that changes in the nine-period day simply allowed all students to experience the enrichment curriculum formerly offered only to a few students.

Finally, some schools, such as Kammerer Middle School in Louisville, Kentucky, introduce heterogeneous grouping into their schools as a "pilot project." They begin with only part of the school and encourage the most experienced and enthusiastic teachers to pioneer new practices. By introducing heterogeneous grouping in tandem with outstanding classroom practices, these schools present parents with an offer they cannot refuse. Ultimately, these schools find that the demand for the heterogeneous program is so great that they can move to blend classes throughout the school (Jennings 1993).

Professional Development and Support

Staff development for teachers is essential to the success of untracking. In fact, asked what they might do differently if they were to begin again, many principals emphasize, "More staff development!" In particular, many stress the need to provide teachers with more direct exposure to learning theory and classroom techniques that pertain to teaching heterogeneous groups. In their schools, professional development takes three major forms:

1. Staff development to plan for whole-school change and to strengthen organizational structures that promote taking risks and ongoing planning, including attention to teacher beliefs about the nature of intelligence.
2. Training in effective classroom instructional strategies, including cooperative learning, for working with diverse students.
3. Training to implement specific curricula that are new to the school and its teachers.

Within this framework, professional development in untracking schools may include building teachers' skills in participatory planning and team-building; reviewing methods for communicating high expectations to all students; discussing research on cognitive development and multiple intelligences in relation to teachers' beliefs about intelligence; developing skills in mastery learning, cooperative learning, and complex instruction; implementing "high-content" curricula; or designing curriculum-embedded assessment strategies.

In many schools, professional development for untracking begins with a discussion of teachers' beliefs about learning. For example, Wellesley Middle School geared much of its professional development toward helping teachers rethink an unstated but accepted belief that some teachers are more capable than others of teaching certain kinds of children. Thus staff development first focused on developing teachers' commitment to and capacity for teaching all students.

During weekly meetings before and after school, staff became familiar with research on tracking, expectations and motivation theory, and cooperative learning. And teachers had the chance to try out new techniques that they would use as the school phased in heterogeneous grouping. Underlying this strategy was the understanding that, if taking risks was a trait the school wanted to encourage in students, the climate in the school needed to reflect that trait, and teachers had to take risks themselves as part of their own learning about working with different groups of students.

Above and beyond specific initiatives, early staff development efforts recognize the importance of establishing a safe, professional climate that allows teachers to flounder as they try new approaches in heterogeneous classes. As Pep Jewell, principal of Helena Middle School in Helena, Montana, remarks:

> Inservice is an investment in the experienced professional. A professional growth strand as part of the evaluation process gives teachers permission to take the risk to be less than perfect in trying something new. Student and teacher teaming during the process gives support.

Principal Chris Lim and project director Ann Hiyakumoro of Willard Junior High School in Berkeley, California, highlight the importance of reforming school structures to support teachers. They cite the needs for "wiping out teacher isolation in the school building" and for added support for teachers "in every way possible, including extra preparation periods, paid curriculum development time, paid staff development time, good materials, and tutors for students." With these conditions in place in untracking schools, staff development may become less a formal event than an accepted part of the school culture that treats teachers as professionals who must keep up with current issues in their field.

In untracking schools, staff development often is intensive, especially in the early stages, and may include study groups, summer institutes, all-day training, staff retreats, visits to other schools, conferences, modeling, coaching, and consultations. For example, at the Rutland Middle School in Vermont, all staff participated in a focused series of paid professional workshops designed to meet Rutland's own goals of schoolwide heterogeneous grouping, as well as state goals related to the education of all children, including students with disabilities, in heterogeneous classrooms. In addition, teachers attended the University of Vermont Middle Level Summer Institute to plan for implementing heterogeneous grouping in their own classes.

In Lowell, Massachusetts, the Bartlett School used funds from the state's dropout-prevention program to hire a "change facilitator" to work directly with teachers, to arrange for teacher visits to other schools, to identify innovative programs, and to help teachers assess whether such programs could be incorporated into Bartlett. Other schools have turned to such resources as the Association for Supervision and Curriculum Development (ASCD) videotapes on cooperative learning (Johnson et al. 1990) or have exploited partnerships with local institutions of higher education to introduce faculty to innovative practices.

Planning for Change

Successful untracking depends on planning for change. Administrators and a representative group of teachers need to debate and discuss new routines, schedules, teaching approaches, curricula, and relationships. Planning in these groups may take place schoolwide, in each grade or department, or in a "house" or teacher team within the larger school.

Successful planning begins with broad agreement about the school's mission. It involves all participants — teachers, parents, and administrators — in thinking about what they expect all students to know and to be able to do. School staff members regularly review data to determine how close they are to realizing these goals. Over time, the attention to comparing "where we are" with "where we want to be" becomes a habit among all members of the school community.

In planning for change, participants are especially attuned to recent findings of education research. Susan Masek, principal of Sierra Middle School in Tucson, Arizona, explains, "We set out to adopt the practices known to benefit our students. Heterogeneous grouping was one of those." As teachers learn to apply research to school practices, they become accustomed to inquiry. Sandra Caldwell, principal of the Middle School for the Kennebunks in Kennebunkport, Maine, reports, "We question practically everything. We ask whether our practices align with research; and when we find gaps, we work team by team to figure out action plans to close them."

In many schools, untracking follows a research-based, data-driven, problem-solving process that is not a one-shot event but becomes a norm of school culture. This process involves developing a vision, gathering data, setting targets, and finally revisiting the vision (Hergert, Phlegar, and Perez-Selles 1991). Some schools begin their planning with a "consciousness-raising" period, during which principals flood staff with data and teachers read current research articles related to tracking and cognitive development. During this time, teachers visit heterogeneous classrooms in other schools to understand the benefits and challenges of mixed-level grouping. Groups of teachers also may conduct research on specific grouping and curriculum changes, make decisions about new directions, and plan staff development to ensure that these changes are effective.

Whatever the model, the process of untracking takes place over several years, sometimes spanning a five- to eight-year period. However, while some schools that initiated untracking in the early or mid-1980s have taken up to eight years to untrack, principals of these same schools emphasize that it need not take so long in the 1990s. "We now have much better evidence documenting the harm of tracking," says Janet Altersitz, whose school dismantled more than 30 instructional levels during a seven-year period and became one of Arizona's exemplary schools in the process. She adds, "Given what we know from research and the resources now available to develop alternative approaches to curriculum and instruction, schools should be able to make great gains in three years."

Phase-in Process of Implementation

Successful untracking does not take place overnight. While untracking schools accept change as a norm, they make changes systematically, often introducing the changes in stages. They follow no formula. However, typically schools implement changes in one grade, department, cluster, or team at a time. Sandra Caldwell reports:

> You have to understand that different people have different comfort levels. We don't expect everyone to do everything at the same time. We have always, with everything, piloted with teachers who felt comfortable. We have never made major changes overnight, but we need to allow people who are ready to go to go ahead, piloting, starting small.

The process of phasing in alternatives depends on the complexity of existing tracking practices, the degree of teachers' investment in change, the availability of resources and support to develop alternatives, and other circumstances. These conditions vary from school to school.

Eliminating the bottom tracks sometimes results in the unexpected benefit of freeing teachers who have worked exclusively with remedial, Chapter 1, or special education classes to work in heterogeneous classrooms, either on their own or paired with other teachers. For example, in Wellesley, once students were succeeding in heterogeneous classes at "Level 2," teachers no longer were needed for "Level 3" classes. The "extra" teachers co-taught heterogeneous, grade-level classrooms; remedial or special-education teachers were matched with "regular Level 2" teachers. Students in these classes had to master more complex material than they had been accustomed to, but they also had the resource of an extra teacher to support them.

Policies that Support Untracking

Untracking begins first at the school level. However, a district-level or state policy can reinforce progress, provide support, and establish a broader climate for change. It is not enough to have only a paper policy that discourages tracking. What is needed is the formal message of a policy advisory, position statement, or implementation guidelines from key decision makers. These can create a climate that increases tolerance for difficult changes and makes the going easier for innovators at the school level. Deborah Meier, co-director of New York's Central Park East Secondary School, notes:

> What the "system" can do is create the structural conditions that encourage people to want to change and give them sufficient autonomy to do so, and that provide support and encouragement even when they blunder in the course of creating their interpretation of the "good school." But in the end the change must be home-grown. (Meier 1991, p. 339)

District-level policies are important, Monica Nelson, director of curriculum in Burlington, Vermont, reports that the curriculum committee of the school board spent one year reviewing research on tracking and discussing the pros and cons of student-grouping practices. Following this dialogue, the board adopted the curriculum committee's "grouping motion" in March 1991. This policy calls for heterogeneous grouping to be implemented within a three-year time frame, and each school must submit an initial plan of action to address alternatives to ability grouping. In addition, Burlington's policy includes directions to the board itself, the superintendent, and the curriculum director to take steps to support schools' untracking efforts. As Nelson explains: "I told the curriculum committee, 'A small but vocal group will always think this is the pits. If they're going to retire in seven years, they'll say you can do it in eight. If you really want anything to happen, you need to set a date'."

State-level policy statements can create momentum for untracking across a state. For example, the Massachusetts Board of Education's 1990 policy advisory, *Structuring Schools for Student Success: A Focus on Ability Grouping*, provided a push to untracking and set the stage for local school reform. Two years later, 69% of the state's middle-grades principals reported a decrease in tracking and increase in heterogeneous grouping at their schools (Massachusetts Board of Education 1993).

The most important feature of the Massachusetts policy is the state's commitment to direct concrete resources to schools — especially those in high-poverty districts — that adopt heterogeneous grouping. Dan French, director of the Division of Instructional Services and administrator of the state's discretionary dropout prevention and remedial grants, asserts:

> We *do* know that heterogeneous grouping has more positive impact on student achievement than homogeneous grouping. Since we want to tie our funding to educational approaches that work, we direct our resources to schools that are working to adopt good practice. In awarding both dropout and remedial grants, we've included heterogeneous grouping of students as one of our required objectives.

State support also includes on-site technical assistance and professional development opportunities to schools adopting heterogeneous grouping, including statewide conferences and regional seminars and the pairing of schools with others that may be "a little further along" in untracking. "Many districts need incentives to try something new, especially if it's controversial," French insists. "A state policy promoting heterogeneous grouping can supply a necessary safety net for districts willing to take the risk, but linking resources to change is what really boosts the credibility of the effort."

Caught in the Middle, a report published by the California Department of Education in 1987, included recommendations for substantial reduction of tracking and the advice that no student in grades six, seven, and eight should be tracked according to ethnicity, gender, general ability, primary language, or handicap. This was a broad initiative directed at reforming the state's middle-level schools, but it established a vehicle for transforming the reform agenda into practice: a partnership involving local school districts, institutions of higher education, and the California Department of Education to develop 100 state-of-the-art middle schools throughout the state.

The Office of Middle Grades Support Services at the California Department of Education invited all middle-level schools to participate in regional networks. Within each network, schools reviewed *Caught in the Middle* and selected the reforms they would pursue in their individual schools.

From the beginning, the major issues among networks concerned untracking and equal opportunity. Schools shared strategies for heterogeneous grouping through monthly meetings of principals, visits to "sister schools," newsletters, directories, telecommunications networks, and collaborative staff-development days. In addition, a summer symposium on "Equal Access" featured workshops on expanding the access of low-income and ethnic minority students.

Belonging to a larger network of schools offers principals the encouragement and support to take risks. "The partnership gave me the courage to speak out," explains Donald LeMay of Valley Junior High School in Carlsbad, California. "It put me in contact with others who were thinking along similar lines. It gave me leverage to be able to say to skeptics in my district that we were not alone."

When Tracking No Longer Makes Sense

The principles that undergird untracking schools are not new. They formed the core of the school-reform movements of the 1980s, and a number of schools that have untracked successfully identify with one or more of these movements. Some of the reform movements that have led to tracking are the Accelerated Schools Project, the Effective Schools Movement, the Coalition of Essential Schools, John Goodlad's Partnership for School Renewal, Mortimer Adler's Paideia Proposal, the Montessori Movement, and the middle school movement.

For example, the Accelerated Schools Project is a comprehensive approach to school change that renders tracking and rigid ability grouping useless. Accelerated schools enroll large numbers of students who risk school failure because of a mismatch between the resources and experiences they get at home and the expectations they encounter at school. Schools that follow this reform movement promote the benefits of an enriched, challenging learning environment over a remedial one in order to bring all students into the education mainstream.

The Burnett Accelerated Middle School in the San Jose (California) Unified School District was heavily tracked when it adopted the accelerated-schools philosophy. The administrators and teachers at Burnett realized that tracking was not compatible with their goal of equal educational opportunity for all students. As teachers experimented with heterogeneous grouping in their classes, individual staff members became major forces for change. For example, teacher Connie Posner began experimenting on her own with untracking in her English-as-a-Second-Language (ESL) classes. Instead of creating low, medium, and high groups, Posner mixed the three groups. She found that all students progressed more rapidly and were able to enter regular classes more quickly. Teacher Steve Novotny realized that he was giving the students in his "lower" classes less exciting opportunities and experiences in the computer lab than he was giving "higher" classes. He assigned the "fun, challenging" projects in programming and robotics to all his classes and was thrilled as he observed the positive results.

Is It Worth It?

Untracking is not a trouble-free undertaking, but staff and students in schools where the process has begun say that it is worth the effort. Many schools report that achievement is up for the "low" and "average" students, while undiminished and sometimes improved for the "high" students. They report that discipline improves dramatically, including the behavior of special-education students. And they report noticeable improvements in the school climate and teacher morale.

Some schools have documented the effects of their untracking efforts on student grades, test scores, and course placement, as well as attendance, discipline, and graduation data. For example, at Castle High School in Hawaii, heterogeneously grouped clusters of students were compared with matched groups of students to assess differences in outcomes. After one year, the school found:

1. Only 7% of the students in the heterogeneous core team had 10 or more absences per quarter, compared with 23% in the control group.
2. One-third of the students in the heterogeneously grouped team were rated "exemplary" in academic performance, compared to 18% in the control group; 34% were rated "below standard," compared to 56% in the control group.
3. Discipline referrals to the principal have been "greatly reduced" in the heterogeneously grouped team, with teachers reporting that discipline "is not the time- and energy-consuming process it was in the past."

Other schools compared the achievement of entire grades or groups of students from one year to the next. For example, the Wayland Middle School in Massachusetts invited teachers from two neighboring districts to act as assessors of student performance before and after implementation of heterogeneous grouping in English classes. The observers compared papers written by seventh-graders in heterogeneously grouped classes to papers written by advanced-level seventh-graders of the year before, when students had been grouped homogeneously. The quality of the compositions written during the second year was equal to or higher than the quality of papers written the previous year.

Educators describe the changes they observe in their students' behavior and social skills. For example, Margaret Bray explains that when

41

Ferndale Middle School in High Point, North Carolina, abolished tracking in science and social studies, the improvements were so dramatic that teachers wanted to untrack everything immediately. In fact, the greatest rewards in untracking schools come from the changes that staff observe in students' achievement, discipline, sense of self-worth, and commitment to the school community. As Sue Galletti reports:

> What I've *stopped* seeing is very talented, bright children feeling they're not worth a bit of salt because they haven't made it into an elitist program for students labeled "gifted." I'm seeing all kids realize there are lots of kids who can contribute to learning.

The Road to Improved Teaching and Learning

Educators are challenging entrenched practices in order to release their students' best learning through untracking. They have taken a hard look at outmoded assumptions about intelligence. They have built trust and confidence among staff, parents, and students so that they could weather mistakes; and they have learned about the nature and timing of changes that staff, students, and parents can accept.

Untracking extends the meaning of school reform to the process of teaching and learning itself. As teacher Marcia Lile of Kammerer Middle School insists, "We are not about . . . just mixing. We are talking about raising the level of instruction, raising the expectations for all students." A purposeful, focused approach to change can bring about reforms in grouping, instruction, curriculum, and school organization that benefit all students and strengthen the whole school as a community of learners.

References

Hergert, L.F.; Phlegar, J.M.; and Perez-Selles, M.E. *Kindle the Spark: An Action Guide for Schools Committed to the Success of Every Child.* Andover, Mass.: Regional Laboratory for Educational Improvement of the Northeast and Islands, 1991.

Jennings, M. "Seeking the Right Track: Schools with 'Blending' Say It Works." *Louisville Courier-Journal*, 16 May 1993, p. A23.

Johnson, D.; Johnson, R.; Slavin, R.; and Vasquez, B.T., program consultants. *Cooperative Learning Series*. Videotapes. Alexandria, Va.: Association for Supervision and Curriculum Development, 1990.

Massachusetts Board of Education, Division of School Programs and Division of Educational Personnel. *Magic in the Middle: A Focus on Massachusetts Middle Grade Schools.* Malden, Mass., 1993.

Meier, D.W. "The Little Schools that Could." *The Nation* (23 September 1991): 331, 338-340.

Oakes, J. "Can Tracking Research Inform Practice? Technical, Normative, and Political Considerations." *Educational Researcher* 21, no. 4 (1992): 12-21.

Superintendent's Middle Grade Task Force. *Caught in the Middle: Educational Reform for Young Adolescents in California Public Schools.* Sacramento: California Department of Education, 1987.

Wheelock, A. *Crossing the Tracks: How "Untracking" Can Save America's Schools.* New York: New Press, 1992.

IS IT POSSIBLE TO LIVE WITH TRACKING AND ABILITY GROUPING?

BY PAUL S. GEORGE

During the last half-century, educators found ways to celebrate differences within the school building but to eliminate those differences
inside individual classrooms. The assumption seems to have been that
diversity in the school building is desirable, but that a wide range of differences inside individual classrooms may make teaching more difficult. If learning proceeds more effectively when teachers are able to
match curriculum and instruction to the needs of learners, then a wide
range of needs — a great diversity of readiness and motivation —
would be more difficult to accommodate than a narrower range of such
factors.

One method chosen to deal with this situation is known as ability
grouping. Ability grouping, as used here, means:

> . . . any school or classroom organization plan that is intended
> to reduce the heterogeneity of instructional groups; in between-
> class ability grouping, the heterogeneity of each class for a given
> subject is reduced, and in within-class ability grouping, the het-
> erogeneity of groups within the class (e.g., reading groups) is
> reduced. (Slavin 1990*b*, p. 471)

Some people argue that ability grouping is a logical and reasonable
method for dealing with the increasing diversity of the student population

in American public schools. If children differ in their ability, motivation, and speed of learning, it would be folly to pretend that such differences did not exist. Instead, educators ought to identify the differences that characterize students, organize students according to those differences, and match curriculum and instruction to those differences. Under such circumstances, students ought to learn much more effectively, their perceptions of themselves as learners ought to become more positive, and they should have greater motivation to learn.

In the real world of public schools, unfortunately, there often is great divergence between what is intended and what actually occurs. Teachers, already overworked, may fail to provide the necessary differentiation in instruction. Administrators, beset by demands from parents and policy makers, may permit seemingly reasonable ability-grouping plans to be implemented in unfair and inequitable ways. Students' readiness, motivation, and behaviors may be affected by their perceptions of the group placements they receive. When real-world pressures conflict with theoretical grouping plans, the result may not resemble what was intended (George and Rubin 1992).

In the real world, the identification and placement of students may be neither fair nor accurate (Oakes 1985). Once placed in groups, students may be "locked" in those groups (Dentzer and Wheelock 1990); and perceived ability may be more important than effort (Stevenson and Lee 1990). Academic achievement may not rise, or may rise for only one group (Slavin 1990b). Racial segregation, intentional or otherwise, may occur within the school (George and Rubin 1992). The sense of community, inside and outside the school, may be damaged irreparably (Gamoran and Berends 1987).

Because of these and other problems, some observers have concluded that ability grouping should be dismantled totally and immediately. Unfortunately, doing so may bring its own set of problems. For example, advocates and parents of gifted and talented students may perceive heterogeneous grouping as a danger to the opportunity for excellence for such students. When these advocates and parents believe that the education of gifted and talented students may be diminished, they will act vigorously to derail such efforts. In fact, these critics may be right. It may be difficult to meet the legitimate needs of gifted and talented students in the heterogeneous classroom, especially given the dismal funding in many school districts.

There are other sizable obstacles to untracking. It may be difficult to find the space and time to schedule desirable alternatives. Effective staff development that permits teachers to change to heterogeneous grouping in confident and competent ways is costly and time-consuming. Directives from the central office or school board may provide insufficient time for careful planning. Principals who have been poorly trained as change agents may be pressured in ways that neutralize their leadership.

Ability grouping, as it usually is practiced, clearly seems unfair, inequitable, and ineffective. However, wholesale change to heterogeneous grouping may be so difficult that even the most enthusiastic and energetic change efforts come to naught. What follows are suggestions from research and experience that may help educators live with ability grouping, but fairly.

Strategies for Living with Ability Grouping — Fairly

Become acquainted with the research. Educators are obligated to learn where ability grouping is likely to be most unfair. That means educators must become acquainted with the research, and there are hundreds of studies dealing with ability grouping. Broad, balanced reviews are offered by: Allen (1991), Gamoran and Berends (1987), Goodlad and Oakes (1988), Henderson (1989), Kulik (1992), Oakes (1985), Oakes and Lipton (1992), Rogers (1991), and Slavin (1987, 1990*a*, 1990*b*). Unfortunately, the claims and counter-claims about the research are so confusing and contradictory that practitioners must come to their own conclusions about the most reliable generalizations that can be drawn.

Conduct a local school or district self-study. Once they have reviewed the research, educators should investigate how ability grouping is implemented least equitably in their own school or district. Such a study also should identify areas in which the process seems to be working quite fairly and effectively. This self-study should highlight the difficulties of placing students into ability groups fairly and accurately. It also should look at the flexibility of local grouping practices, grade distributions within and among various tracks, sources of student behavior problems, tracking of minority students, teacher preferences and planning, and a number of other factors. For suggestions about conducting a local study, see *How to Untrack Your School* (George 1992).

Postpone the beginning of between-class ability grouping as late as possible. Elementary schools should be encouraged to use within-class ability grouping. Between-class grouping and "departmentalization" should be delayed as long as possible. Between-class grouping occurs when an entire grade level is divided into ability groups and different teachers instruct different groups. Departmentalization occurs when teachers divide the responsibilities for various subjects so that one teacher has all the math, for example, and the students are ability grouped and scheduled into that teacher's class at various times. Under such arrangements, students may spend substantial portions of their day organized into grade-level homogeneous groups.

Improve the criteria for identification and placement. Educators must abandon arbitrary, single, or narrow criteria for grouping students, such as reliance on the scores of intelligence or general achievement tests. Instead, data on performance in specific subject areas, teacher and counselor recommendations, and even parent and student input must be used. An index of criteria would be best.

It is important to limit the degree to which parents are able to affect the placement of their children. Grouping practices are grossly unfair when placements are made as a result of political, rather than pedagogical, criteria. Educators must be able to demonstrate that it is the characteristics and needs of the children that influence placement, rather than the "pull" of their parents.

Restrict grouping to subjects that are overtly hierarchical in nature. McPartland and Slavin recommend that educators "limit tracking in the later grades to those basic academic subjects where differences in students' prior preparation are clear detriments to whole class instruction" (1990, p. 20). Ability grouping is considerably more fair in such subjects as acceleration in mathematics and foreign language than it is for such subjects as social studies, art, or science.

Decrease practices in early grades that lead to ability grouping in later years. There seems to be little evidence that retention in grade contributes to the improved achievement of retained students; but it does contribute to greater ranges of achievement in later grades, increasing the pressure for ability grouping. Within-class ability grouping, practiced almost universally in elementary school, may be necessary and can be effective; but it also may produce negative outcomes that are realized only in later years. The differences that initially separate learners in such intra-classroom groups may grow greater each day until the achievement levels in top and bottom groups represent years rather than months of achievement. Once placed in such groups, students remain locked in; and such relatively permanent groups then structure the sort of friendships and social networks that continue to influence individual motivation and performance.

Make certain that authentic and substantial differences in curricula distinguish various levels. It is important to distinguish between acceleration and enrichment. Ensure that acceleration of advanced students does not lead to "deceleration" of less-advanced students. While it may make good sense for many advanced eighth-graders to study algebra, this does not imply that others should be repeating the arithmetic of earlier years. All students can benefit from and deserve learning opportunities that enrich their study. There is no support in the research literature for grouping that restricts such experiences to the advanced students.

Be sure all students spend a large part of the day in heterogeneous situations. Placements must be for specific skills groupings only; grouping must never be reduced to a single, day-long assignment. Fairness in ability grouping requires that students spend most of their day in heterogeneous groups. For example, if students participate in a seven-period school day and spend two periods in homogeneous classes, with the remainder of the day in mixed-ability settings, a substantial degree of fairness may be ensured.

Make placement a flexible process. It is necessary to reassess student placements annually. Fairness requires that students, especially in secondary school, be able to move from one group or track to another without barriers. If the only movement from one track to another is to a lower track, then it is possible that some factors may unfairly discourage students from exceeding their previous achievements. School must not function as a tournament where one "loss" means forever dropping out of competition.

Keep the number of groups to a minimum. It may be difficult or unnecessary to eliminate all groups in a particular subject, but it is desirable to cut back on the number of such groups. For example, if a middle school has five levels of mathematics, it can reduce the number to two or three levels. This will make it possible to retain an advanced or honors section, and it will eliminate the less productive lower sections, folding them into regular sections. Doing so will maintain the support of parents, students, and teachers.

Be absolutely certain that classes or levels do not "load" by race, ethnic group, or economic level. Isolation of identifiable groups is illegal under Title VI of the Civil Rights Act of 1964. The Office of Civil Rights (OCR) of the United States Department of Education may terminate federal funding to school districts found to be engaging in such discriminatory practices. Educators must ensure a reasonable racial balance in each classroom. If a school has a sizable group of minority students and high-track classes contain predominantly majority-culture, upper-middle-class students, the school is likely to be in violation of the law.

Educators can remedy such a situation in several ways (see George 1992). One strategy is simply to eliminate the lowest remedial sections in the school's schedule. Another strategy for reintegrating the classroom is to use consulting and co-teaching practices that bring together regular classroom teachers and special educators. School leaders should re-examine the placement of the school's minority students to select those students who have been misidentified. Many such students, especially when matched with teacher-mentors, succeed in higher sections when given the opportunity and the encouragement to do so. In a school of 500 students, changing the placement of 25 to 50 students can have a large effect on the demographic composition of ability-grouped classes without eliminating all grouping.

Be sure that grouping procedures satisfy other legal requirements. It is a good idea for the grouping procedures to be endorsed as policy by the school board. The school or district should be able to demonstrate that the outcomes of grouping are evaluated and that specific grouping practices are altered or eliminated when they are found to be ineffective. The district should spell out the specific goals that grouping strategies are intended to achieve. The district also should take steps to inform all parents about the selection procedures and the programs and potential future benefits of groupings in which their children are involved. Students and their parents should be informed of their due-process rights and the procedures for seeking changes in grouping assignments. (For more details, see Bryson and Bentley 1980.)

Emphasize effort; de-emphasize ability. Many researchers (for example, Stevenson and Lee 1990) argue that the reason Asian nations such as Japan, Korea, and China are able to produce such high academic achievement is that they constantly emphasize effort, endurance, and diligence, and consistently downplay the role of innate ability. Indeed, on my visits to Japanese schools, the word I have heard constantly is *gambaré*, which translates roughly as "endure with enthusiasm." Japanese psychologists with whom I have spoken are convinced that the 10-point gap in IQ scores separating their children from ours is due entirely to the perseverance of their students in test-taking situations. There is no ability grouping of students in Japan until the 10th grade (George 1989).

Recent research on how children learn makes it clear that it is productive for students to think of "ability as an acquirable skill that can be increased by gaining knowledge and competencies" (Bandura 1992, p. 18). Children who view ability in this way do far better on learning tasks than do other children. They seek challenges. They learn from their mistakes. They are not easily rattled by difficulties. "They judge themselves in terms of personal improvement rather than by comparison against the achievement of others" (Bandura 1992, p. 18). They have a much stronger sense of "self-efficacy"; they believe in themselves and act accordingly.

The astounding test results achieved in Los Angeles by the students of master teacher Jaime Escalante testify to the importance of effort (Mathews 1988). Educators who wish to ameliorate the less desirable effects of ability grouping will make use of every opportunity to celebrate and reinforce the importance of effort.

Monitor language and other communications that unfairly label or stigmatize groups of students. The "Bluebirds," "Blackbirds," and "Redbirds" may no longer exist in many classrooms, but other ways of discrediting the backgrounds, learning styles, preferences, or accomplishments of individual students and groups of learners still are embedded in the communication patterns of some schools. Even the term "honors" seems to imply the existence of its opposite, "dishonors," somewhere in the school; and some observers might think that having special groups for gifted children means that most children have no special gifts. Examining the language used in school assemblies and honor rolls and the procedures for extending special privileges will help to eliminate some of the more subtle inequities.

Instruction across levels should vary in style, pace, or depth, but not in quality. In too many schools, the differences in instruction mean less depth in the lower sections than in higher ones. In schools where ability grouping is implemented fairly, teachers differentiate instruction appropriately. In the lower sections, reliance on quiet, unimaginative, and repetitive seatwork is rejected. Less successful students receive instruction that is active, concrete, hands-on, highly structured, and both visual and auditory. It is delivered by teachers who are positive, energetic, enthusiastic, and warm and who have more than average skill in classroom management.

Being fair with ability grouping means that teachers must take instructional risks with their lower sections, as well as with the higher ones. Many teachers introduce new and untried curricula or try state-of-the-art instructional strategies in what they believe to be "safe" situations, with students whom they believe can manage the ambiguity or lack of precision that might accompany such innovation. Consequently, the advanced sections often get to be involved in the things about which the teacher is most excited. In schools that practice fair ability grouping, these kinds of curricula and teaching also are used in the low sections.

51

Provide staff development that helps teachers become more effective with both high and low sections. Teachers need training in dealing with homogeneous grouping. Workshops on the effects of teacher expectations on student motivation and achievement will help them overcome the tendency to demand less work from students in lower sections. Training that increases teachers' sensitivity to cultural diversity and their comfort level in multicultural situations will help them develop more positive and productive relationships with students. Insights into such factors as learning styles will enable them to diversify their instruction from one level to another. Inservice education that prepares teachers to implement instruction that is active, concrete, structured, and enriched will serve them in homogeneous as well as in heterogeneous classrooms. In short, fairness in the use of ability grouping requires that teachers receive training that helps them match instruction to the learning needs of students in all sections.

Establish and enforce policies that ensure balanced distribution of teaching talent and other learning resources. One significant and readily available way to continue with ability grouping but to do so fairly is to apportion the teaching talent and other learning resources in an equitable manner. At all levels of schooling, but perhaps especially in high school, the assignment of teachers to various classes may be as much a political process as it is a pedagogical one. Charged with motivating their teaching staff, many principals assign the best or most experienced teachers to the advanced students and the least successful or inexperienced teachers to the students who need the most help (Darling-Hammond 1988).

This practice often is motivated by the need for principals to pacify politically powerful or influential parents. In schools it appears that an unspoken obligation of the principal is to keep angry parents away from the central office. Too many angry, influential parents pounding on the superintendent's door will limit the principal's career. Thus, when certain parents ask that their students have specific teachers, the principal may be receptive.

For whatever reason, students perceived as having less potential for successful learning often are grouped together and have teachers without a record of success in teaching. Recent research indicates that when inexperienced teachers are assigned a heavy load of low-track classes, a pattern of lower achievement for these students results (Sanders 1992). Maintaining ability grouping is more defensible in schools where procedures ensure that all teachers share the duties of teaching both high and low sections. Fairness demands that all students have opportunities to be taught by the best teachers the school can offer.

Provide opportunities for student interaction and involvement across groups. If students seem to be isolated because of ability grouping, the negative potential can be softened by vigorous efforts to bring students together for activities and experiences that go beyond the regular classroom. In the elementary school, teachers can work together to ensure that students engage in heterogeneous activities. In the middle school and high school, mixed-ability, advisor-advisee, and mentor groups can spend regular time together, exploring interpersonal relationships and building a sense of unity. Intramural programs organized around these groups also can help build that sense of community.

Emphasize the development and maintenance of an inclusive climate. Identification, placement, and isolation in low tracks may be related to a devaluation of school, self, and others. Low-track students may come to see their school work, and themselves, as having little merit. They may find themselves part of a negative, anti-school crowd bent on damaging the value of the school experience for others (Gamoran and Berends 1987). Retaining ability grouping requires that educators create a climate in which all students say, "I am an important part of an important group." Researchers call this "decreasing the sense of marginalization" felt by low-track students (Kramer Schlosser 1992).

Moving toward such a "learning community" requires, first of all, an organizational structure built on the concept of "smallness within bigness." Large schools must be organized so that students and teachers experience a "sense of smallness." Some school leaders break a large school into smaller houses, or schools-within-a-school. These houses then are divided further into teams, clusters, or blocks of four to five teachers and 125 to 150 students. These teams continue the process by being subdivided into advisory or mentor groups of approximately 20 students and one teacher. Some schools also use nongradedness, multiage grouping, or "student-teacher progression" to organize teachers and students so that they remain together for more than one year. These organizational strategies make it possible for teachers to know their low-track students as persons, to understand the forces that affect their school lives, and to sustain the energy necessary to teach in ways that make a difference. (For further discussion of this organizational process, see George and Alexander 1993).

Experiment with new ways of involving more students in upper-level, challenging courses. Some middle and high schools involve students in choosing their tracks or ability groups. Interesting grading options, such as pass-fail or extra credits for certain offerings, encourage students to take the risk of choosing an "honors" track (McPartland and

Slavin 1990). Other schools combine honors and regular sections into single classrooms but permit students to choose an honors or regular "contract" on the basis of differentiated curricula, assignments, grade standards, or other criteria.

Make the time requirements of some courses more flexible. A few schools have begun to identify certain "gatekeeper" courses, such as Algebra I, and make it possible for students to complete the requirements for the course in more or less than the standard academic year. Larger numbers of less successful students might attempt such a course if they were virtually assured of passing it, provided they are willing to give it the time it requires. Three semesters might be a more reasonable time allotment for some students; for others, one semester might be adequate.

Study versions of tracking that work. At least three different ability-grouping strategies seem to work better than most. These three are named after the cities where they were first implemented. The Baltimore Plan emphasizes stratified ability grouping within each grade level in an elementary school, so that each class has thirds of its students from the high, middle, and low achievement ranges, but no class is composed of only one level. The Winchester Plan organizes middle school students into heterogeneous interdisciplinary teams but subdivides the students on a team into 10 levels, assigning no more than two levels at a time to any one class. Students spend most of their day in heterogeneous groups, but teachers never have to deal with the full range of achievement represented on the team. The Joplin Plan emphasizes nongraded, multi-age, large groups, with grouping by achievement across grade levels in such subjects as reading and mathematics. (For further information on these plans, see George 1992.)

Develop a culture of detracking. In spite of the need to live with ability grouping for now, many school leaders would prefer, eventually, to move beyond tracking. Oakes and Lipton (1992) argue that progress toward such inclusive academic environments must begin with the presence of an inclusive climate among the adults in the school. Such an adult "culture" would emphasize shared decision making. It would focus on a process of continuous school improvement that recognizes that ability grouping, even when implemented as fairly as possible, is less desirable than more heterogeneous alternatives. Such a culture would facilitate staff development about heterogeneous classroom arrangements. It requires school leaders who are capable of taking risks and persisting in the face of difficult odds.

Conclusion

If public schools are to remain viable over the next decade, the struggle to balance the demands for both equity and excellence must be successful. Doing away with tracking and ability grouping in a hasty, ill-conceived fashion might lead large numbers of upper-middle-class, majority-culture students to abandon the public schools in favor of new and attractive private schools. The resulting public pauper schools would surely be unattractive.

On the other hand, to continue to practice ability grouping as it has been done may lead to elite, quasi-private, but publicly funded academies for gifted and advanced students within the public schools. Exciting and enriching educational experiences for the few and very different, less satisfying experiences for others is equally unacceptable. Educators must find alternatives to rigid and unfair tracking and ability grouping; but these options, at least for the near future, may include living with ability grouping fairly.

References

Allen, S.D. "Ability-Grouping Research Reviews: What Do They Say About Grouping and the Gifted?" *Educational Leadership* 48, no. 6 (1991): 60-65.

Bandura, A. "Perceived Self-Efficacy in Cognitive Development and Functioning." Paper presented at the annual meeting of the American Educational Research Association, San Francisco, April 1992.

Bryson, J.E., and Bentley, C.P. *Ability Grouping of Public School Students: Legal Aspects of Classification and Tracking Methods.* Charlottesville, Va.: Michie, 1980.

Darling-Hammond, L. "Teacher Quality and Educational Equality." *The College Board Review* no. 148 (1988): 17-23.

Dentzer, E., and Wheelock, A. *Locked In/Locked Out: Tracking and Placement in Boston Public Schools.* Boston: Massachusetts Advocacy Center, 1990.

Gamoran, A., and Berends, M. "The Effects of Stratification in Secondary Schools: Synthesis of Survey and Ethnographic Research." *Review of Educational Research* 57, no. 4 (1987): 415-35.

George, P.S. *The Japanese Junior High School: A View from the Inside.* Columbus, Ohio: National Middle School Association, 1989.

George, P.S. *How to Untrack Your School.* Washington, D.C.: Association for Supervision and Curriculum Development, 1992.

George, P.S., and Alexander, W.M. *The Exemplary Middle School.* 2nd ed. Forth Worth, Texas: Harcourt Brace, 1993.

George, P.S., and Rubin, K. *Tracking and Ability Grouping in Florida: A Status Study.* Sanibel: Florida Education Research Council, 1992.

Goodlad, J.I., and Oakes, J. "We Must Offer Equal Access to Knowledge." *Educational Leadership* 45, no. 5 (1988): 16-22.

Henderson, N.D. "A Meta-Analysis of Ability Grouping Achievement and Attitude in the Elementary Grades." Doctoral dissertation, Mississippi State University, 1989. Dissertation Abstracts International, 50, 873A.

Kramer Schlosser, L. "Teacher Distance and Student Disengagement: School Lives on the Margin." *Journal of Teacher Education* 43, no. 2 (1992): 128-40.

Kulik, J.A. *An Analysis of the Research on Ability Grouping: Historical and Contemporary Perspectives.* Storrs, Conn.: National Research Center on the Gifted and Talented, 1992.

Mathews, J. *Escalante: The Best Teacher in America.* New York: Henry Holt, 1988.

McPartland, J.M., and Slavin, R.E. *Policy Perspectives: Increasing Achievement of At-Risk Students at Each Grade Level.* Washington, D.C.: U.S. Department of Education, 1990.

Oakes, J. *Keeping Track: How Schools Structure Inequality.* New Haven, Conn.: Yale University Press, 1985.

Oakes, J., and Lipton, M. "Detracking Schools: Early Lessons from the Field." *Phi Delta Kappan* 73, no. 6 (1992): 448-54.

Rogers, K.B. *The Relationship of Grouping Practices to the Education of the Gifted and Talented Learner.* Storrs, Conn.: National Research Center on the Gifted and Talented, 1991.

Sanders, C.S., Jr. "The Effects of High School Staffing Patterns on Low-Achieving Students." Doctoral dissertation, University of Florida, Gainesville, Florida, 1992. *Dissertation Abstracts International* 54, 52A.

Slavin, R.E. "Ability Grouping and Student Achievement in Elementary Schools: A Best-Evidence Synthesis." *Review of Educational Research* 57, no. 3 (1987): 293-336.

Slavin, R.E. "Ability Grouping, Cooperative Learning, and the Gifted." *Journal for the Education of the Gifted* 14, no. 3 (1990): 3-8, 28-30. a

Slavin, R.E. "Achievement Effects of Ability Grouping in Secondary Schools: A Best-Evidence Synthesis." *Review of Educational Research* 60, no. 3 (1990): 471-99. b

Stevenson, H.W., and Lee, S.Y. *Contexts of Achievement: A Study of American, Chinese, and Japanese Children.* Chicago: University of Chicago Press, 1990.

56

SECTION II

Striving for Inclusiveness in Schools and Classrooms

MORE THAN MEETS THE EYE: LINKS BETWEEN TRACKING AND THE CULTURE OF SCHOOLS

BY JEANNIE OAKES

Tracking supports a nearly century-old belief that a crucial job of schools is to prepare workers with varied knowledge and skills. Thus academic classes prepare students heading for jobs that require college degrees, while more rudimentary academic classes and vocational programs ready students for less-skilled jobs or for post-high school technical training. Policy makers, educators, and the public believe it is fair and appropriate for schools to track students for different work lives according to the perceived differences in students' intellectual abilities, motivation, and aspirations.

Tracking is connected closely with testing, since many tests were created during the early part of the century for the purpose of sorting students "scientifically" into different tracks. The development of standardized tests for placement persuaded most people to view tracked curricula as functional, scientific, and democratic. Tracking is perceived as an educationally sound way to accomplish two important tasks: 1) to provide students with the education that best suits their abilities and 2) to provide the nation with the array of workers it needs.

---

*This chapter will appear, in adapted form, in an upcoming issue of the *Peabody Journal of Education*.

Despite this perception of legitimacy, there is no question that tracking — and the assessment practices that support it — limit many students' opportunities for education and in life. These limits affect children from all racial, ethnic, and socioeconomic groups. However, schools far more often judge African-American and Latino students to have learning deficits and limited potential. Thus schools disproportionately place these students in low-track, remedial programs that provide them with restricted opportunities.

Educators justify these placements by pointing out that children from these groups typically perform less well on commonly accepted assessments of ability and achievement. Moreover, conventional school wisdom holds that low-track, remedial, and special education classes help these students, since they permit teachers to target instruction to the particular learning deficiencies of low-ability students. However, research about human capacity and learning suggests that typical placement tests measure only a very narrow range of students' abilities. These tests provide little information about students' higher-order cognitive abilities, such as how well they generate ideas or solve problems, or about how well they can accomplish real-world tasks (Wigdor and Garner 1982). Furthermore, students do not profit from enrollment in low-track classes as much as students with similar skills profit from heterogeneous classes. Students in low-track classes have less access than other students to knowledge, engaging learning experiences, and resources (see Oakes, Gamoran, and Page 1991).

In this essay I first describe the complex links among race, tracking, and the culture of schools that make tracking practices so difficult to change. Then I suggest factors to which policy makers and schools need to pay attention if schools are to become places where tracking no longer makes sense.

The Links Among Race, Tracking, and School Culture

Testing and tracking often begin before students enter kindergarten. Over the past decade, a growing number of local school systems have begun to administer "readiness" tests to select some five-year-olds for the academic demands of kindergarten, others for a less academic pre-kindergarten class, and still others to stay home and wait another year. Many systems use such tests to guide placement decisions about first-graders. Because children's prior academic learning opportunities have considerable influence on their scores, it is not surprising that children with academically rich preschool and school-like home environments do better on such tests and are more likely to be judged as developmentally "ready" for "regular" kindergartens and suited for high-ability first-grade classrooms. Thus these tests place low-income children, a group in which most minority children fit, at a clear disadvantage, since most of them have fewer educationally advantaged preschool opportunities.

On average, minority children score less well on "readiness" tests than white students do (Ellwein and Eads 1990). Therefore, it is no surprise that we find disproportionate numbers of young minority children in special "transitional" classes, in separate programs for "at-risk" children, and in other types of low-ability primary classrooms. Even more troubling, these "readiness" tests are not sufficiently accurate to be used as a basis for placement decisions. They were not designed to predict whether children will succeed in a particular placement, and they do not predict children's success well (Shepard 1990).

Tracking propels children through the system at different speeds — even though the goal for the slower-paced groups is to have them "catch up." In reading, for example, the low groups spend relatively more time on decoding activities, whereas high groups move on to consider the meanings of stories and progress further in the curriculum. High-group students do more silent reading and, when reading aloud, are less often interrupted than are low-group students. The high-group advantage presumably accumulates as the years pass, and students with a history of membership in high-ability groups are more likely to have covered considerably more material by the end of elementary school.

In this way, tracking in the elementary grades determines much of what happens later. Differences in pace through a sequenced curriculum (particularly in mathematics and reading) lead to differences in coverage. Coverage differences result in some children falling further behind and in receiving increasingly different curricula. These differences further stabilize students' track placements. Before long, students in slower groups lack the prerequisite curricular experiences to qualify (that is, to score well on tests) for faster groups or to succeed in faster or higher groups. Moreover, they are likely to have internalized the judgment that they are less able and less likely to succeed and, as a consequence, are no longer eager to put forth the hard work it might take to do well in a higher-ability class (Rosenholtz and Simpson 1984).

Early in the middle school years, there begins an intentional shift away from the goal of propelling kids through the same curriculum at different speeds (with the illogical intention that slower students will "catch up"). Instead, middle schools — still relying on slow, special,

61

and remedial classes — change their intentions for students. Not only is the speed different, so is the direction. Rather than being propelled through the same curriculum at different speeds, albeit with much omitted for those in slower groups, students are pulled intentionally through different curricula toward different "end-points" — different high schools and different post-high school expectations.

Increasingly, these different destinations influence judgments about appropriate placements and courses. There are different courses with different names — sometimes prefixed with "basic," "regular," "pre-," "honors," or "gifted" — and clearly different in content and rigor (for example, slower-track students might take a "crafts" elective instead of a foreign language). In middle school, the differentiated curriculum conforms to a larger social purpose — preparing students for alternative futures — and creates even greater curricular differences than would be expected from variances in pace and consequent losses in coverage.

As students proceed through middle and high school, increasingly disproportionate percentages of African-American and Latino students enroll in low-ability tracks (Braddock 1989; Oakes 1990; Oakes, Gamoran, and Page 1991). For example, I found that all-minority secondary schools enroll far greater percentages of their students in low-track classes compared to all-white schools; and in racially mixed schools the concentration of minority students in low-track classes is dramatic. Indeed, 66% of the science and mathematics classes with disproportionately large minority enrollments (compared to their representation in the student body as a whole) were low-track, compared with only 5% of the disproportionately white classes. In contrast, only 9% of the disproportionately minority classes were high-track, compared to 57% of the disproportionately white classes (Oakes 1990). These findings were echoed in a recent study of the effects of middle school tracking in six minority, urban districts. According to this research, minority students were over-represented in low-track math classes (23% compared to only 8% of the white students) and under-represented in high-track classes (36% of the minorities compared to 56% of whites) (Villegas and Watts 1991).

In part, these disproportionate placements stem from real differences in minority and white students' opportunities and achievements in elementary school — differences that are often a consequence of earlier tracking. These differences — and disproportionate placements — are exacerbated by schools' reliance on standardized tests in making tracking decisions. Even though such tests underestimate minority students' capabilities, they typically carry more weight than information about students' past classroom performance or teachers' recommendations, particularly when students move into new schools where counselors may have little or no contact with students' former teachers (Oakes et al. 1992; Villegas and Watts 1991).

At least two additional, related factors play a role in creating the racially skewed pattern of track placements. One is the pervasive, stereotypical expectations that society and schools hold for students of different racial and ethnic groups. These stereotypes can negatively influence the placement of minority students with marginal test scores (for example, "Latino parents don't care much about their children's school achievement and are unlikely to help their children at home"). A second is "politicking" by savvy parents who want their children placed in the best classes. Although such parents are not exclusively white, in most schools white parents, especially middle-class white parents, better understand the inequalities in the school structure and feel more confident that the school will respond positively to their pressure (Oakes et al. 1992; Useem 1990). Students from different backgrounds sometimes receive different information, advice, and attention from counselors and teachers. While many secondary schools claim that students "choose" their tracks, low-track, minority students most often report that others made decisions for them (Villegas and Watts 1991).

Why does this matter? Low-track courses consistently offer less demanding topics and skills, while high-track classes typically include more complex material. Teachers of low-track classes give less emphasis than teachers of other classes to such matters as basic science concepts, students' interest in math and science, their developing inquiry and problem-solving skills, their learning mathematics and science ideas, and the preparation of students for further study in these subjects (Oakes 1990). These differences cannot be construed as fine-tuning of the curriculum to accommodate individual differences. These goals need not depend on students' prior knowledge or skills. To the contrary, math and science educators increasingly see these goals as essential for all students — regardless of their current skill levels. High-track teachers in all subjects often stress having students become competent and autonomous thinkers. By contrast, low-track teachers place greater emphasis on conformity to rules and expectations (Oakes 1985).

Teaching strategies differ in ways consistent with this pattern of curricular disadvantage. Teachers allocate less time to instruction (as opposed to routines, discipline, and socializing) in low tracks; and learning activities more often consist of drill and practice with trivial bits of information, seatwork, and worksheet activities. When technology is introduced in low tracks, it is often in conjunction with low-level tasks, such as computation. For example, computer activities often mimic texts and worksheets (Oakes, Gamoran, and Page 1991). Low-track teachers tend to maintain tight control over students' opportunities, activities, and interactions. Furthermore, while these disadvantages affect all students in the class, low-track minority students may be especially disadvantaged, because teachers may treat them even less favorably. For example, Villegas and Watts (1991) found that in racially mixed, low-track classes, teachers focused their interactions with minority students on behavioral rather than educational concerns (six times more often than with whites), both telling students what to do (three times more often for minorities than for whites) and criticizing them (five times more often).

Since many schools track their teachers as well as their students, low-track students have less exposure to well-qualified teachers. While some schools rotate the teaching of low- and high-ability classes, it is more typical for teachers to jockey among themselves for high-track assignments or for principals to use class assignments as rewards and sanctions. Such political processes work to the detriment of low-track students, because the least-prepared teachers usually are assigned to low-track students. For example, teachers of secondary low-ability science and mathematics classes are usually less experienced, are less likely to be certified in math or science, hold fewer degrees in these subjects, have less training in the use of computers, and less often report themselves to be "master teachers" than their colleagues in upper-track classes. These differences are particularly troublesome for students in schools with large minority and low-income populations, because these schools have fewer well-qualified teachers to begin with. In such schools, for example, low-track students frequently are taught math and science by teachers who are not certified to teach those subjects, if they are certified at all (Oakes 1990).

These track-related differences have pernicious consequences stemming from conceptions and judgments about human capacity and individual differences that connect with students' race and social class. These inequalities are not educationally appropriate adaptations to variation in students' learning aptitude, speed, or style. Not surprisingly, the combination of separating students into different groups and providing different knowledge and learning conditions to these groups affects achievement. When schools track, low-track students — disproportionately African-American and Latino — get less and learn less. Moreover, tracking systems signal very loudly that the school regards minorities as less intelligent than whites, judgments that students often internalize.

What We Need to Pay Attention to in Detracking

Tracking is just one of many problematic school structures and practices. Tracking supports and is supported by much else that is wrong with schools — thin, skills-based curricula; passive, teacher-dominated instructional strategies; and standardized, paper-and-pencil assessment, to name just a few. As a consequence, detracking requires far more than the development of new grouping and scheduling strategies. Simply mixing students into heterogeneous classrooms cannot begin to provide diverse groups of students with the opportunities and supportive environment they need to learn well.

Neither can a single new technique pave the way. Training teachers in cooperative learning methods, for example, is typical of detracking efforts. As helpful as this teaching method is, teachers still confront disconnected subject areas, fragmented curricula, norm-referenced assessments, inadequate support for special needs, isolation from their colleagues, and related problems. Since these practices frustrate efforts to develop high-quality heterogeneous classes, detracking will not work unless these other practices also are reconsidered and made compatible with the new grouping structure. An outcome, now largely unanticipated, is that such changes should improve the quality of schooling for all children — even those now receiving the "best."

Schools that attend to these concerns have invented and adapted an array of practices that provide enormously helpful illustrations for other schools (Wheelock 1992). Nevertheless, the schools themselves should not be considered "models" to be copied, but rather purveyors of more general lessons. The most important lesson they teach is that creating a culture of detracking is more important than particular organizational arrangements, curricula, or instructional strategies, as necessary as these are. More important, these accounts of schools that are grappling with detracking probably will emphasize that such schools move beyond an exclusively "practical" focus on school programs and classroom strategies and attend to values and beliefs. This process restructures their thinking and allows them to build political support for school cultures in which tracking no longer makes sense.

A second lesson from these schools is that, while new technologies are necessary, they are clearly insufficient to bring forth change. Alternative practices must make sense to educators and their communities before they can be fully implemented and sustained in schools. Such sense-making occurs when the values and beliefs on which tracking rests are challenged and replaced with new norms that support heterogeneous grouping and the other school and classroom practices that it requires.

Challenging norms is essential because the underlying assumptions of any practice provide the intellectual infrastructure that protects it from change. Though increasingly obsolete, the norms that support tracking are conventional conceptions of intelligence, as well as deep-seated racist and classist attitudes and prejudices. These norms — consciously and unconsciously — drive the day-to-day educational practices mentioned above. Tracking also conforms to the deeply ingrained bureaucratic notion that any process can be made more efficient when it is divided into hierarchical levels and specialized categories.

Another norm that bolsters and legitimizes tracking is the American emphasis on competition and individualism over cooperation and the good of the community — a norm that suggests that "good" education is a scarce commodity available only to a few winners. Although the American system of public education was designed to promote the common good and to prepare children for participation in a democratic society, more recent emphasis has been placed on what a graduate can "get out" of schooling in terms of income, power, or status. Obviously, efforts to detrack schools must reach beyond the technical, day-to-day functions of the school and address the way in which our society views such matters as human capacities; individual and group differences; fairness, efficiency, and competition; and what the goals of public education should be.

A third lesson drawn from these schools is that reformers must address pressures from the social-political milieu that holds tracking in place. Political concerns grow out of the norms that undergird tracking and, at the same time, have a strong influence on technical decisions at the school and district levels. The pressure placed on educators by savvy parents who want their children enrolled in the "best" classes is no doubt the most obvious such political factor. Parents of high-track students are clearly advantaged — both in educational opportunities and status — by the current arrangement. And in a competitive system that offers only a small percentage of students slots in the high-track classes, these parents have few options but to push to have their children better educated than other children.

Administrators rightfully worry that attempts to do away with tracking will lead to a loss of support from these involved parents and a lower enrollment of children from the most advantaged families. This latter concern has been fueled by advocates for high-achieving students and those who have qualified for state and local gifted-and-talented programs. They perceive the research on tracking and the response it has engendered as a serious threat to high-quality education for their constituents. They fear that detracking will sap the opportunities now available to high achievers. Because all schools need political support — not only for funding and physical resources, but also for credibility — a policy that allows some tracking (such as maintenance of separate gifted-and-talent programs) often is exchanged for the political credit that more advantaged and involved parents bring to a school.

The pressure from more affluent and better-educated parents to keep tracked schools and to have their children placed and kept in the highest-level courses certainly reflects a competitive, individualistic attitude toward the purpose of schooling. But in racially mixed schools it can take on another dimension. Because race, class, assessed ability, and track placements interrelate, heterogeneous ability grouping may mean racial integration in classes where none previously existed. Fearing that minority-student enrollment leads to lower educational standards, white and wealthy parents often lobby for their children's enrollment in more racially and socioeconomically homogeneous gifted-and-talented programs or honors courses within desegregated schools. Most truly believe that their children will receive a better education in a homogeneous classroom. Given what we know about teacher expectations for students in different tracks and the resulting level of difficulty of the work teachers assign to students in those tracks, these parents are correct.

Therefore, successful detracking will depend on building supportive communities both within and outside the school. This political dimension asks, "How might such competing interests as advocates for the gifted, for disadvantaged, and for minorities redefine their roles and create a collective advocacy for all children?" Building such new communities requires the political leadership of educators. This leadership is likely to emerge from reasoned and critical inquiry, based on research, self-study, and democratic values. And it must be built on new norms, on new confidence in the intellectual capacities of all children, and on new confidence in the capacities of schools to provide for all a far richer and more meaningful education than that now reserved for only those in the top tracks.

Schools currently undergoing detracking provide both inspiration and sobering insight. It is likely that none of these schools has resolved all its tracking problems; many are still vulnerable to social and political forces grounded in old norms regarding race, class, ability, and competition for the "best" education. What matters here is that these schools bear witness to the most essential lesson about altering schools in ways that serve all children well. That lesson is that, at the same time schools entertain new techniques, they also must recognize and be willing to confront the fact that tracking is simply a structural manifestation of norms deeply rooted in the culture of schooling and the political forces driven by these norms.

References

Braddock, J.H., II. *Tracking of Black, Hispanic, Asian, Native American, and White Students: National Patterns and Trends*. Baltimore: Johns Hopkins University, Center for Research on Effective Schooling for Disadvantaged Students, 1989.

Ellwein, M.C., and Eads, G.M. "How Well Do Readiness Tests Predict Future School Performance?" Paper presented at the annual meeting of the American Educational Research Association, Boston, April 1990.

Oakes, J. *Keeping Track: How Schools Structure Inequality*. New Haven, Conn.: Yale University Press, 1985.

Oakes, J. *Multiplying Inequalities: The Effect of Race, Social Class, and Tracking on Opportunities to Learn Mathematics and Science*. Santa Monica, Calif.: Rand Corporation, 1990.

Oakes, J.; Gamoran, A.; and Page, R.N. "Curricular Differentiation." In *Handbook of Research on Curriculum*, edited by P.W. Jackson. New York: Macmillan, 1991.

Oakes, J.; Selvin, M.; Karoly, L.; and Guiton, G. *Educational Matchmaking: Academic and Vocational Tracking in Comprehensive High Schools*. Santa Monica, Calif.: Rand Corporation, 1992.

Rosenholtz, S.J., and Simpson, C. "The Formation of Ability Conceptions: Developmental Trend or Social Construction?" *Review of Educational Research* 54, no. 1 (1984): 31-63.

Shepard, L. "Readiness Testing in Local School Districts: An Analysis of Backdoor Policies." *Journal of Education Policy* 5, no. 5 (1990): 159-79.

Useem, E. "Social Class and Ability Group Placement in Mathematics in the Transition of Seventh Grade: The Role of Parent Involvement." Paper presented at the annual meeting of the American Educational Research Association, Boston, April 1990.

Villegas, A.M., and Watts, S.M. "Life in the Classroom: The Influence of Class Placement and Student Race Ethnicity." Paper presented at the annual meeting of the American Educational Research Association, Chicago, April 1991.

Wheelock, A. *Crossing the Tracks: How "Untracking" Can Save America's Schools*. New York: New Press, 1992.

Wigdor, A.K., and Garner, W.R., eds. *Ability Testing: Uses, Consequences, and Controversies*. Washington, D.C.: National Academy Press, 1982.

TRACKING AND ITS EFFECTS ON AFRICAN-AMERICANS IN THE FIELD OF EDUCATION

BY JANE A. PAGE AND FRED M. PAGE, JR.

In the past decade educators, administrators, and sociologists have been concerned with the marked decline in the number of African-American teachers and teacher-education students. This decrease in the number of African-American teachers is accompanied by a large increase in the number of African-American public school students, which may reach 40% of the total student population by the year 2000 (Graham 1987). For example, in Georgia African-American students already constitute 40% of the public school population while the percentage of African-American teachers in Georgia is 20% and declining yearly. In fact, colleges and universities in Georgia produce fewer than one African-American teacher per school system each year (Professional Standards Commission 1991). Trends at the national level are even more disturbing.

This decline is primarily the result of a diminishing number of African-American students entering teacher education. But that is not the only factor. According to a report by the Metropolitan Life Foundation (1988), minority teachers are far more likely than majority teachers to leave the profession.

In a survey of 285 African-American teachers in 36 school systems in southeast Georgia, respondents reported generally positive views of factors related to the teaching career but were not likely to encourage their own sons and daughters to enter the profession (Page and Page 1990). When asked whether they would urge an interested daughter to pursue teaching, only 19.9% (compared to 25.9% of Caucasian teachers) responded affirmatively and 33.2% said "no." Even fewer (15.8%) would encourage an interested son to pursue teaching; 24.8% said they would "possibly" encourage a son to enter teaching, 20.1% said they would "doubtfully" do so, and 39.2% said "no." Perhaps even more discouraging were these teachers' responses to the question: "If you could start all over again, would you choose teaching as a career?" Only 20.4% stated that they would choose teaching. Others responded with possibly (31.9%), doubtfully (18.6%), and no (29.1%). A comparison with Caucasian teachers from the same geographic area shows that African-American teachers are significantly more negative in the evaluation of their career choice and in their willingness to encourage their own children to consider teaching.

In-depth interviews with African-American college students and educators have shed light on the problem of their declining numbers in the profession (Page and Page 1991; Page, Page, and Battle 1993). The college students in these interviews included those with majors in computer science, accounting, business management, mechanical engineering, history, finance, communication arts, and marketing, as well as education. The educators in the study included an education professor, five elementary school teachers, four middle school teachers, two high school teachers, a counselor, a retired administrator, and a central office administrator. Career experience for these interviewees ranged from one to 34 years.

Data collected through these interviews were initially analyzed through the qualitative categorization approach. Some of the concerns about teaching careers expressed by the African-Americans in this study coincided with problems suggested by the literature on the shortage of minority teachers, including insufficient salary, lack of financial support to attend college, and overemphasis on the testing of teachers. However, the primary factors cited by many of the interviewees were related to practices in school systems that diminish opportunities for African-American students and teachers. All the predominant negative factors could be associated with a single detrimental practice: tracking.

An Ulterior Motive for Tracking

After desegregation was mandated by federal courts in the late 1960s and early 1970s, schools in the South often were organized in a manner that would limit contact of African-American teachers with Caucasian children. Some of these educators were given assignments as "roving teachers" who would visit classrooms and teach one subject. Others were assigned positions in remedial resource classrooms. African-American principals were reassigned as assistant principals in the integrated schools and usually were put in charge of "disciplining" (paddling) students. When the courts discontinued close monitoring, schools in the region became increasingly resegregated through the use of tracking, with the majority of African-American students assigned to lower tracks and the majority of Caucasian students assigned to higher tracks (Deever 1992).

Teachers reported that, as the older African-American teachers retired, they were replaced by Caucasian teachers. When an African-American teacher was hired, that teacher usually was assigned to a low-level class. Traditionally, lower levels are assigned to beginning teachers and assignments to higher levels are given to experienced teachers. However, veteran African-American teachers seldom were successful in "working their way out" of the lower track. The reason given was that they could "relate" better to these students and were more successful in disciplining them.

Comments from Educators

Following are quotations from interviews by Page, Page, and Battle (1993). These quotations are representative of the problems related to tracking as identified by educators. A school counselor commented:

> The problem that really bothers me doesn't relate as much to the placement of teachers as it does to the placement of children. I see many children misplaced. Children who come to school without the enrichment experiences which encourage learning the alphabet and numbers are labeled as "slow" and are never given a chance. Some children do struggle and somehow make it. But many of them feel so discouraged about "schooling" that education is not a career consideration. My daughter told me, "Mama, I would never want to teach. I know what the kids are like. And I also know which kids I would get."

A retired administrator, responding to a question about the declining numbers of African-Americans entering the profession, stated:

> Going back to the days of integration, and in particular in the Southern states, it was difficult for black educated males and females to get a position. They were not hired unless they had some

extraordinary skill or talent. When hired, they were given the worst assignments, lower-ability students for most of their courses, and positions requiring little or no intelligence. These same individuals are now the parents of our current generation of college students. These parents don't want their children to have to undergo this unfair treatment. I guess the parents are continuing to feel hurt and anger because of past treatment.

An elementary Chapter 1 teacher remarked about the tracking of low-achieving students in her former position in New York and her current position in Georgia:

> They eat together, play together, attend special classes (art, music, physical education) together; they never get a chance to interact with "average" students. They feel like they are different, and I think we are responsible for that because of ability grouping. To me, it is a travesty. When I look at these children, they are intelligent; but they think they lack intelligence, and many of their parents feel the same. As teachers, we treat them like they are different.

A Case Study

One of the in-depth interviews of a high-school teacher provided data for a case study (Page and Page 1991), which may be representative of many teachers in the area. The name and some identifying information have been changed to ensure anonymity.

When Connie Parrish was a teenager, she knew that she wanted to do something special with her life. She wanted to go to college. Most of her friends in her small, south-Georgia town were not planning to go to college. Either they were going to work or vocational school or they already were raising children. But Connie had worked hard to make good grades in her college-prep classes, and she was intent on achieving her goal. In 1979 she enrolled in a small junior college near her hometown, where she was one of only a handful of African-American students. Public schools in Georgia had only recently achieved full implementation of court-ordered desegregation, and this private college had just begun to receive and accept applications from African-Americans.

Connie graduated with an associate degree after two years and transferred to a large senior college. She continued to work hard and maintained a high grade-point average. In 1983, she received a B.A. in biology, her favorite subject; and she was convinced that she wanted to spend her life making science as exciting for other young people as it had been for her. Connie was going to be a teacher.

Connie moved with her new husband to a community where he worked in a local factory. The community was near a college, and Connie taught school while pursuing certification. After earning her teaching certificate, she continued her education and received a master's degree in 1986. When Connie's husband received a better job offer in another community, she obtained a position at the local high school.

Connie was told by the administrator that new teachers in the school usually taught the lower levels. After each year, teachers could make requests for certain classes, grades, and levels. Connie observed that only 10 of the 98 teachers in the school were African-American, though 40% of the students were black. She also observed that the African-American teachers taught lower-level classes. Connie was very dedicated and strived to motivate the young people in her classes, who were mostly African-American students.

The system had tracked most of these students into the low level when they were in the first grade, and they had remained there. Although they seemed to like and respect Connie, they were not interested in learning about science. In fact, they did not seem to care about much of anything to do with school. Most of them said they were just waiting to drop out. This was very discouraging for Connie.

At the end of the year, Connie asked that she be given some upper-level classes along with the lower classes. This request was not granted. However, at the end of the next year, she was more persistent. She was told that she may be given some upper-level classes but would not be given any "advanced" classes. After further investigation, Connie realized that there were students assigned to the advanced level who could go all the way through school without ever having an African-American teacher.

The following year a new, young, Caucasian teacher was hired. She was inexperienced and asked Connie for assistance. Connie provided her with help in planning and gave her materials. The young teacher was most appreciative of the help received throughout the year. At the beginning of the next year, the young teacher was told that she would be assigned to teach the advanced biology classes. She objected and said that she did not feel ready to do this. However, she was told by the administrator that, since the teacher who taught these classes the previous year was gone, she had no choice. Of course, Connie was very disheartened. When she asked the principal about her request to teach these classes, he told her it had been misplaced and he had forgotten about it.

Another year, the principal told Connie that the advanced class would be too stressful for her because she was pregnant.

Finally, the principal admitted that there were some students whose parents would not want them to have a black teacher. "If you don't like it, then maybe you don't belong here." This comment was made to her at 8:30 one morning. Connie wanted to walk out. But she had students waiting for her. She went back to her classroom.

Because Connie dared to question the way she was treated and the system's practice of tracking children in the first grade, she felt that remarks were made to her by the principal to humiliate her. Some of the faculty also began to treat her differently.

Connie's three-year-old son was denied admittance to the school's preschool program. She was told that it was because she did not sign him up when he was born. However, the new Caucasian coach got his child into the class in his first year at the school.

Connie wanted to quit. But she loved to teach and she needed the money. She wanted to initiate a lawsuit. But legal fees were outrageously high. She wanted to cry. And she did.

Conclusions

Tracking serves to limit the number of African-American teachers who enter and remain in the profession in two ways. First, tracking limits the number of African-American students who enter college. The large number of minorities who are tracked in the early grades never are provided with opportunities in school that would lead to preparation and readiness for college. Therefore, education competes with business and industry for a small number of potential candidates. If the barriers that inhibit college preparation for minorities were removed, a larger pool of candidates would enter college, some of whom probably would choose to enter the teaching profession.

Second, the tracking of students also allows administrators to track teachers. The consistent assignment of African-American teachers to low-ability tracks (with all the problems inherent with these tracks) does not provide an enticing future for those considering teaching as a profession. A recent report by Metropolitan Life (1992) indicated that teachers who work with large numbers of minority and low-income children are significantly more likely to leave the profession in the first five years.

As we compare advantages and disadvantages of moving away from strict ability grouping and tracking, we must think first of our children.

However, we also should be aware that the procedures we use in our schools affect the lives of teachers and the future of our profession. Tracking is detrimental to both populations. A move away from this practice should help to ameliorate many of the problems we have in recruiting and retaining minority teachers.

References

Deever, B. "Desegregation in a Southern School System, 1968-1974: Power/ Resistance and the Discourse of Exclusion." *Journal of Education* 174, no. 3 (1992): 66-88.

Graham, P.A. "Black Teachers: A Drastically Scarce Resource." *Phi Delta Kappan* 68, no. 8 (1987): 598-605.

Metropolitan Life Foundation. *The American Teacher*. New York, 1988.

Metropolitan Life Foundation. *The American Teacher*. New York, 1992.

Page, F.M., Jr., and Page, J.A. "Teachers' Perceptions of the Teaching Profession and Educational Reform." Paper presented at the annual meeting of the American Educational Research Association, Boston, April 1990.

Page, J.A., and Page, F.M., Jr. "Gaining Access into Academe: Perceptions and Experiences of African-American Teachers." *Urban League Review* 15, no. 1 (1991): 27-39.

Page, J.A.; Page, F.M., Jr.; and Battle, D.A. "The Plight of African-American Teachers in the Deep South: An Analysis of Case Studies." Paper presented at the annual conference of the Association for Supervision and Curriculum Development, Washington, D.C., March 1993.

Professional Standards Commission. *Profile of Georgia Public School Personnel, 1985-1990*. 3rd ed. Atlanta, 1991.

HOLISTIC EDUCATION LEADERSHIP AND THE TRACKING CONTROVERSY

BY MALCOLM KATZ

Leaders need to ask what impact tracking has on the culture of the school. For example, does tracking bring with it an undue emphasis on differentiated learning potential? Is there a general belief in tracked schools that "some kids can learn, some can't," along with the behavioral norms that accompany that belief? Are the norms for teacher behavior in the tracked school based on the assumption that, since children "earn" their placement in groups, it is the students' fault when they seem unable to learn and little can be done by the teachers to change it? Are supervisory behaviors in tracked schools focused on teaching strategies for each of the special subpopulations, rather than on principles of teaching for all children?

Does tracking affect the beliefs and assumptions of the children beyond just their self-esteem? Do children in tracked schools believe that what is important is the group they are in, rather than what they are learning?

The perceptions and expectations of parents and other adults can be powerfully influenced by tracking. Do the processes that determine placement in a group become a central concern of parents? Will parents' expectations of the school and their images of sound educational practice be shaped by the philosophy and the organizational realities of the tracked school? Also, will tracking cause the local board of education to give excessive concern to the progress of such subgroups as gifted students and slower learners, rather than to the progress of all students?

Answering these large questions is critical to understanding tracking issues. That they have not been pursued with vigor is no surprise. One part of the problem is our historically narrow, simplistic approach to serious questions in education. As the tracking issue exemplifies, it has been the norm in education for discussions about school improvement to proceed from a premise that there is some "one thing" that needs to be changed. For example, class size, parent involvement, and time-on-task, as well as grouping, are familiar issues that have been examined as individual problems.

However, we now are witnessing the ascendance of four important new ways of looking at change: the restructuring movement, the effective schools/school improvement movement, the school-cultures movement, and the new inquiry into education demographics. All of these attempt to explain what goes on in schools by systems approaches, rather than by controlled-variable, cause-effect models of education research.

The restructuring movement is concerned with tracking because of its effects on the way schools are governed and managed. Tracking mechanisms affect site-based management. The formal organization of a school into tracks can create informal teacher subsystems within the school. When principals create decision-making teams, they might use such groupings of teachers as a basis for appointment to committees in order to represent all ability levels by those who teach them. In this way, the organizational pattern becomes a major determinant of the process through which teacher empowerment takes place.

The effective schools movement has shown that, while each of the correlates of school effectiveness is critical, the successful implementation of any one factor will not produce significant improvement in pupil performance if the other correlates are not simultaneously put into place. Systemic changes are prerequisite to any real gains in the classroom (Lezotte 1981). One of the correlates of the effective schools movement is that teachers' behaviors convey the belief that all children can learn. Tracking contradicts that correlate.

Those concerned with school culture also should be concerned about tracking. School culture is "built through the everyday business of school life. It is the way business is handled that forms and reflects the culture" (Saphier and King 1985, p. 72). The norms, beliefs, and assumptions in a tracked school help create the culture of that school.

Will the development of artifacts, stories, and traditions in a tracked school support collegiality among all faculty, or will they support informal subgroups based on the tracking system? Will beliefs about children and learning support a common endeavor, or will those beliefs be applicable only to subgroups of students?

A fourth major movement is concerned with the social conditions that shape the child's experience before starting school and during the school years. External conditions have a significant impact on what happens inside schools. Education leaders need to examine the interrelations between demographic factors and tracking.

The holistic approach grows out of systems organizational theory, developed by Easton (1965) and others. Systems theory posits that each element of a system, including schools, is interactive with the others and with certain aspects of the environment beyond the system, such as the neighborhood and the community, state and nation, employment and demography, and so on. We are able to understand events in the education arena only by understanding the interaction among the elements of the system.

However, most school leaders rarely use systems theory as the basis for thought and action. Their earliest learning about the scientific method, their training in education research as undergraduates, their graduate-school writing and dissertation work, and the research literature they read as practitioners have equated research and improvement strategies with carefully controlled, cause-and-effect modes of inquiry. Most professionals have not internalized a way of synthesizing this traditional research with systems theory. While administration texts today tell about systems, behavior is based on a conception of change that parallels academic training, which emphasizes controlled experiments.

Old Improvement Model, New Improvement Model

The problem with the older model arises when a well-researched strategy does not bring about the desired result or produces results too limited to answer a need. For example, we still see enormous class and race differences in pupil achievement despite our best efforts to improve the technology of the classroom. Apparently, changing the events within the classroom or school, while helpful, is insufficient to produce noteworthy gains for students. The important implication is that, if we persevere in this model of improvement, we may be responsible for perpetuating a pattern of insufficient results.

The "new" model is characterized by strategies that are more inclusive, harder to define, and much less likely to be demonstrated by a traditional quantitative research study. If the new model becomes the norm, it will bring three major arenas for change in education leadership: changes for the practitioner, changes for the researchers, and changes for the preparation of practitioners through higher education and staff development.

Changes for the Practitioner. A continuing dilemma concerns the focus of the leadership role: Is it to be instructional leadership or institutional management? The new model suggests that neither will be sufficient. The reform movement of the 1980s called for instructional leadership as the preeminent role. But the role of the leader in the 1990s will be much broader. It will embrace all the subsystems of the organization, not merely the instructional; and it will attend more consciously to factors beyond the school. The education administrator increasingly will see himself or herself as the executive leader of the entire enterprise and view that enterprise as existing within an environment that strongly affects it. When the scope of the leadership role is broadened, the decision structure of the school or system will be realigned so that teachers and others also will lead — convene, chair, plan, recommend, evaluate progress, and facilitate group process. In short, teachers will perform the activities and engage in the processes normally associated with the leader role.

Two implications follow from these changes. First, managing shared leadership requires improved skills of delegation, supervision, and control or follow-up. Second, the administrative leader will need to work through the issue of what decision areas he or she "keeps." Mission, goals, strategic planning, major personnel processes and decisions, evaluating program quality, resource allocation, and school-community relations are some of the task areas that may continue to be — or come to be — handled primarily by the executive leader. Other areas may be delegated. Among these will be teaching methodology, materials selection, and working with individual student or parent problems.

The new model will emphasize the leader's role as a culture builder directly responsible for creating with others an environment that encourages teaching and learning. The new model sees the elements of culture, such as those identified by Saphier and King (1985), as an interrelated and synergistic whole, which requires a more holistic approach to leadership than we have practiced in the past.

The new model suggests that education leaders will serve as brokers and bridge builders between the school and other agencies that serve youth. Because the conditions of youth are powerful factors in learning, the schools must take an activist role in mitigating these influences or risk continued failure. Tomorrow's principals and superintendents will work with health agencies concerned with prevention and treatment of communicable diseases and teen pregnancy, with social agencies to address child abuse and family dysfunction, and with welfare agencies in matters of poverty and jobs (Kirst 1991). This will be a continuing role, rather than an occasional or special-project activity. Consistent with this role will be a revival of the community-school movement and re-emphasis of parent and citizen education.

A caveat is in order. There will be objections from those who contend, with good reason, that the school cannot and should not take on all the services to children and youth. But the point is that social and demographic factors are critical variables in the solution of school problems, and there is growing public recognition of the connection. Education leaders will work more directly with other community agencies precisely because the schools cannot take on the role as sole providers of comprehensive youth services.

Finally, it seems likely that education leaders will come to use systems organizational theory, whether consciously or not, as a framework for action. They will become more aware of how the subsystems in education relate to one another. For example, teacher selection will be based on the organizational mission and goals and through teacher-involved committees. The new leader will become more aware that demands for uniform procedures and behavior may negatively affect efforts to extend creativity and experimentation. Education leaders will recognize that initiatives are sometimes "contraindicated," to borrow the physicians' term, and that steps may need to be taken to lessen the impact of one action or program on others. In sum, education leaders will act more holistically and will understand that important actions, events, or processes within the system are interactive; and they will take steps to capitalize on synergy or minimize a negative outcome.

Changes for Research. The new model suggests that research on the interrelated elements of organization or on elements affected by a single variable, such as the research of Blumberg and Greenfield (1986) on the work of principals, holds high promise for addressing school problems. Naturalistic research designs provide "an emergent plan for a highly interactive process of gathering data from which analysis will be developed" (Owens 1987, p. 294).

The new model strongly suggests that the changes that are important to school improvement are not discovered through traditional experimental and quasi-experimental, cause-and-effect research. One of the delusions of the empirical research model is that children's learning can be understood as a series of isolated schooling events. But we know that pupil readiness and motivation are conditioned, in part, by what happens in their lives outside the school. Another delusion is that in-classroom events are unrelated to the rest of the life of the school. A third is that school improvement can be treated without any consideration of school system conditions (Katz 1987). One of the reasons that superintendents and principals have been largely untouched by much education research is that they intuitively sense this inconsistency between the reality of the school or system and the research design on which the proposed improvement is based (Heller, Conway, and Jacobson 1988).

Changes in the Professional Preparation of Education Leaders. Three kinds of change might take place as a result of more holistic conceptions. The first is a movement toward a more integrated approach to the graduate curriculum in education leadership. For example, Murphy (1990) recommends that such a program feature interdisciplinary experiences and that a significant problem of practice, not a specific discipline, be the organizing dynamic.

A second change may be the broader use of the case method and other treatments of school leadership that promote the study of situations and solutions reflecting the total reality of the specific problem being examined. This contrasts with the traditional approach of dissecting professional practice according to subdisciplines, such as school law, personnel, and supervision. We also may see a change in the kinds of problems that students choose for papers, theses, and dissertations. Our academic tradition has been to reshape the student's proposal to fit the cause-effect model, to restrict the student's interest, to narrow and isolate the topic, and then to inquire into the effects of the controlled variable. While such studies will continue to be essential for building the knowledge base, studies that pursue a naturalistic design will grow alongside them. Increasingly, the aim will be to discover from reality and to experiment with intervention models consisting of several elements, as in the work of Pajak and Glickman.

A third change will be the development of programs to prepare education leaders to work with those in other fields who serve the school population, such as health care, social work, mental health, recreation, and religion. Kirst (1991) suggests that "universities have a major role in designing interprofessional preparation through interprofessional courses, continuing education, and interprofessional policy analysis" (p. 617). He notes that Ohio State University has been offering such a program for more than a decade.

Summary

As a result of four major movements that were central to education during the late 1980s and early 1990s, there has been a change in the way education leaders think about improving schools, a new orientation to thought and action. These four movements concern: 1) restructuring, 2) effective schools and school improvement, 3) the "school as culture," and 4) demography. These movements are causing educators to think about school problems as sets of interrelated elements, both within and beyond the schools. Although school leaders historically have been taught to see education problems as isolated series of discrete variables and to seek solutions that reflect rationalistic research, they have been suspicious of research findings based on studies so controlled as to bear little resemblance to the realities they faced.

These four movements will affect education leaders in three ways. First, they will see problems and solutions, such as learning deficits and tracking, as multiple and integrated, rather than as isolated and focused. They will view their role as that of an executive leader of the system, rather than as either institutional manager or instructional leader. Brokering and building bridges with other community agencies will become regular, rather than special, parts of their job. And culture building will become one of their central preoccupations.

Second, research on leadership will become more inclusive. Qualitative studies and case histories, among other types of naturalistic research, will gain respectability. Holistic approaches will be seen as potential sources of major improvement in achieving educational outcomes. Rationalistic research will be seen as just part of the larger, naturalistic picture. Variables in the environment of the schools will become, through naturalistic research designs, legitimate topics of education research. The results of research will become more credible to education leaders as research designs more closely reflect the conditions of practice.

Third, the professional preparation of education leaders will change as the curriculum and methods of instruction shift toward the integration of the disciplines, rather than their isolation. The preparation of education leaders will include content and training that will help them to enter into their roles with other community agencies.

As the profession moves in these directions, it will become better equipped to put the pieces of the puzzle together, to integrate theory and practice, and to adopt a more holistic approach to education leadership. In such a context, administrators facing decisions on tracking will seek out research findings and problem-solving approaches that go beyond the old model of narrowly conceived experimental designs and problem-solving strategies. They will examine criteria that go beyond test results and self-esteem measures. Holistic education leaders will ask about the effects of tracking on the culture of the school, on practice within the school, on the formal and informal decision-making structures in the school, and on the groups outside the school that play such an important role in shaping events within it.

References

Blumberg, A., and Greenfield, W. *The Effective Principal: Perspectives on School Leadership*. 2nd ed. Boston: Allyn and Bacon, 1986.

Easton, D. *A Framework for Political Analysis*. Englewood Cliffs, N.J.: Prentice-Hall, 1965.

Heller, R.W.; Conway, J.A.; and Jacobson, S.L. "Here's Your Blunt Critique of Administrative Preparation." *The Executive Educator* 10, no. 9 (1988): 18-30.

Katz, M. "Superintending for Effective Schools." *The Effective School Report* 5, no. 7 (1987): 2-3, 6.

Kirst, M.W. "Improving Children's Services: Overcoming Barriers, Creating New Opportunities." *Phi Delta Kappan* 72, no. 8 (1991): 615-18.

Lezotte, L.W. "Climate Characteristics in Instructionally Effective Schools." *Impact on Instructional Improvement* (Summer 1981): 26-31.

Murphy, J.F. "Restructuring the Technical Core of Preparation Programs in Educational Administration." *UCEA Review* 31, no. 3 (1990): 4-5, 10-13.

Owens, R. *Organizational Behavior in Education*. Englewood Cliffs, N.J.: Prentice-Hall, 1987.

Pajak, E.F., and Glickman, C.D. "Dimensions of School District Improvement." *Educational Leadership* 46, no. 8 (1989): 61-64.

Saphier, J., and King, M. "Good Seeds Grow in Strong Cultures." *Educational Leadership* 42, no. 6 (1985): 67-74.

BEYOND TRACKING, WHAT? DISCURSIVE PROBLEMS AND POSSIBILITIES

BY BRYAN DEEVER

This is a speculative essay on the genesis and sustenance of tracking, or grouping by ability or achievement, and the possibilities for practical change. It is an essay full of "what ifs," not a presentation of "scientific data." The terms *tracking* and *grouping* are used as synonyms in this essay. Therefore, when I use *tracking*, it should be understood to encompass all differentiating practices. I am not ignorant of the fact that the two actions are usually separated in terms of their focus — one on student organization, the other on the differentiation of curriculum content — but I argue that the same assumptions inform and support both practices. In this sense, when we differentiate between tracking and grouping, we are merely talking about different ends of the same horse.

Tracking, through its construction of rigid social and epistemological hierarchies, is an inherently undemocratic educational practice (Giroux and McLaren 1988; Oakes 1985). The deleterious effects of tracking, particularly on minority cultures, have been clearly documented (Banks and Banks 1989; Nieto 1991; Oakes 1990*a*, 1990*b*; Oakes and Lipton 1990).

This book considers a future beyond tracking. A review of the program of the Phi Delta Kappa Leadership Skill Institute that spurred the development of this book reveals scholarly emphases in such areas as alternative forms of classroom instruction, metacognition, peer relations, curriculum reform, and classroom organization (*Beyond Tracking*, 1992). However, these various emphases share one common characteristic: Each addresses embedded problems in tracking. Oakes, Gamoran, and Page (1992) cite three issues that consistently have held center stage in the public and academic debate about tracking: Does it work? Is it fair? Does it enhance or compromise our ability to transmit the knowledge and values we want our students to appropriate? Although these questions and others regarding the effects of tracking should be addressed vigorously, they are but symptoms of a deeper problem.

If one were to bracket out or somehow mitigate the negative consequences of tracking — as many have attempted to do through alternative forms of pedagogy and curricular organization — what argument would then exist for its elimination? None. The bulk of our interaction with tracking lies in consideration of its effects on students, but we fail to consider the assumptions supporting its pedagogy. It is on this point that I wish to focus. And, in this regard, I pose two questions:

1. What are the assumptions that endorse tracking as a legitimate form of educational practice?
2. Why does tracking seem to make sense to so many people?

Tracking is a protrusion, a visible point of application that is supported by a larger system of unstudied assumptions about schools and schooling. These assumptions lie deeply embedded in the language and rationale of daily education work and take the form of commonsense truths, bypassing any need for education workers to question their validity. But what if the "truths" are flawed? What if they are inherently exclusionary? Will eliminating practices based on these assumptions change the assumptions themselves? My response is, probably not. By continuing to focus almost exclusively on tracking practices and not their supporting rationale, we are treating the symptoms rather than the disease.

Discursive Problems

The Structures of Discourse. I want to draw a very clear understanding of *discourse* as a closed system of words and the application of words within particular social and ideological contexts that simultaneously define a specific constellation of meaning and exclude other closed systems (Deever 1991, p. 73). The discourse of schooling, as it currently exists, endorses the practice of tracking. In fact, the dominant language of schooling is a language of differentiation and exclusion. In a sense, these are internally coherent sets of assumptions ("truths") that frame ideas and act as practical referents for social action.

On this discursive terrain are constructed the frameworks of meaning that support all education work. Ultimately, these meanings become articulated in such practices as tracking. Therefore, practice is inseparable from the supporting discourse that supplies both a rationale for its existence and a set of boundaries for its application. No matter how benevolent or detached the assumptive rationale, the substantive results of tracking are still the same: the social stratification of individuals and the creation of hierarchies of knowledge and resources.

As a comprehensive system of thought interwoven with ideological and epistemological suppositions, discourse is complete and self-sustaining. What we call "truth" is really "discursive truth," which exists only within the framework of the discourse. However, given the closed nature of discursive systems, such truths appear to be transcendent. This is a critical point. Practice is built on this framework.

Discursive Practice. If all social action is grounded in assumptions that provide referents for daily life, then these referents act as orientation points for discursive practice. The nature of this practice articulates the essential beliefs of the supporting discourse. The relationship between discourse and practice is symbiotic. Not only do practices receive their genesis in the discourse, but the results of those actions affect the discourse itself. These effects might take the form of reinforcing and reifying the basic assumptions, or they might produce some modification in one or more assumptions. Discourse is a dynamic and fluid universe of meaning — constructed, mediated, and capable of being modified through social action.

Discourse and Schooling. The dominant discourse of schooling is a hybrid of meanings held together by a perennial epistemology and a positivist gestalt. The positivist domain supplies us with a universe in which reality is orderly, observable, and generalizable. This leads to the construction of discursive forms emphasizing standardization and empirical verification. The perennial epistemology provides a basis for the construction of an absolute, finite body of eternal truth/knowledge that transcends both history and context.

Since meaning is fixed in this dominant discourse, pedagogy must center on the transmission of that truth/knowledge. The positivist influence dictates that this transmission be done efficiently. Robert Hutchins summed up the relationship between these epistemological assumptions and pedagogy when he wrote: "Education implies teaching. Teaching implies knowledge. Knowledge is truth. Truth is everywhere the same. Hence education should be everywhere the same" (1962, p. 66).

Thus discursive truth supports the construction of discursive forms. Three particularly powerful discursive truths support the practice of tracking: native ability, transcendent truth, and commodity knowledge.

Native ability is the belief that our intelligence is individually measurable and has finite limits. These predetermined limits might be culturally or ethnically based. If this is true, then (discursively speaking) it is sensible to group students by their levels of ability in order to facilitate the most efficient learning.

The concept of transcendent truth posits that truth and knowledge are discrete and timeless entities separate from the confusion of human experience. Truth/knowledge, in this form, is affected neither by time nor by context. Because of its relatively stable nature, truth/knowledge can be organized into discrete parcels to be dispensed to students in some standardized manner. The result is a decontextualized and de-politicized view of curriculum content as inherently neutral and value-free. Its worth is measured through accumulation and application.

This leads to the discursive assumption of knowledge as commodity. If schools exist primarily as reproductive sites where extant knowledge is transferred to succeeding generations, it might be argued that the process of education simply revolves around the accumulation of the commodity being offered. As with other forms of consumption, the surest method of control is in the allocation of the commodity resource. In schools, students compete for larger shares of the inequitably allocated knowledge product. Fortunately, at least from the perspective of those in power, we have the discursive means available to regulate this process and to ensure that each group receives the amount of commodity knowledge appropriate to its predetermined abilities. Such a plan is necessary if the transmission of knowledge is to be efficient and orderly, for waste is intolerable in schooling. Whether it be time, "human resources," or knowledge, thrift through effective management is the order of the day.

Grouping as Discursive Form. The frameworks of meaning that compose discursive forms draw their existence from discursive truth. Let us explore grouping as an example. The two primary grouping differentiations are ability and achievement. Ability grouping draws largely on the discursive truth of native ability and the positivist rationale. Native ability supplies the argument that there are finite, measurable

90

limits to our learning capabilities, while the positivist rationale provides for a whole series of "objective scientific tests" to measure those limits. Grouping by achievement would seem, on the surface, to be a more equitable discursive form. In fact, it appears to be antithetical to grouping by ability. But in looking beyond the surface, one discovers the same set of flawed assumptions.

Although specifics might be debated, the grounding assumption is clear: mastery of a discrete body of organized "truth." Thus we are brought back to underlying discursive beliefs in transcendent truth and commodity knowledge. If truth/knowledge is, in fact, the same for everyone, then surely we can measure the relative amount of the commodity one has been able to accumulate. Achievement, therefore, is superior to consumption and digestion (in the sense that one is able to synthesize and apply). Therefore, it must be argued that whether one engages in grouping by ability or achievement, one still proceeds from the same flawed assumptions.

Discursive Possibilities

Little can be done to mitigate the powerful effect that this discourse exerts on the landscape of schooling. However, it is possible to engage in an informed, systematic process of interrogating and revising the discursive assumptions informing educational work. The final form such a revised discourse might take is pure conjecture at this point, but there are two possible revisions we might visit at this time.

Concerning the positivist belief in a measurable and generalizable social universe, what if the reverse were true? What if, in fact, social reality were a relative concept defined not *for us*, but rather *by us* as individuals? Consider the effects on the discursive truth. Native ability would no longer carry its predetermined eugenic power. The tenets of standardization would become suspect, mitigating the unquestioned acceptance of "scientific" tests and measurements. Education might begin to be perceived as an open-ended process, rather than a closed course, thus rendering obsolete our emphasis on benchmarking and the transmission of truth/knowledge in predetermined doses at predetermined times to predetermined groups. The entire emphasis might shift from control to exploration.

What then of perennial epistemology? Is it possible to envision an approach to schooling that is built on something other than the transmission of transcendent truth/knowledge? What if, in fact, we are both producers and consumers of knowledge? What if knowledge is a highly individualized construct that is mediated by each of us through our personal experiences? How then could knowledge be a commodity? Knowledge acquisition would become a highly subjective enterprise. Is it possible that we are, in fact, engaged in such a subjective enterprise at this time, while camouflaging our actions under the guise of objectivity? I would argue that we are, much to the detriment of those we seek to educate.

If we were to eliminate these two sets of assumptions, the entire framework of established "truth" that supports tracking would be destabilized. It would no longer be necessary to attempt to reduce the negative impact of tracking, nor to eliminate it as a field of application; the rationale for its very existence would collapse.

This is important. If tracking is eliminated but the supporting rationale is left untouched, then I suspect that other, equally negative forms of practice would rise to fill the void. Thus the discourse must be articulated. The flawed assumptions must be expressed. And we must eradicate tracking at its source. We must remove the thing that gives it sustenance. We must rewrite the discourse.

References

Banks, J.A., and Banks, C.A. *Multicultural Education: Issues and Perspectives*. Boston: Allyn and Bacon, 1989.

Beyond Tracking. Official program from the Phi Delta Kappa Leadership Skill Institute, Savannah, Ga., November 1992.

Deever, B. "Critical Pedagogy: The Concretization of Possibility." *Contemporary Education* 61, no. 2 (1991): 71-76.

Giroux, H.A., and McLaren, P. "Reproducing Reproduction: The Politics of Tracking." In *Teachers as Intellectuals: Toward a Critical Pedagogy of Learning*, edited by H.A. Giroux. Granby, Mass.: Bergin and Garvey, 1988.

Hutchins, R.M. *The Higher Learning in America*. 1936. Reprint. New Haven, Conn.: Yale University Press, 1962.

Nieto, S. *Affirming Diversity: The Sociopolitical Context of Multicultural Education*. New York: Longman, 1991.

Oakes, J. *Keeping Track: How Schools Structure Inequality*. New Haven, Conn.: Yale University Press, 1985.

Oakes, J. *Lost Talent: The Underparticipation of Women, Minorities, and Disabled Persons in Science*. Santa Monica, Calif.: Rand Corporation, 1990. a

Oakes, J. *Multiplying Inequalities: The Effects of Race, Social Class, and Tracking on Opportunities to Learn Math and Science*. Santa Monica, Calif.: Rand Corporation, 1990. b

Oakes, J.; Gamoran, A.; and Page, R.N. "Curriculum Differentiation: Opportunities, Outcomes, and Meanings." In *Handbook of Research on Curriculum*, edited by P.W. Jackson. New York: Macmillan, 1992.

Oakes, J., and Lipton, M. "Tracking and Ability Grouping: A Structural Barrier to Access to Knowledge." In *Access to Knowledge*, edited by J.I. Goodlad. New York: Teachers College Press, 1990.

THE DILEMMA OF TRACKING AND GROUPING IN EARLY CHILDHOOD AND MIDDLE GRADES: ARE WE SPEAKING THE SAME LANGUAGE?

BY JAMES J. BARTA AND
MICHAEL G. ALLEN

This chapter presents a brief dialogue between an early childhood specialist and a middle-grades specialist on the relative merits of academic tracking and ability grouping. The interchange depicts a critical discussion of the impact of each person's perceptions and school-based practices on the other. Blame is directed and fingers are pointed. Yet by sharing individual perspectives, these two educators discover a common ground for a more fruitful interchange that leads to an action plan for breaking the academic and psychological bonds of ability grouping and academic tracking. The focus of this session is on eliciting a shared commitment to changing such school-based practices in early childhood and the middle grades.

The Dialogue

Mike: Jim, we both know that the volume of research on academic tracking and ability grouping demands some sort of reasonable response. I know you were not happy with my point the other day that you early childhood folks hand us a *fait acompli* in that all students are effectively tracked academically by the time they enter the middle grades.

Jim: No, you completely misunderstand! Tracking is not an invention of early childhood educators wanting to decide young children's academic — and I might add, social — fate. The pressure to fill them with gross amounts of decontextualized and fragmented facts comes from misguided middle-grades teachers who are far more concerned with training than educating.

Mike: I disagree. Look at the reading, writing, and computational skills these kids have when they leave you. We in the middle grades are forced to track in an effort to prepare students for the intellectual rigors of high school. On top of this, we are challenged to address the developmental realities of early adolescence as well as to extend academic and social-skill learning.

Jim: You have just said it yourself. In speaking of reading, writing, and computational skills, what aspects of the child have you considered in your quest to train for high school? Mike, I believe our system of education, whether you agree with me or not, is blindly focused on academic excellence for a few and very willing to disregard those who are assessed as "less able." Education seems to be defined as something only for training the intellect, rather than as a vehicle for promoting a more holistic perspective of education.

Mike: Wow! That's a mouthful. You have my attention. It sounds like we may share more in common than I thought.

Jim: Tracking has served the limited definition of education well. Its purpose is to sort those students who seemingly "have" from those who seemingly "have not" early on in their education careers. Once tracked, particularly in the lower-ability groups, students receive inadequate education that expands the gap between them and those judged to be more capable. Simply stated, once placed there, they usually remain at that "level," regardless of academic performance.

Like Oakes (1986), I believe the drive to track permeates the entire system, and even greater pressure is exerted in the upper grades. This "top-down" pressure, again accentuating academic achievement to the exclusion of other aspects of the whole child, tends to dictate the grouping and academic-tracking practices elementary educators follow.

Certainly academics are vital but not to the exclusion of all that childhood represents. We do not meet children's needs when we view some children as disposable or as simply young people to prepare for the next grade level. In our haste to accomplish this goal, we lose something very precious. We become so entrapped in the ritual of education that we have closed our eyes to what is really happening.

Mike: Jim, I am intrigued by your perspective on grouping and tracking, since you raise the very same issues that challenge us at the middle-grades levels when you speak of academic pressure and developmental needs. I am reminded of a statement in a book I read years ago that is still in my professional library. I think Hullfish and Smith (1961) captured your perspective when they wrote about the education processes we follow. [Mike reads from the book]:

> We are in no doubt about the end we seek. We are simply not clear that this end must be given meaning in the daily run of life's activities and used there as a principle against which to judge the adequacy of what may seem at the moment to be more demanding ends. In consequence, we have developed practices, under the guise of proper housekeeping and in the name of efficiency, which now seem so normal that we fail to see that our acts deny our words. (p. 16)

Jim: That's great! Just my point. Let me offer a few more specific examples, apologizing in advance if I sound as if I am preaching. Developmentally appropriate practice with preschool children embraces a curriculum that encourages active discovery, choice, social learning, and creativity. Few raise a stink with this style of education at this level because of what really is at stake. When children enter formal education, starting in the first grade, the focus takes on an academic intent that seems to open the doors to improper pedagogical and organizational practices like ability grouping and academic tracking.

Why we suddenly switch gears and move from a child-centered approach to one where children are often passive recipients of facts and information is a question I puzzle over. We in early childhood stress the importance of allowing all aspects of the child to expand and flourish. In our classrooms we must respect and nurture the social, physical, and emotional needs of children, as well as their intellectual needs.

We, too, want our children to master certain skills and knowledge, not so much for the fact that these skills and knowledge will prepare them for the adult world, but so they will flourish in their "child" world. Let us give the children what is rightfully theirs, namely a special time free from undue stress and pressure to explore and discover, to question and search, as we guide all children to achieve their own excellence. Let us educate them for the future by respecting where they are now and helping them to grow and learn. I do not argue that one of the goals of education is the continued development toward the adult citizen, but are we not sacrificing much that is "childhood" in the meantime?

Mike: Yes, I guess we are. And it sounds as if we in the middle grades need to listen to other teachers more closely. Jim, I think you would make a fine middle school teacher. When I consider what research states about appropriate middle-grades education, I realize that many of the same tenets are being promoted at both levels. Curricular changes adapted to the needs of middle-schoolers, rather than the other way around, are being designed and implemented. Active discovery, hands-on learning, heterogeneous grouping, and cooperative groups are promoted.

Jim: I have been thinking about the discussion we had a few days ago and honestly feel that, when compared, the desires of the developmentally centered elementary teacher and those of the middle school teachers really are not that different. Rather than blame one another for causing inappropriate grouping and tracking practices, the solution lies in coming together.

We face many of the same difficulties as we educate our children. Seeing our students as a shared treasure is the first step in beginning the dialogue that derails ability grouping and academic tracking and revives equitable education for the whole child. If we can come together and dream our dreams as one, realizing that we share our students as they grow and mature, perhaps at long last we can truly educate our children.

Mike: You have captured what I have been saying about middle-graders for the past 26 years. I am frankly amazed at the parallels between our two professional worlds.

Jim: There is even more we can do, Mike. Fundamental change must occur as we collectively lobby for a major redefinition of education. These changes, however drastic they may appear, are not mystical or beyond reach.

Interestingly, the roots of many promising practices lie in the ideas promoted by past education thinkers such as Deutsch, Dewey, and Piaget. We do not have to reinvent the wheel, for much of what we need is currently available. What is clearly called for is a return to a philosophical orientation that respects the child as a whole person with talents to expand and gifts to share. This hinges on a new and dynamic perspective.

Mike: You make many excellent points, Jim. Let's search for some common ground between us that we might build on. First, you need to understand that when your students enter the middle grades, it is a dramatically different sociocultural environment from elementary school. Additionally, they themselves are changing in important ways. You pass them on to us at a developmental point that changes daily, if not hourly!

These kids are beginning to experience physical, social, emotional, and intellectual changes that, when complete, produce young adults. All this happens at a time when academic expectations increase substantially. It strikes me that your students, too, experience a degree of heightened academic expectations and are coping with their own developmental challenges. I guess I am left with the question, "What can we do?"

Jim: I suggest that we share the information we recently challenged each other to secure on the issue of ability grouping and academic tracking. Then we can briefly relate those findings to our respective areas of responsibility.

Mike: Sounds good, Jim. Why don't you go first?

Jim: Okay. I'll share my findings on ability grouping and the young child.

Ability Grouping and Tracking of the Young Child

Tracking does two things: It promotes elitism, and it facilitates segregation. It is an instructional practice from the past that damages students in the name of education. It condones a very narrow definition of education that places greater value on some than others. Very often these "others" receive a less complete education and are viewed as less capable learners. We track because our current education structure is unable or simply unwilling to address each child's multifaceted potential.

Current tracking and grouping processes are grounded in basic assumptions that include the following:

1. Education should focus on academic achievement. Social, emotional, and physical development is of secondary importance.
2. Young children can be accurately and appropriately assessed and instructionally placed, often using limited formal assessment that may include data from subtests from a standardized test battery.
3. Tracking benefits all children.
4. Children with seemingly lower ability levels need a slower learning pace and a curriculum with less content.
5. Children of average or low ability impede the academic achievement of more academically gifted children.

The National Association for the Education of Young Children, America's largest organization of early childhood educators, states that we must meet the needs of our children by teaching them in ways that are developmentally appropriate (NAEYC 1987). Developmentally appropriate practice (DAP) involves two key aspects:

1. Instruction must be individually appropriate: Every child is a multifaceted embodiment of abilities, experiences, culture, and learning styles.
2. Instruction must be age appropriate: The special abilities of young children and their maturational development must be respected and understood. Instruction must equally address the physical, social, emotional, and intellectual domains of young children while helping them learn how to learn. These domains are complexly integrated and do not exist in isolation.

We must adapt our instruction to meet the needs of children. Childhood is indeed a very special time. The practices of ability grouping and tracking devalue all but the purely academic. A curriculum that focuses on academics while minimizing other aspects of the whole child is educating only a small portion of the child. The NAEYC states that the relevant principle related to instruction is that teachers of young children must be cognizant of the whole child.

Using DAP, young children are viewed as individuals with a wide variety of skills, abilities, interests, and needs. These differences are to be expected and respected. In fact, some researchers claim that within any group of children similar in age, there may exist a range of abilities from 12 months to two years.

Assessing young children should involve more critical observation and recording at regular intervals. This allows us a holistic picture of the child and provides meaningful data upon which to plan further instruction addressing individual needs. The inappropriate practice of tracking measures a child's worth based on a narrowly defined perspective of group expectations.

Young children have few opportunities to experience standardized tests. Asking them to do their best using formal assessment instruments that are foreign to their experience and that focus on basic facts and rote learning typifies education thinking that is completely out of touch with the developmental realities of early childhood.

Tracking simply does not benefit all children. In fact, it can be argued that it benefits no one. If I am working with a young child who is experiencing difficulty in a particular area, such as reading, and I place that child in a group with only poor readers as models, how will that child ever know what fluent, effective reading is all about? Teachers of children, particularly in lower ability groups, will admit that they hold lower expectations for their students and believe that they cannot take the children as far or as fast. This almost certainly dooms the children to that level of learning, perhaps for the remainder of their school lives. What hope is there that these children will ever be brought "up to speed"?

Socially, developing a child's self-esteem and positive feelings toward learning and others is critically important. We live in a world where the solutions to many of the monumental problems facing our communities, our nation, and our world will be brought about only through cooperation. We can no longer afford to lose some children along the way. Each child must be viewed as potentially the person who will help us discover a cure for AIDS or derive a solution to some political, social, or environmental problem we face.

Research proves that mixed-ability grouping improves achievement in children previously classified as having low or average ability. Further, for those labeled academically gifted, research shows that their achievement is not diminished as a result of heterogeneously mixed groups. Social benefits for all levels of children no longer enslaved in the inappropriate practice of tracking are numerous.

When children are placed in mixed groups where critical, divergent thinking is promoted, anyone can derive a unique solution to a problem. Children learn that each person possesses a unique perspective to be respected and accepted.

Simply stated, tracking is wrong. Realizing this is the first step toward truly educating young children. I have stated this once before but wish to say it again: We must respect children and teach them at their levels. Soon enough, they will grow up to assume adult roles. We must nurture and foster their current development. We do not need to reinvent the wheel to accomplish this, since instructional practices exist that meet the various needs of the young child.

Briefly, such practices include the following:

1. Cooperative groups, where children collectively improve their academic achievement while fostering positive social reliance and collaboration.
2. Multi-age classrooms, where the wide range of abilities that do exist among children are accepted and children learn at their own level, rather than at the arbitrary levels defined by specific grade-level expectations.
3. Integrative curriculum using themes and concepts as our frame of reference, where children learn to make sense of their world by

realizing the rich, complex relationships that exist among virtually all the things we study.

4. Guided and unguided discovery learning, teamed with structured critical thinking, problem solving, and decision making, where diversity is acknowledged.

Children are natural-born scientists, always searching and seeking. Let's encourage their development of these essential skills while they are young. Let's nurture their natural excitement about learning by inviting active participation in the process, rather than merely forcing them into narrow academic paths.

Mike: Now it is my turn, Jim. I see major parallels to the middle grades. Since you have covered the basics of ability grouping and academic tracking and their underlying assumptions, I will not replow that ground. However, I will try to relate how we might reframe such practices to come closer to meeting the unique developmental and educational needs of early adolescents.

Meeting the Needs of Middle-Level Students

One of the keys to changing grouping practices at the middle-grades levels is ITO — Interdisciplinary Team Organization. Within the ITO structure, all students are placed in heterogeneously organized teams, each of which represents a microcosm of the total school population. Such characteristics as age, gender, socioeconomic status, race, and academic ability (as measured by a wide variety of means) are taken into account.

ITO grouping options in middle grades that might mitigate against the worst excesses of ability grouping and academic tracking include the school-within-a-school concept, multi-age grouping, and student/ teacher progression. Each form of student grouping may be instituted independent of academic achievement, reflecting the multiplicity of student characteristics in a given school. Also, within any of these grouping arrangements, learning in cooperative groups is an excellent way to mix and match students of different academic abilities and personal interests.

Now that the middle school movement has achieved a measure of acceptance and credibility and revolutionized organizational patterns at this grade level, we need to focus on curriculum. Specifically, the integrated curriculum best reflects the essence of reality and how most of us learn. An integrated, thematic approach to subject matter at this level

102

is an excellent way to promote integration within diverse student groups.

Finally, I agree completely that more guided and unguided discovery learning, based on structured critical-thinking, problem-solving, and decision-making opportunities, is vital to supporting academic diversity and student learning of essential skills for life and living. At this point, we need to join together in putting forth our closing arguments.

Final Thoughts

The challenge is clear. The various solutions are equally apparent. We must begin to make major inroads toward altering traditional practices of ability grouping and academic tracking. The evidence points to a myriad of detrimental effects of such age-old practices.

We have attempted to frame the various arguments in the context of both early childhood and middle grades, since the practices are not unique to either level. While understanding is the first step to resolving the issue, communication among educators at both levels is essential if we expect to change one of the most entrenched aspects of the education structure. We trust that, on reflection, readers also might conclude that such a dialogue is a fruitful step in the direction of improving the quality of the educational experience for all students.

References

Deutsch, M. "A Theory of Cooperation and Competition." *Human Relations* 2, no. 2 (1949): 129-52.

Dewey, J. *The Child and the Curriculum.* 1902. Reprint. Chicago: University of Chicago Press, 1950.

Hullfish, H.G., and Smith, P.G. *Reflective Thinking: The Method of Education.* New York: Dodd, Mead, 1961.

National Association for the Education of Young Children (NAEYC). *Developmentally Appropriate Practice in Early Childhood Programs from Birth Through Age 8.* Washington, D.C., 1987.

Oakes, J. "Keeping Track, Part I: The Policy and Practice of Curriculum Inequity." *Phi Delta Kappan* 68, no. 1 (1986): 12-17.

Piaget, J. *The Psychology of Intelligence.* London: Routledge and Kegan Paul, 1950.

10

IDEAS AND PROGRAMS TO ASSIST IN THE UNTRACKING OF AMERICAN SCHOOLS

BY HOWARD D. HILL

As most educators are now aware, ability grouping (tracking) is the separation of students by ability into academic or career paths based on standardized test scores or past school performance. Students who score well on these indicators track into college and professional paths, while those who fare poorly enter tracks that stress vocational and general skills. Classroom activities for these "low-track" students generally entail worksheets and related mundane tasks that do little to challenge them along social, personal, or academic lines.

No matter how similar students may appear on the surface, each is unique. Each has different interests, abilities, and ways of learning. With this kind of diversity in today's classrooms, it is essential that teachers possess flexible, adaptable tools that permit students to learn at a comfortable pace in their own ways. Teachers must find ways to challenge students of different abilities in the same classroom. Toward this end, teachers must discover exciting new ways to stimulate student curiosity, encourage exploration, and meet individual needs. Teachers cannot afford to do less.

This chapter has two primary purposes: first, to indicate that the separation of children in schools on the basis of perceived ability does not achieve its intended purpose of improving the delivery of education and, second, to describe six distinct program activities that make a difference in students' classroom performance and achievement.

Since most teachers know that tracking is harmful to student progress, one might wonder why they continue to track students on the basis of ability. The answer is that many teachers do not have a repertoire of resources from which to plan and carry out activities for learners. Some teachers have not had the opportunity to shift their thinking from ability grouping to more desirable and meaningful educational approaches.

Ability Grouping: A Misguided Educational Effort

Data provided by the National Education Longitudinal Study of 1988 indicate that grouping students by ability worsens the academic prospects of low-achieving students while doing nothing to improve those of higher-achieving ones. Moreover, ability grouping also appears to lessen the chances that tracked students will relate well to children of different ethnic and racial groups. Given the segregative impact of ability grouping; the negative effects of grouping on such outcomes as self-esteem, delinquency, and dropping out; and the anti-egalitarian nature of the practice, there is little reason to maintain the between-class ability-grouping practices that are so prevalent in American middle and high schools and not uncommon at the elementary level (Schmidt 1992).

The study also found that low-track eighth-graders were much more likely to end up in non-college-preparatory programs in the 10th grade than were low-achievers who had not been tracked, suggesting that being placed in a low-ability track effectively slams the gate on any possibility that a student can take the courses leading to college. Low achievers who had been tracked indicated they felt less control over their fate than did their untracked counterparts (Schmidt 1992).

Oakes (1985; see also Oakes et al. 1990) reports a growing body of research on tracking and ability grouping that shows there are substantial harmful effects on low-income and minority students, who are over-represented in low tracks and face an unequal distribution of learning opportunities that favors the privileged. Oakes also found that high-track students have access to "high-status" content, including literature, expository and thematic writing, library research, and higher-order mathematical thinking, while their peers in lower tracks typically face workbooks and kits, low expectations, and exercises in language mechanics and computation. Students in the high track generally have more time to learn and greater exposure to effective teaching. Lower-track students, by contrast, receive the least time for learning and the lowest-quality instruction.

An obvious question must be raised: "Does tracking or ability grouping work?" After reviewing a complex body of literature on the topic, Oakes (1985) concludes that there is little credible evidence to support any of the assumptions about the merits of tracking and ability grouping. Indeed, the effects of tracking on student outcomes have been widely investigated, and the bulk of this work does not support commonly held beliefs that tracking increases student learning. Although existing tracking systems appear to provide advantages for students who are placed in the top tracks, the literature suggests that students at all ability levels can achieve at least as well in heterogeneous classrooms. The net effect of tracking is to exaggerate the initial differences among students, rather than to provide the means to accommodate them to a larger extent.

However, the greatest concern over ability grouping is the relationship between group or track placement and race, language, class, gender, and special-education background. The disproportionate numbers of poor and minority students in lower-ability classes suggest that student differences are misunderstood and that individual strengths are overlooked when ability groups are formed. The segregation of poor and minority students denies them the opportunity to participate in the mainstream of education and to achieve their full academic potential. In effect, ability grouping and tracking mirror and perpetuate social and economic inequalities (Massachusetts Board of Education 1990).

Ideas to Consider When Moving Away from Tracking

Very often competent, capable teachers experience failure, especially in the area of teaching academically marginal or at-risk students. In part, this happens because it is extremely difficult for teachers to turn around patterns of failure that involve the entire life experience of some students. Many students today, including most at-risk children and youth, do not learn well through traditional educational approaches.

Following are six ideas and programs to enable teachers to "reach" students so that all learners will achieve their full potential in the social and academic activities provided by the school. In order for teachers to move from ability grouping and tracking, they must refine their attitudes, behaviors, and skills. Unless one adapts instruction to an environment that nurtures learners, marginal outcomes will prevail, thereby reducing teacher efficacy and the desire of students to achieve. Alternatives that have the potential to alter attitudes, behaviors, and professional skills needed for successful teaching and enhanced student achievement are: 1) student empowerment, 2) teaching for multiple intelligences, 3) IEPs for all students, 4) home visits, 5) cohort/affinity groups, and 6) the parent university.

Student Empowerment. Educators must believe that academic achievement gains for minority students can be facilitated through the use of instructional strategies that: 1) encourage the sharing of control over the instructional process among teachers and students, 2) involve a high degree of interaction among students, and 3) focus on higher cognitive processes, rather than on skills practice and factual recall. Examples of this type of instruction include cooperative learning, peer tutoring, whole-language approaches to literacy, the use of interactive computer networks, and in some cases, academies for black males.

Cummins (1989) presents specific recommendations for empowering minority students. He assigns a central role to three inclusive sets of interactions or power relations: 1) the classroom interactions between teachers and students, 2) relationships between schools and minority communities, and 3) the intergroup power relations within the society as a whole. This framework assumes that the social organization and bureaucratic constraints in schools reflect not only broader policy and societal factors, but also the extent to which individual educators accept or challenge the social organization of the school in relation to minority students and communities.

The central tenet of the framework is that students from "dominated" groups are "empowered" or "disabled" as a direct result of their interactions with educators. Further, students who are empowered by their school experiences develop the ability, confidence, and motivation to succeed academically. They participate competently in instruction as a result of having developed a confident cultural identity as well as appropriate school-based knowledge and interactive structures. Students who are disempowered or "disabled" by their school experiences do not develop this type of cognitive/academic and social/emotional foundation. Student empowerment is regarded as both a mediating construct influencing academic performance and as an outcome variable itself (Cummins 1983).

Cummins (1989) cites four structural elements in the organization of schools that contribute to the extent to which minority students are empowered:

1. Cultural/linguistic incorporation. Students' language and culture must be incorporated into the school program. The adjust-

ment of cultural patterns must take culturally conditioned learning styles into account. The incorporation of minority students' culture and language will in no way impede academic progress.

2. Community participation. When educators form a partnership with minority parents, parents seem to develop a sense of efficacy that is picked up by their children with positive academic effects in the students' performance. Most parents of minority students have high hopes and expectations for their children's success in school and in life and do wish to be involved in the promotion of their academic progress.

3. Pedagogy. Too often the instruction of minority students convinces them that what they have to say is irrelevant or wrong. The failure of this method of instruction is then taken as an indication that the minority student is of low ability, a verdict frequently confirmed by assessment procedures. Empowering teaching will help students to become independent learners and to overcome their learning handicaps by being active in the generation of their own knowledge. A teaching model allowing for reciprocal interaction among students and teachers represents more gains than one where teaching/learning is confined to a passive role and induces a form of "learned helplessness" on the part of students.

4. Student assessment. Though not deliberate, many educators, school psychologists, and other support personnel extend the disempowering of minority students from transmission-model teaching to discriminatory assessment practices. For example, they manage "to find" a disability "to explain" a student's apparent academic problems. An alternative role for special educators and school support personnel is for them to de-legitimize the traditional function of psychological assessment in the educational disabling of minority students by becoming learner "advocates." In this role, they must locate "the pathology within the societal power relations between dominant and dominated groups, in the reflection of these power relations between students which takes place in classrooms." (p. 30)

Teaching for Multiple Intelligences. If teachers were to be honest with themselves, they would fast come to the conclusion that students are taught mainly through two-dimensional areas of instruction: logical/mathematical and verbal/linguistic. However, instruction is provided at other times in specialized classes, such as art, physical education, music, and the practical arts.

Many students hate school because they dislike the way teachers teach, what they are expected to learn, the concepts on which they are "tested," and the idea that all they should learn comes mainly from lectures, textbook presentations, or unfulfilling exercises. For a large percentage of students, education has a negative image. When their achievement is determined by scores on the ACT, SAT, BSAP, and the like, they tend to feel they have little control over academic subject matter or how it relates to their needs.

Today's youth are different from any other generation in the history of organized education. They have to deal with life and school situations that their parents and grandparents could not predict they would face: the AIDS epidemic, school violence, child abuse, teenage pregnancy, wayward fathers and dysfunctional families, negative peer pressure, exit exams for high school graduation, absentee parents, and rap music with lyrics of violence, sadism, and explicit sex.

It will be difficult for the school to alleviate many of these social ills. The school is a microcosm of society. Nevertheless, teachers can alter the way they present instruction and invite students to be active participants in it. The school really needs to embrace a concept put forth by Howard Gardner (1983) called "multiple intelligences." Lazear (1992) indicates that "Gardner, director of Harvard University's Project Zero, coined the phase 'multiple intelligences' to describe multi-knowing capacities. His research suggests that we all possess at least seven intelligence areas or ways of knowing" (p. 9). These are: 1) verbal/linguistic, 2) logical/mathematical, 3) visual/spatial, 4) body/kinesthetic, 5) musical/rhythmic, 6) interpersonal, and 7) intrapersonal (Gardner 1983).

Walters and Gardner (1985) state that:

> Multiple Intelligences theory . . . pluralizes the traditional concept [of "intelligence"]. An Intelligence entails the ability to solve problems or fashion products that are of consequence in a particular cultural setting. The problem-solving skill allows one to approach a situation in which a goal is to be obtained and to locate the appropriate route to that goal. The creation of a cultural product is crucial to such functions as capturing and transmitting knowledge or expressing one's views or feelings. The problems to be solved range from creating an end to a story to anticipating a mating move in chess to repairing a quilt. Products range from scientific theories to musical composition to successful political campaigns. (pp. 3-4)

Students bring a wealth of personal talents and intelligences into the classroom. If a lesson concept is best understood by some students through a visual/spatial presentation, this is the way it should be taught to them.

IEPs for All Students. Setting up Individualized Education Plans (IEPs) for all students may appear to be an awesome teaching assignment. However, if teachers possess the desire to use an approach that lessens the likelihood of ability grouping, this is it. The real gains from using IEPs are so great that the extra time is worth it. This approach also helps teachers make sure that each student achieves in ways ability grouping will not and cannot manage. IEPs require that all participants in the education process be diligent in anticipating student needs, requesting resources, developing appropriate goals, and providing support systems.

Because the diversity of students in today's classrooms often is already very great, cooperation is essential. Parents, teachers, and students must promise to work together to accomplish the goals of instruction. Parents, for example, state what they can do, have done, and will do to assist with learning activities in the home. Students will have their own goal sheets: a simple format for the youngest learner, more sophisticated and advanced activities for older learners. Teachers must use IEPs systematically to foster respect and cooperation for the nature of learning and the individual accomplishments to be realized.

IEPs must be developed for all students, including the gifted and talented. The plans must specify what learners should learn. Sometimes that will mean that a given student will be learning different things from others in the classroom. The teacher's job, of course, is to arrange instruction that benefits all students. For example, students in an economics class may be at different points of achievement depending on their level of interest and depth of involvement in the course. One student might be analyzing the federal budget put forth by the President to see how it stimulates the economy through private-sector initiatives. Another might be examining ways that the federal government could significantly reduce the deficit by the year 2000. A group of students might be engaged in a cooperative-learning activity, discussing the meaning of various economics terms. The teacher will be able to help each student accomplish the goals specified in his or her IEP.

Good teachers maximize the opportunities for all students, even though they may be learning at different levels. In general, good teachers help students accomplish as many of the IEP-related activities as feasible and function just as closely as possible to the way their classmates function. If ability grouping occurs in this classroom arrangement, it is strictly by chance.

Home Visits. An abundance of information is available on strategies for teachers and families to join together in planning the goals and objectives of the school. Since an unfavorable home environment hinders a child's progress at school, there is a great need for teachers to help parents become aware of factors that make for student success in school. Years ago, home visitation was an important part of a teacher's working schedule (Burney 1971). However, today many teachers make home visits only when a child has become a serious problem. This change in practice seems to have widened the gap between the parents and teachers of educationally disadvantaged children.

When teachers engage in selected home visits, they generally discover the reasons for a child's poor performance at school and can then adjust the child's placement and curriculum. Often, the causes of a student's failure to succeed cannot be alleviated by the school alone. Astute and observant teachers and administrators will work with parents to obtain resources outside the school.

Teachers who make home visits often comment on the enlightenment they received from meeting parents and viewing home situations. It made a positive difference in the way they related to the child, and vice versa. Reasons listed by teachers for their reluctance to make home visits include: 1) fear of the parents or their neighborhood — that the home visit may be "a risky venture," 2) lack of training about how to make home visits, and 3) lack of interest (Johnson 1992). When possible, school leaders should help teachers to overcome such obstacles. The values that can be achieved include:

1. Parents are impressed. They get more involved, especially in coming to future parent-teacher conferences. They see teachers in a new, more positive light.
2. The teachers gain a better understanding of the pupils, their parents, and their home life, which helps the teacher to better serve the child.
3. The lower achieving student's performance in class usually improves (Davis 1986, pp. 198-199).

Should parents be unreceptive to a home visit, arrangements can be made to meet them in the school or at some other site in the community. Bringing reluctant parents into the schooling process can lessen the likelihood that their children will not receive the full range of opportunities provided by the school.

Cohort/Affinity Groups. The cohort/affinity group (CAG) concept has not yet made its way into the broader education literature. It is a concept similar to cooperative learning in that it involves students in group arrangements and teams to promote achievement. The unique characteristic of the cohort/affinity-group concept is that it operates mainly on an informal, outside-the-classroom basis. Students of different ages (10-18), grades (middle-high school), and socioeconomic groups may form CAGs. In addition, students may participate in more than one CAG to benefit from interactions with several groups.

Cohort/affinity groups are developed and operated for the well-being of members in the group. There is an adult mentor who supervises activities for each group. (Sometimes there may be two mentors, as when a husband and wife team is involved.) A *cohort* is a group united in a common struggle; *affinity* refers to the natural attraction of the group members to one another.

Why develop cohort/affinity groups? Schooling is stressful for many students, particularly those who do not live in families where education is valued and supported through family and community traditions. The formation of CAGs involving five to seven students per mentor can serve useful in-school and out-of-school purposes. A typical CAG curriculum might include:

A. Character development.
   1. Role modeling.
   2. Family relations.
   3. Behavior at school.

B. Career development.
   1. Behavior needed for success in school.
   2. Preparing to attend college.
   3. Part-time jobs/internships.

C. Group survival skills.
   1. Obeying rules of the school.
   2. Avoiding premarital sexual intercourse.
   3. Building healthy peer involvements.

D. Leisure-time activities.
   1. Forming group social outings.
   2. Church activities.
   3. Community-related activities.

E. Handling difficult situations.
   1. Avoiding difficulty with the law.
   2. Steering clear of adolescent pranks.
   3. Averting problems associated with street gangs.

Still other dimensions could be added to the curriculum. CAGs help students feel better about themselves. This, in turn, lessens the stress placed on them by the school. Students who feel good about themselves generally will come close to, reach, or even exceed the expectations teachers have for them, thereby reducing the likelihood they will end up in no-win situations.

Parent University. Schools must take charge of initiatives to acquaint parents with the format and operation of school programs. While the popular media and school public-information directors provide the public with information about school programs, these blurbs do little to help parents understand the complexities of such topics as IEPs, the pros and cons of full inclusion, multicultural education, Afrocentrism, tracking and ability grouping, technology in the classroom, schools of choice, and AIDS education. Parents need a local setting provided by the schools in which they can gain in-depth knowledge about topics currently discussed by educators and policy makers. The outcome of the experiences provided by a "parent university," staffed by educators and others who are competent to teach about current education issues, would be parents who are better informed about education.

There are numerous benefits to be realized from establishing a parent university. The parent university has the potential to empower parents. Some of the meetings might spawn the development of support groups and family connections. By tackling difficult topics, parents will come to understand them better. A parent university is 1) feasible in any size community, 2) cost effective, and 3) prepares schools, families, and communities to deal with the realities of contemporary schooling.

Viable Instructional Strategies

There are viable educational approaches for those seeking to move away from ability grouping and tracking. If teachers wish to do what is "right" and "just" by students, they need to develop and engage in teaching practices that enhance their classroom routines. For example, they might:

1. Plan learning activities so that all students benefit from the curriculum.
2. Establish clear student performance goals and communicate the goals to students and their parents in a syllabus.
3. Use learning styles that are comfortable for the learners; not all learners should receive instruction in the same manner.

4. Provide opportunities for under-prepared students to receive remediation and cross-age tutoring.
5. Use technology to improve instruction whenever appropriate.
6. Address the issues of student success and self-esteem, recognizing that one success breeds another.
7. Alter classroom arrangements and permit students to engage in collaborative learning activities; some students have a cultural affinity toward group activities, rather than learning in isolation.
8. Use alternative textbooks and resource materials that are appropriate for instruction, because not all standard textbooks are adequate by themselves.
9. Be sensitive to ethnic, cultural, racial, and gender issues that will surface in the classroom, carefully listening to students and their concerns.
10. Set high academic standards for all students and then hold them strictly accountable for meeting those standards.

The shift in practice from ability grouping and tracking will be difficult in some schools where teachers believe that ability grouping is necessary and in the best interest of all students. Slower students are supposed to learn best with other slower students, and accelerated students are thought to learn best when around students with like characteristics. Nothing could be further from the truth.

The research on ability grouping clearly reveals that students taught in heterogeneous classrooms fare much better socially and academically than students taught in classrooms arranged according to perceived ability. In order to move toward greater heterogeneity, educators and parents need to:

- explore their assumptions about ability grouping;
- define the challenges in a socioeducational context;
- define the mission and purpose of changing student-placement procedures;
- locate the human and financial resources needed to carry out newly defined activities;
- develop strategies that will lead to a changes that are acceptable to the majority of the citizenry, realizing that change takes time; and
- commit to an action plan.

The job will not be easy. There must be teams of citizens and educators committed to the compromise. Administrative support for reasonable change must be visible. Advocates for untracking should be alert to unexpected events that could derail hard-won gains. Untracking proponents must keep their goal in sight: to meet the needs of students of different abilities in all classrooms.

References

Burney, V.K. "Home Visitation and Parent Involvement." *Today's Education* 60, no. 7 (1971): 10-11.

Cummins, J. "Functional Language Proficiency in Context: Classroom Participation as an Interactive Process." In *Compatibility of the SBIS Features with Other Research on Instruction for LEP Students*, edited by W.J. Tikunoff. San Francisco: Far West Laboratories, 1983.

Cummins, J. "Empowering Minority Students: A Framework for Intervention." *Harvard Educational Review* 56, no. 1 (1989): 18-36.

Davis, D.R. *School Public Relations: The Complete Book*. Arlington, Va.: National School Public Relations Association, 1986.

Gardner, H. *Frames of Mind: The Theory of Multiple Intelligences*. New York: Basic Books, 1983.

Johnson, C. *Teachers Making Home Visits*. Bloomington, Ind.: Associates in Educational Research, Planning, and Institutional Adaptation, 1992.

Lazear, D.G. *Teaching for Multiple Intelligences*. Fastback 342. Bloomington, Ind.: Phi Delta Kappa Educational Foundation, 1992.

Massachusetts Board of Education. *Structuring Schools for Student Success: A Focus on Ability Grouping*. Boston, 1990.

Oakes, J. *Keeping Track: How Schools Structure Inequality*. New Haven, Conn.: Yale University Press, 1985.

Oakes, J.; Ormseth, T.; Bels, R.; and Camp, P. *Multiplying Inequalities: The Effects of Race, Social Class, and Tracking on Opportunities to Learn Math and Science*. Santa Monica, Calif.: Rand Corporation, 1990.

Schmidt, P. "Tracking Found to Hurt Prospects of Low Achievers." *Education Week*, 16 September 1992, p. 9.

Walters, J.M., and Gardner, H. "The Development and Education of Intelligences." In *Essays on the Intellect*, edited by F.R. Link. Alexandria, Va.: Association for Supervision and Curriculum Development, 1985.

SECTION III

Strategies that Help Meet All Students' Needs

PROVIDING EQUITY FOR ALL: MEETING THE NEEDS OF HIGH-ABILITY STUDENTS

BY SALLY M. REIS

In the current discussion about education reform, many educators involved in gifted education have noted the similarities between the recommendations put forth by the "reformers" and the basic principles of educating gifted and talented students. Key ideas such as thinking skills, product development, product and portfolio assessment, higher standards, teaching to students' strengths and interests, flexible instructional grouping, and numerous other strategies have been suggested by leaders in educating high-ability students for over two decades (Marland 1972; Renzulli 1976, 1977a; Torrance 1962).

Some of the suggestions being offered in the current national dialogue about reform may create problems for all students, and high-ability students in particular (Renzulli and Reis 1991). For example, a standardized national curriculum may result in the specification of minimum standards for able youth. The use of heterogeneous classes all the time in all subject areas may deprive high-ability students of the appropriate challenge they so desperately need. The absence of staff development to help teachers meet the diverse needs of students in a heterogeneous setting creates further problems. The misuse of cooperative learning may result in high-ability students tutoring other students to the detriment of their own achievement gains. The use of group grades in a cooperative-learning situation may result in lower grades for high-ability students.

The "Dumbing Down" of Textbooks

One reason that so many average and above-average students become bored in school and demonstrate mastery of the curriculum is that contemporary textbooks have been "dumbed down," a phrase used in 1984 by then-Secretary of Education Terrel Bell. Chall and Conrad (1991) concur with Bell's assessment, documenting a trend of decreasing difficulty in the most widely used textbooks over a 30-year period from 1945 to 1975. "On the whole, the later the copyright dates of the textbooks for the same grade, the easier they were, as measured by indices of readability level, maturity level, difficulty of questions, and extent of illustration" (p. 2). Kirst (1982) also believes that textbooks have dropped by two grade levels in difficulty over the last 10 to 15 years. Philip G. Altbach, noted scholar and author on textbooks in America, and his associates recently suggested that textbooks, as evaluated across a spectrum of assessment measures, have declined in rigor (Altbach et al. 1991).

Researchers have discussed the particular problems encountered by high-ability students when textbooks are "dumbed down" because of readability formulas or the politics of textbook adoption. Bernstein (1985) summarized the particular problem that current textbooks pose for gifted and talented students:

> Even if there were good rules of thumb about the touchy subject of textbook adoption, the issue becomes moot when a school district buys only one textbook, usually at "grade level," for all students in a subject or grade. Such a purchasing policy pressures adoption committees to buy books that the least able students can read. As a result, the needs of more advanced students are sacrificed. (p. 465)

Chall and Conrad (1991) also cite particular difficulties for the above-average student with regard to less difficult reading textbooks:

> Another group not adequately served was those who read about two grades or more above the norm. Their reading textbooks, especially, provide little or no challenge, since they were matched to students' grade placement, not their reading levels. Many students were aware of this and said, in their interviews, that they

preferred harder books because they learned harder words and ideas from them. Since harder reading textbooks are readily available, one may ask why they were not used with the more able readers, as were the easier reading textbooks for the less able readers. (p. 111)

Repetition in Content

Recent findings by Usiskin (1987) and Flanders (1987) indicate that not only have textbooks decreased in difficulty, but they also incorporate a large percentage of repetition to facilitate learning. Usiskin argues that even average eighth-grade students should study algebra, because only 25% of the pages in typical seventh- and eighth-grade mathematics texts contain new content. Flanders corroborated this find by investigating the mathematics textbook series of three popular publishers. Students in grades two through five who used these math textbooks encountered approximately 40% to 65% new content over the course of the school year, which equates to new material two to three days a week. By eighth grade, the amount of new content had dropped to 30%, which translates to encountering new material only 1½ days a week. Flanders suggests that these estimates are conservative, because days for review and testing were not included in his analysis. He concludes, "There should be little wonder why good students get bored: they do the same thing year after year" (p. 22).

Repetition in content also is reflected by the scores students attain on pretests taken before they open their textbooks. For example, a study conducted by the Educational Products Information Exchange Institute (1980-1981), a nonprofit education consumer agency, revealed that 60% of fourth-graders in the studied school districts were able to achieve a score of 80% or higher on a test of the content of their math texts *before* they had opened their books in September. In a more recent study dealing with average and above-average readers, Taylor and Frye (1988) found that 78% to 88% of fifth- and sixth-grade average and above-average readers could pass pretests on comprehension skills before the skills were taught in the basal reader. The average students were performing at approximately 92% accuracy, while the better readers were performing at 93% on comprehension skill pretests. The mismatch between 1) what students are capable of doing and what they already know and 2) the curricular materials they are expected to study becomes even more disturbing when one considers teachers' heavy reliance on textbooks and the textbooks' declining levels of challenge.

The Mismatch Between Student Ability and Instruction

It is clear that students should be matched with curriculum that is appropriate for their ability level. That is, for learning to occur, instruction should be above the learner's current level of performance. Chall and Conrad (1991) stress the importance of the match between a learner's abilities and the difficulty of the instructional task, stating that the optimal match should place the instructional task slightly above the learner's current level of functioning. When the match is optimal, learning is enhanced. However, "if the match is not optimal [that is, if the match is below or above the child's level of understanding or knowledge], learning is less efficient and development may be halted" (Chall and Conrad, p. 19). It is clear that the current trend of selecting textbooks that the majority of students can read is a problem for high-ability students.

A mismatch seems to exist between the difficulty of textbooks and the repetition of curricular material in these texts, on the one hand, and the needs of our high-ability learners, on the other. It is reasonable to conclude that many of these students spend much of their school time practicing skills and learning content they already know. All these factors may be causing our most capable children to learn less and consequently encouraging their underachievement.

Inadequate Instructional Practices

Three recent studies have analyzed whether the needs of high-ability students currently are being met in classroom settings. This research presents a disturbing picture of what happens to high-ability students in their regular classrooms.

The Classroom Practices Survey (Archambault et al. 1992) was conducted by the National Research Center on the Gifted and Talented (NRC/GT) to determine the extent to which gifted and talented students receive differentiated education in regular classrooms. Six samples of third- and fourth-grade teachers in public schools, private schools, and schools with high concentrations of four different ethnic minorities were selected randomly to participate in this research. More than 51% of this national sample of classroom teachers responded to the survey.

Of the respondents, 61% of the public-school teachers and 54% of private-school teachers reported that they had never had any training in teaching gifted students. The major finding of this study was that classroom teachers make only minor modifications in the regular curriculum to meet the needs of gifted students. This result holds for all types of schools sampled and for classrooms in all parts of the country and for various sorts of communities.

The Classroom Practices Observational Study (Westberg et al. 1992) extended the results of the Classroom Practices Survey by examining the instructional and curricular practices used with gifted and talented students in regular elementary classrooms throughout the United States. Systematic observations were conducted in 46 third- and fourth-grade classrooms. The observations were designed to determine if and how classroom teachers meet the needs of gifted and talented students in the regular classroom. Two students, one gifted and talented or high-ability student and one average-ability student, were selected as target students for each observation day. A Classroom Practices Record (CPR) was developed to document the types and frequencies of differentiated instruction that gifted students received through modifications in curricular activities, materials, and teacher-student verbal interactions. Descriptive statistics and chi-square procedures were used to analyze the CPR data.

The results indicated little differentiation in the instructional and curricular practices, including grouping arrangements and verbal interactions, for gifted and talented students in the regular classroom. Across five subject areas and 92 observation days, gifted students received instruction in homogeneous groups only 21% of the time. More alarming was that the target gifted and talented or high-ability students experienced no instructional or curricular differentiation in 84% of the instructional activities in which they participated. Anecdotal summaries provided poignant glimpses into the daily experiences of high-ability students:

> It should be noted that S#1 (the targeted high-ability student) was inattentive during all of her classes. She appeared to be sleepy, never volunteered, and was visibly unenthusiastic about all activities. No attempt was made to direct HOTS [higher-order thinking skills] questions to her or to engage her in more challenging work. She never acted out in any way. (p. 36)

Meeting the Needs of High-Ability Students in Regular Classrooms

The Curriculum Compacting Study (Reis, Westberg, et al. 1992) examined the effects of escalating levels of staff development on the teaching practices of elementary teachers throughout the country as they implemented a plan called "curriculum compacting" (Renzulli and

Smith 1978; Reis, Burns, and Renzull 1992) to modify the curriculum for high-ability students. Three treatment groups of second- through sixth-grade teachers from across the country received increasing levels of staff development as they implemented curriculum compacting. Three steps are used in curriculum compacting: 1) assessing the content area in which students demonstrate proficiency, 2) eliminating content students have already mastered, and 3) substituting more appropriate alternatives, some of which are based on student interest. A control group of teachers continued with their normal teaching practices. The study included 436 teachers and 783 students.

Students in both control and treatment groups took the next chronological grade-level Iowa Test of Basic Skills in both October and May. When classroom teachers in the treatment group eliminated between 40% and 50% of the regular curriculum for high-ability students, no differences were found between treatment and control groups in reading, math computation, social studies, and spelling. In science and math concepts, students in the treatment group whose curriculum was compacted scored significantly higher than their counterparts in the control group. In some content areas, scores were higher when the elimination of previously mastered content took place. These findings clearly point out the benefits of curriculum compacting insofar as achievement in basic skills is concerned. Analyses of data also indicated that students viewed replacement activities as more challenging than standard material.

Additional findings are based on an examination of the efficiency and effectiveness of the compacting process and the training provided to the three treatment groups. Of the teachers in the study, 95% were able to identify high-ability students and individual student strengths. Curriculum that high-ability students had yet to master, appropriate instructional strategies for students to demonstrate mastery, and a logical mastery standard were established by 80% of participating teachers. The most frequently compacted subject was mathematics, followed by reading, language arts, science, and social studies.

Replacement strategies consisted of three categories of activities for students: enrichment, acceleration, and "other" (including peer tutoring, cooperative learning, correcting papers, and other teacher-assistance tasks). Almost all the teachers (95%) employed enrichment as a replacement strategy; 18% used acceleration. Many teachers said they would have used acceleration more frequently if their school districts' policies had not prohibited them from allowing students to work in textbooks beyond their current grade level. Although the majority of new approaches reflected student interests, needs, and preferences, many of the replacement strategies did not include the types of advanced content from which high-ability students can benefit. Therefore, additional staff development obviously is essential. Teachers confirmed this finding; many said they would like to have inservice education from gifted-education specialists and more assistance in locating and using good enrichment materials.

Teachers in the treatment group that received more extensive staff development used significantly more replacement strategies. A difference in favor of this group also was found with regard to the overall quality of curriculum compacting. A particularly encouraging finding was that a majority of teachers in all treatment groups indicated they would like to continue to compact curriculum once the study had been completed. They also expressed an interest in learning more about the process and in evaluating materials that could be used in replacement activities. Further, many teachers stated that, as the year progressed, they were able to use the process with as many as eight to ten students in their classes, not just the one or two students originally targeted for this study.

What Gifted Education Can Offer the Reform Movement

The Accelerated Schools Model was developed by Hank Levin, one of nine persons recently identified by the *New York Times* as standard bearers in education, leaders who are nationally known for education innovation. In a 1992 interview in *Educational Leadership*, Levin was asked, "What makes the Accelerated Schools Model different from some other programs for at-risk students?" He responded, "'What may be most unusual is that we believe the teaching-learning approach that works best for at-risk kids is a 'gifted and talented' strategy rather than a remedial approach" (Brandt 1992, p. 19). Later in the interview, Levin recalled his initial work on the Accelerated Schools Model:

> Well, I started to do a lot of reading in the research literature, and in the literature on gifted and talented programs and I was convinced that if we exposed all children to the richest experiences . . . we could bring kids into the mainstream. And we would find that a lot of these kids *were* gifted and talented, even in the traditional sense [emphasis in original]. (p. 20)

The extension of activities originally designed for high-ability students to all students is not a new idea. In the 1970s, Renzulli (1976, 1977*a*) advocated the use of various enrichment activities as a way to identify strengths and potential interests in all students. He also stressed the use of general enrichment experiences and group training activities for all students in the original Enrichment Triad Model (Renzulli 1977*b*). He and his colleagues further extended the services normally reserved for gifted students to all students with the Revolving Door Identification Model (Renzulli, Reis, and Smith 1981). This model included provisions for much more flexible identification procedures, the involvement of all students in enrichment opportunities, and the possibility for more intensive follow-up if an interest emerged on the part of any student.

In its relatively short history, the field of gifted education has achieved a rather impressive "menu" of exciting curricular adaptations: thinking-skills programs, independent-study skills, and numerous other innovations. For example, specialists who use the Schoolwide Enrichment Model (Renzulli and Reis 1985) concentrate on identifying students' interests and learning styles. They then offer challenging curriculum experiences to students who need specific services instead of providing identical experiences to all students in a classroom regardless of their previous knowledge of the curriculum. Because of the experience gained in the use of these exciting techniques, many benefits exist when a good enrichment program is implemented.

First, exciting opportunities can be made available to all students. For example, in the Schoolwide Enrichment Model, many enrichment opportunities are provided to all students in an effort to identify those young people in whom a potential exists for talent development. Second, the techniques used for high-ability students by gifted-education specialists often can be extended to a much wider circle of students and, in some cases, to all students. In the curriculum-compacting study cited earlier (Reis, Westberg, et al. 1992), teachers who had participated in the staff development program and subsequently implemented curriculum compacting originally targeted one to two students for the curriculum-compacting process. However, once they had modified the curriculum for these targeted students, they were able to use this strategy with other students who were not identified as gifted. In many instances, the teachers were able to use compacting with 10 to 15 students in their classrooms. Following are specific suggestions of how curricular and instructional strategies often used with gifted students have been or can be extended to a broader population of students.

Creative Alternatives in Curriculum and Instruction. For the last two decades, specialists in education of the gifted have been developing innovative curriculum units and extending the regular curriculum to include a wide variety of creative alternatives. The use of these units and strategies by gifted-education specialists is documented in the professional journals and includes, in addition to curriculum units, thinking and process skills, independent study skills, research skills, and problem solving. Two well-known approaches that often are implemented in gifted-education programs now are used with a much broader range of students: Talents Unlimited (developed from Taylor's multiple-talents theory) and the Enrichment Triad (Renzulli 1977b; Renzulli and Reis 1985).

Calvin Taylor (1967) and Carol Schlichter (1979) suggested the use of various types of thinking skills for all students. The multiple-talent approach to teaching, defined by Taylor (1967), operationalized by Schlichter (1979), and linked to Guilford's (1956) research on the nature of intelligence, is a system for helping teachers identify and nurture students' multiple talents in productive thinking, forecasting, communication, planning, decision making, and academics. In this approach, traditional academic talent helps students to gain knowledge in a variety of disciplines, while the other five talents assist them in processing or using the knowledge to create new solutions to problems. Schlichter (1979) cites four assumptions that underlay the multiple-talent approach: 1) people have abilities or talents in a variety of areas; 2) training in the use of these thinking processes can enhance potential in various areas of talent and, at the same time, foster positive feelings about self; 3) training in particular talent processes can be integrated with knowledge or content in any subject area; and 4) the multiple talents are linked to success in the world of work.

The Schoolwide Enrichment Triad Model (SEM) evolved after 15 years of research and field testing by both educators and researchers (Renzulli and Reis 1985). It combined the previously developed Enrichment Triad Model (Renzulli 1977b) with a much more flexible approach to identifying high-potential students, called the Revolving Door Identification Model (Renzulli, Reis, and Smith 1981). This combination initially was field tested in 12 school districts of various types (rural, suburban, and urban) and sizes. Research indicated positive growth for students, even those who were not identified for gifted-program services (Reis 1981).

In the SEM, a talent pool of 15% to 20% of above-average-ability/high-potential students is identified through a variety of measures, including achievement tests, teacher nominations, assessment of potential for creativity, and task commitment, as well as other alternative entrance pathways (self-nomination, parent nomination, etc.). High scores on achievement and IQ tests automatically include a student in the talent pool, enabling those students who are underachieving in their academic work to be involved.

Once students are identified for the talent pool, they are eligible for several services that also are extended to other (non-identified) students in numerous situations. First, interest and learning-styles assessment are used with talent-pool students. Informal and formal methods are used to identify students' interests and to encourage the further development and pursuit of interests in various ways. Second, the curriculum is modified by eliminating portions of previously mastered content. Third, the Enrichment Triad Model offers three types of enrichment experiences. The first two types of enrichment experiences are available to all students. These include general exploratory experiences that are designed to expose students to new and exciting topics and ideas not ordinarily covered in the regular curriculum and instructional methods and materials that are created expressly to promote the development of thinking, feeling, research, communication, and methodological processes. The third level of enrichment, defined as investigative activities and artistic productions in which the learner assumes the role of a first-hand inquirer, is usually more appropriate for students with higher levels of ability, interest, and task commitment.

Modification of the Regular Curriculum

Because so many high-ability students need their curriculum modified in some way, gifted-education specialists have developed a number of strategies that also can be used with other students. Curriculum compacting is one service that can be extended to many students other than those who achieve at a high level. In the compacting process, classroom teachers modify the regular curriculum for students who already know some or much of the content or who can master the content at a more rapid pace than others.

Time saved through curriculum compacting is used by the teacher to provide a variety of enrichment or acceleration opportunities for the student. Enrichment strategies might include self-selected independent investigations, minicourses, advanced content, mentorships, and alternative reading assignments. Acceleration might include the use of material from the next unit or chapter, the use of the textbook for the next grade level, or the completion of even more advanced work with a tutor or mentor. Alternative activities should reflect an appropriate level of challenge and rigor that is commensurate with the student's abilities and interests.

In addition to curriculum compacting, which has been used successfully with a broad segment of the population, a number of other strategies that often are used with high-ability students can be extended to all
students. For example, Kaplan (1986) advocates the use of thematic
units and has devised a system for developing these units. An underlying theme (such as power and conflict) can be expanded, and more
complex extensions can be made for students interested in pursuing advanced content.

The focus of gifted education has always been the identification and
development of talent in young people. The field of gifted education
has emphasized the development of student strengths and the encouragement of student interests. Specialists in education of the gifted have
stressed the use of individual education plans to eliminate work that
students already have mastered and to find the time for students to pursue their individual interests and talents. Others who are not directly
involved in gifted education now suggest that many of the strategies
developed by researchers and practitioners in gifted education should
be used as a method of school improvement (Brandt 1992). Rather than
allowing the reform movement to institute practices that might have a
negative impact on high-ability students, such as the elimination of all
advanced classes, the programs and practices in gifted education can be
used to benefit *all* students.

References

Altbach, P.G.; Kelly, G.P.; Petrie, H.G.; and Weis, L. *Textbooks in American
Society.* Albany: State University of New York Press, 1991.

Archambault, F.X., Jr.; Westberg, K.L.; Brown, S.; Hallmark, B.W.; Emmons,
C.; and Zhang, W. *Regular Classroom Practices with Gifted Students: Re-
sults of a National Survey of Classroom Teachers.* Storrs, Conn.: National
Research Center on the Gifted and Talented, 1992.

Bell, T.H. Speech delivered at the annual conference of the American Association of School Administrators, Las Vegas, February 1984.

Bernstein, H.T. "The New Politics of Textbook Adoption." *Phi Delta Kappan*
66, no. 7 (1985): 463-66.

Brandt, R. "Building Learning Communities: A Conversation with Hank
Levin." *Educational Leadership* 50, no. 1 (1992): 19-23.

Chall, J.S., and Conrad, S.S. *Should Textbooks Challenge Students? The Case
for Easier or Harder Textbooks.* New York: Teachers College Press, 1991.

Educational Products Information Exchange Institute. *Educational Research
and Development Report* 3, no. 4 (1980-1981).

Flanders, J.R. "How Much of the Content in Mathematics Textbooks Is New?"
Arithmetic Teacher 35, no. 1 (1987): 18-23.

Guilford, J.P. *Fundamental Statistics in Psychology and Education.* New York: McGraw-Hill, 1956.

Kaplan, S.N. "The Grid: A Model to Construct Differentiated Curriculum for the Gifted." In *Systems and Models for Developing Programs for the Gifted and Talented,* edited by J. Renzulli. Mansfield Center, Conn.: Creative Learning Press, 1986.

Kirst, M.W. "How to Improve Schools Without Spending More Money." *Phi Delta Kappan* 64, no. 1 (1982): 6-8.

Marland, S.P. *Education of the Gifted and Talented: Report to the Congress of the United States Commissioner of Education.* Washington, D.C.: U.S. Government Printing Office, 1972.

Reis, S.M. "An Analysis of the Productivity of Gifted Students Participating in Programs Using the Revolving Door Identification Model." Doctoral dissertation, University of Connecticut, 1981. *Dissertation Abstracts International* 43, 123A.

Reis, S.M.; Burns, D.E.; and Renzulli, J.S. *Curriculum Compacting: The Complete Guide to Modifying the Regular Curriculum for High-Ability Students.* Mansfield Center, Conn.: Creative Learning Press, 1992.

Reis, S.M.; Westberg, J.; Kulikowich, J.; Caillard, F.; Hébert, T.; Purcell, J.H.; Rogers, J.; Swist, J.; and Plucker, J. *An Analysis of Curriculum Compacting on Classroom Practices.* Technical Report. Storrs, Conn.: National Research Center on the Gifted and Talented, 1992.

Renzulli, J.S. "The Enrichment Triad Model: A Guide for Developing Defensible Programs for the Gifted and Talented, Part I." *Gifted Child Quarterly* 20, no. 3 (1976): 303-26.

Renzulli, J.S. "The Enrichment Triad Model: A Guide for Developing Defensible Programs for the Gifted and Talented, Part II." *Gifted Child Quarterly* 21, no. 2 (1977): 227-33. a

Renzulli, J.S. *The Enrichment Triad Model: A Guide for Developing Defensible Programs for the Gifted and Talented.* Mansfield Center, Conn.: Creative Learning Press, 1977. b

Renzulli, J.S., and Reis, S.M. *The Schoolwide Enrichment Model.* Mansfield Center, Conn.: Creative Learning Press, 1985.

Renzulli, J.S., and Reis, S.M. "The Reform Movement and the Quiet Crisis in Gifted Education." *Gifted Child Quarterly* 35, no. 1 (1991): 26-35.

Renzulli, J.S.; Reis, S.M.; and Smith, L.H. *The Revolving Door Identification Model.* Mansfield Center, Conn.: Creative Learning Press, 1981.

Renzulli, J.S., and Smith, L.H. *The Compactor.* Mansfield Center, Conn.: Creative Learning Press, 1978.

Schlichter, C.L. "The Multiple Talent Approach to the World of Work." *Roeper Review* 2, no. 2 (1979): 17-20.

Taylor, B.M., and Frye, B.J. "Pretesting: Minimize Time Spent on Skill Work for Intermediate Readers." *The Reading Teacher* 42, no. 2 (1988): 100-103.

Taylor, C.W. "Questioning and Creating: A Model for Curriculum Reform." *Journal of Creative Behavior* 1, no. 1 (1967): 22-23.

Torrance, E.P. *Guiding Creative Talents*. Englewood Cliffs, N.J.: Prentice-Hall, 1962.

Usiskin, Z. "Why Elementary Algebra Can, Should, and Must Be an Eighth-Grade Course for Average Students." *Mathematics Teacher* 80, no. 6 (1987): 428-38.

Westberg, K.L.; Archambault, F.X., Jr.; Dobyns, S.M.; and Salvin, T.J. *Technical Report: An Observational Study of Instructional and Curricular Practices Used with Gifted and Talented Students in Regular Classrooms*. Storrs, Conn.: National Research Center on the Gifted and Talented, 1992.

PROMOTING GIFTED BEHAVIOR IN AN UNTRACKED MIDDLE SCHOOL SETTING

BY THOMAS O. ERB, STEPHEN O. GIBSON, AND SUZANNE E. AUBIN

For most of this century educators have attempted to meet the needs of diverse learners by separating students into different academic classes based on what appeared to be ability. Students learned at different rates, and some students learned more than others. By the time students entered junior high, some were functioning on the 11th-grade level while others languished at the third-grade level. All the variance appeared to result from an inherent, unchangeable characteristic of youngsters — intelligence. And intelligence appeared to be the best predictor of students' ability to achieve in school. The system seemed to be working fairly well.

However, over the years a body of research appeared that demonstrated that the intended outcomes of across-class ability grouping and tracking seldom were realized. Students in tracked classes did not tend to do better academically and students in the lowest tracks clearly did more poorly than those students in heterogeneously grouped classes (Slavin 1990). Neither did student self-esteem tend to be better in tracked classes than in untracked ones. The very students who were supposed to benefit from being placed in "remedial," "slow," and "basic" classes received a dumbed-down curriculum and were taught by the least-experienced teachers, with the least-successful teaching strategies, and in the worst learning environments (Goodlad 1984; Oakes 1985; Wheel-ock 1992).

Others who studied human intelligence and learning suggested that "ability" was only one factor that affected achievement. Learning styles and self-concept may have more to do with how a student learns than does ability. Sternberg (1990) has argued that thinking and learning styles are every bit as important as ability in explaining student learning. Beane and Lipka (1987) and March, Byrne, and Shavelson (1992) have documented that youngsters' self-concepts as learners have a more powerful impact on student achievement than does ability. The practice of grouping students by ability to reduce heterogeneity in classrooms is being increasingly criticized.

Another line of attack also has challenged the notion that what you see is what you get when it comes to ability. Sternberg and Davidson (1985) believe that the importance of IQ in predicting success in the classroom is overestimated, because studies of intelligence virtually never control for the correlates of IQ. For example, measures of IQ correlate very highly with socioeconomic status (Humphreys 1985). Baldwin (1987), who decries the under-representation of minority youth among the high scorers on tests of IQ, has confirmed the overlap between ethnic background and measures of intelligence.

At this time it seems that, unless one deliberately wants to keep America's classrooms segregated by class and ethnicity, there is no defense for the practice of across-class ability grouping or tracking. Even if one wanted to create homogeneous environments for learning, the task is impossible. Certainly, in middle-grades classrooms where teachers encounter perpetual pubertal metamorphoses, a homogeneous classroom is an oxymoron.

So what are educators to do? Children are different from each other. It does not make sense to put together a heterogeneous group of young adolescents and teach them all in the same way. In successful heterogeneous classrooms all students do not get the same treatment, though they are exposed to the same basic curriculum. There are a whole host of teaching practices that have emerged to allow different learners to encounter appropriate learning activities in a classroom of diversity: interdisciplinary thematic teaching, cooperative-group investigation, authentic assessment, independent-study contracts, and class-within-a-class, to name a few. But what about those students who really want to get beyond the basic curriculum and delve deeply into the study of some topic or issue? Even the highly motivated, creative, and intelligent — some might call them "gifted" — students can have their unique learning needs met in an otherwise heterogeneously grouped middle school.

Unlike the traditional notions of "giftedness" that are linked to high scores on IQ tests, there are newer conceptions of giftedness that are developmental in nature. Rather than focus on some measure of general intelligence, developmental views suggest that giftedness is as varied as the fields in which human beings pursue excellence (Feldman 1979). In other words, there are many ways to display gifted behavior. Not only would one have to look in many places to find gifted performance, but gifted performance itself is multifaceted. One of the most highly developed conceptions of giftedness was proposed by Renzulli (1978, 1986), who viewed giftedness as being composed not only of above-average (but not necessarily superior) intelligence, but also creativity and task commitment. Renzulli goes on to suggest that these three components of giftedness can be applied to 11 general performance areas (such as mathematics, visual arts, life science, and music) and scores of specific performance areas (such as cartooning, biography, poetry, fashion design, navigation, wildlife management, film criticism, and child care).

To get students involved in appropriate learning activities using Renzulli's model, one does not administer an IQ test or ask for teacher recommendations to put a child into a special class to be treated differently. Instead, students are guided into appropriate learning experiences based on information from a variety of sources collected over an extended period of time. Students are invited to participate in three types of learning activities, the first two of which are open and appropriate for all learners. Renzulli's (1977) Type I activities are called "General Exploratory" (see also Reis and Renzulli 1985; Renzulli and Reis, 1985). These are learning activities designed to bring learners into touch with the kinds of topics or areas of study that they may have an interest in pursuing. These might include field trips, guest speakers, interviews, publications, videos, or artistic performances. The Type II activities are referred to as "Group Training" and consist of methods, materials, and instructional techniques that are mainly focused on the development of thinking and feeling processes.

The Type III activities are the in-depth projects that Renzulli calls "Individual and Small-Group Investigations of Real Problems." At this stage, students become investigators of real-world problems and employ the methods of inquiry appropriate for a professional in a given field of study. These projects require a great deal of independence and perseverance. These requirements distinguish Type III work from the independent-study projects that less committed students might undertake.

Getting appropriate students engaged in these Type III activities requires the collection of information about student performance that is acquired over time. The first-level identification requires four types of data:

1. *Psychometric Information* from traditional tests of intelligence, aptitude, achievement, and creativity;
2. *Developmental Information* from teacher, parent, and self-nomination and rating scales;
3. *Sociometric Information* from peer nominations and ratings; and
4. *Performance Information* from examples of previous accomplishments in school and non-school settings (Reis and Renzulli 1986, p. 276).

A second-level identification consists of collecting "action information" that is based on student performance in Type I and Type II activities. This action information grows out of the interests of children, rather than being based on some standardized measure. Though this process of meeting the needs of students may seem to be complicated, it really meshes well with the curriculum.

This Renzulli system has been working well for several years in Howard County, Maryland. In the Howard County middle schools, students are grouped into disciplinary teams. It is in these teams that the Howard County students engage in the three types of activities that Renzulli has proposed. For this chapter, we focus specifically on Patapsco Middle School, which has undergone a successful transition allowing all students to exhibit "gifted behavior."

Patapsco Middle School is located in a suburban community consisting of a wide range of socioeconomic classes. For several years the school followed the practice of grouping students for instruction on the basis of "ability." Little regard was paid to other factors that affect student performance. The school was ripe for change. About 15 years ago, Patapsco, along with most junior high schools in the district, made the sweeping change from junior highs to middle schools in both name and practice. This radical change brought a structure that departed from a departmental, discipline-centered organization to one based on interdisciplinary teams, allowing a more student-focused environment to be created.

Not long after this change in organizational structure, the county found itself in a population boom. The county and the school system were growing at such a rate that the building of schools could barely keep pace with the overall growth. With this tremendous influx of new students came increasing pressure from parents of so-called gifted students to establish a separate magnet middle school for the "Gifted and Talented." After a long battle, the school system rejected the magnet proposal and adopted the "Triad Model" (Renzulli 1977), somewhat modified to incorporate "talent-pool" classes in English, science, social studies, and math. Although talent-pool classes were created to permit acceleration or enrichment of the curriculum for students who met the entrance criteria, these classes did not become an excuse for denying other students opportunities to display gifted performance.

How does this program allow for "addressing giftedness in an untracked middle school setting"? As a result of the varied facets of the Renzulli model, more students than ever before at Patapsco Middle School have been given the opportunity to explore, investigate, and realize that they can truly display gifted behavior. Patapsco students at all grades are given the opportunity to engage in Type I activities as described earlier. It is wonderful to see the delight of youngsters as they engage in activities with people ranging from snake-handlers to museum curators, from artists to skydivers, from computer programmers to story-tellers. Students are able to interact with the presenters in a number of different ways. At times that may mean a question-and-answer period or an opportunity to use a special piece of equipment.

Last school year during a Type I presentation, the vocal music teacher had the unique opportunity to play a musical instrument called a video harp. At the time, this video harp was one of only seven such instruments in the world. Although the opportunity to play this instrument did not lead to the purchase of a video harp, it did turn on a light bulb in that teacher's head. He believed he could greatly enhance the school's music curriculum by the purchase of a computer and a media system that would allow students considerable freedom and creativity to compose original music. Students of all academic abilities were then able to write original music scores. Born out of one of these Type I activities, students and their teacher have been given the opportunity to display truly gifted behavior in the fine arts. In the old traditional structure for addressing gifted behavior, it is likely that only students who were perceived as having high ability in music would have been exposed to this activity. Under the Triad Model, students of all abilities are exposed to a wide range of activities.

Type II activities can be integrated into every content area in the middle school. All students possess intellectual strengths, and Type II projects are designed to stimulate creative thinking, research, communication, and critical skills. In essence, these types of activities are designed to teach students the skills and habits necessary to engage successfully in independent inquiry. For example, after the entire class read Jean George's novel, *My Side of the Mountain*, students were able to choose among a wide range of projects, such as diary entries, models, and scrapbooks created to portray a character's experiences. Because extensive reading experiences are necessary to enhance an individual's reading skills, students also were required to do outside reading daily and to respond to creative, divergent questions using a journal or reader's response log.

Given the opportunity to perform, all students — not just those students who are labeled "gifted and talented" — possess insights and ideas. Type II activities permit students to tap their strengths and apply them in different ways. This allows all students to have opportunities to develop as active learners.

Although Type I and Type II activities extend gifted-behavior opportunities to all students, it is through Type III activities that we begin to see students of all levels of perceived academic ability display truly gifted behaviors. As noted earlier, Type III activities are those in which individual students or small groups engage in investigation of real-world problems. Students who are excited about a specific topic or subject are encouraged to report to the gifted-and-talented resource room where they are asked to fill out a "light-bulb" form. After completing this form, a six-step module is set into place:

1. Introduction to the Enrichment Triad Model.
2. Development of a Knowledge Base.
3. Problem Finding and Focusing.
4. Determination of a Product/Audience.
5. Research and Data Collection.
6. Production.

These six steps allow students to become deeply involved in their chosen topics and force students to become creative and critical thinkers, which in and of itself is a fairly good definition of gifted behavior.

Students at Patapsco have used this format to create a wide variety of products and services under the umbrella of the Triad Model. It would be impossible to list many of the Type III projects, but here are a few of the projects that students have developed over the last two years:

1. *Soup to Nuts:* A local restaurant guide was designed to offer parents choices of places to dine out with their children.
2. *New Student Survival Guide:* A booklet was designed by students who were new to school with the purpose of aiding future new students.

3. *Memory Book:* This completely student-driven publication recorded the events and pictures of the eighth-grade class.
4. *Bike Helmet Law:* Following the death of a fellow classmate, a group of students at Glenwood Middle School, another Howard County middle school, lobbied successfully to have the nation's first Bike Helmet Law enacted.
5. *Piffer School House:* An old, abandoned, one-room schoolhouse was saved from demolition because of the efforts of several students, who researched the history of this structure and garnered enough support and capital to have the schoolhouse moved to another location, thus preserving it for future generations.
6. *Patapsco Middle School Directory:* A computer-generated school directory was created on the HyperCard program. The directory includes pictures of staff members, layout of the school building, and complete teacher schedules.

These projects are just a sample of the wonderful things that all kinds of students can accomplish when there is a program in place to allow gifted behavior on a wide variety of subjects.

Students of varying abilities can demonstrate gifted behavior, because gifted performance is only partially dependent on ability. Other traditionally overlooked factors contribute to academic success: self-confidence, learning style, motivation, and student priorities. Not only does gifted performance depend on a lot more than ability, but the concept of ability is much more domain-specific than is acknowledged in traditional conceptions of giftedness.

Instead of only one way to be gifted, there are many ways. Some students may progress to Type III activities only once in the three years they spend in middle school. Others may engage in such activities on an almost continual basis. However, no child is denied the opportunity to produce gifted performance because of rigid tracking practices. All students can pursue self-selected parts of the curriculum as far as their talents, priorities, interests, learning styles, and motivation will allow them. Patapsco Middle School is living proof.

References

Baldwin, A. "Undiscovered Diamonds." *Journal for the Education of the Gifted* 10, no. 4 (1987): 271-86.
Beane, J.A., and Lipka, R.P. *When the Kids Come First: Enhancing Self-Esteem.* Columbus, Ohio: National Middle School Association, 1987.

Feldman, D. "Toward a Nonelitist Conception of Giftedness." *Phi Delta Kappan* 60, no. 9 (1979): 660-63.

Goodlad, J.I. *A Place Called School: Prospects for the Future*. New York: McGraw-Hill, 1984.

Humphreys, L.G. "A Conceptualization of Intellectual Giftedness." In *The Gifted and Talented: Developmental Perspectives*, edited by F.D. Horowitz and M. O'Brien. Washington, D.C.: American Psychological Association, 1985.

March, H.W.; Byrne, B.M.; and Shavelson, R.J. "A Multidimensional, Hierarchical Self-Concept." In *The Self: Definitional and Methodological Issues*, edited by T.M. Brinthaupt and R.P. Lipka. Albany: State University of New York Press, 1992.

Oakes, J. *Keeping Track: How Schools Structure Inequality*. New Haven, Conn.: Yale University Press, 1985.

Reis, S.M., and Renzulli, J.S. *The Secondary Triad Model: A Practical Plan for Implementing Gifted Programs at the Junior and Senior High School Levels*. Mansfield Center, Conn.: Creative Learning Press, 1985.

Reis, S.M., and Renzulli, J.S. "The Secondary Triad Model." In *Systems and Models for Developing Programs for the Gifted and Talented*, edited by J.S. Renzulli. Mansfield Center, Conn.: Creative Learning Press, 1986.

Renzulli, J.S. *The Enrichment Triad Model: A Guide for Developing Defensible Programs for the Gifted and Talented*. Mansfield Center, Conn.: Creative Learning Press, 1977.

Renzulli, J.S. "What Makes Giftedness? Reexamining a Definition." *Phi Delta Kappan* 60, no. 3 (1978): 180-84, 261.

Renzulli, J.S. "The Three-Ring Conception of Giftedness: A Developmental Model for Creative Productivity." In *Conceptions of Giftedness*, edited by R.J. Sternberg and J.E. Davidson. New York: Cambridge University Press, 1986.

Renzulli, J.S., and Reis, S.M. *The Schoolwide Enrichment Model: A Comprehensive Plan for Educational Excellence*. Mansfield Center, Conn.: Creative Learning Press, 1985.

Slavin, R.E. "Achievement Effects of Ability Grouping in Secondary Schools: A Best-Evidence Synthesis." *Review of Educational Research* 60, no. 3 (1990): 471-99.

Sternberg, R.J. "Thinking Styles: Keys to Understanding Student Performance." *Phi Delta Kappan* 71, no. 5 (1990): 366-71.

Sternberg, R.J., and Davidson, J.E. "Cognitive Development in the Gifted and Talented." In *The Gifted and Talented: Developmental Perspectives*, edited by F.D. Horowitz and M. O'Brien. Washington, D.C.: American Psychological Association, 1985.

Wheelock, A. *Crossing the Tracks: How "Untracking" Can Save America's Schools*. New York: New Press, 1992.

UNTRACKING YOUR MIDDLE SCHOOL: NINE TENTATIVE STEPS TOWARD LONG-TERM SUCCESS*

BY PAUL S. GEORGE

Middle school educators have long championed an approach to curriculum planning and school organization that places the characteristics and needs of early adolescents above other criteria, such as the structure of academic disciplines or ease of scheduling. Thus it should not be surprising that middle school leaders and teachers are in the forefront of educators who are expressing concerns about grouping arrangements. Over the past five years, I have acted as a participant-observer in dozens of middle school situations where teachers, administrators, and parents were involved in attempts to "untrack" their schools. When the process has proceeded smoothly and has been implemented successfully, it appears to have followed a number of relatively distinct steps:

Step 1: Make certain an exemplary middle school organization already exists.

---

*Portions of this chapter were published previously in P.S. George, *How to Untrack Your School* (Alexandria, Va.: Association for Supervision and Curriculum Development, 1992).

Middle school improvement happens in programs that already demonstrate certain other fundamental features to meet the needs of early adolescent learners. It seems to me that middle school educators have learned that there are some program and organizational components that must come first in order for others to be added effectively. The move to untrack the middle school curriculum will occur most effectively where adviser-advisee programs and interdisciplinary-team organization have been established and internalized. There is a student-centered mindset associated with these arrangements that, if absent, will almost certainly diminish any effort at diversifying curriculum and instruction. This is a tall order; but if we are interested in long-term improvement, we might as well admit at the outset that no innovation will take root and blossom in the absence of the fertile educational soil provided by appropriate middle school concepts and organization.

Step 2: Carefully consider the formidable odds against successfully detracking the school.

A number of important problems are associated with the development of more-inclusive middle schools, each one serious enough to derail any poorly planned effort to institute greater heterogeneity. Practitioners with experience in the change process know that attempts to implement a more inclusive model by administrative fiat are unlikely to succeed. Such haste damages both credibility and effectiveness, since neither teachers nor parents will be prepared properly for the change. Parents must be persuaded that detracking is the correct thing to do and that, at minimum, their children will not be harmed by the changes. Teachers want to do their best with their students and must see that a more inclusive school and classroom is a way to do that. Teachers rarely have been trained for success in a real middle school, let alone the heterogeneous classroom; both preservice and inservice education are needed.

Similarly, in a move toward greater heterogeneity, middle school leaders — especially principals — will be heavily pressured from all sides. Some parents will exhort the person charged with the transition to scuttle the plan; other parents will encourage the person in charge to make the change more quickly. Some middle school teachers will react negatively to moving away from ability grouping, while others will make the principal feel guilty for not having ended the practice years earlier. The central office will expect everything to be done with a minimum of disruption and an absence of controversy. To persist in such circumstances takes considerable courage on the part of the school principal; to succeed takes both competence and careful planning. Both the political and the pedagogical climate must be right for the process to move forward successfully.

To the uninitiated, change may seem like a simple reorganization of who learns with whom; but such is not the case. Moving to a more inclusive school can be an expensive process. Creating a climate for change means pulling together a great deal of research and experience; disseminating the information takes time and effort. However, all this will pale compared to the costs of preparing a faculty for the actual implementation of heterogeneous classrooms with confidence and competence. Remember, few teachers can put such programs into practice at a moment's notice; fewer still have been properly trained to do so. Thus staff development will require significant time and money.

Racial, ethnic, and social-class issues also must be considered. Various researchers (for example, MacLeod 1987) make clear that such prejudice plays an influential role in determining how schools are organized and operated. Especially in districts and communities where ability grouping has come to act as a proxy for racial and social-class segregation, attempts to change the situation may be met with hostility and brazen attempts to shout down carefully planned, child-centered school practices. This may even be the case in otherwise cosmopolitan — even "liberal" — communities. Subtle prejudice frequently surfaces around the detracking issue in school districts where the student population is bimodal (a significant number of poor, minority children and an equivalent number of upper-middle-class, high-achieving, majority-culture students).

Change agents also must demonstrate that any new school organization will continue to meet the needs of gifted and talented students. This is not just because it is politically expedient (although it is), but also because these students are children with real educational needs. No middle school parents, including those of gifted and talented students, should be expected to sit idly by and accept the sacrifice of their child's learning on the altar of social or educational experimentation. Parents of gifted and talented students must be involved and must be satisfied that equity and excellence issues are met.

Step 3: Establish a culture of detracking.
Jeannie Oakes advises the development of what she wisely describes as a "culture of detracking." Practitioners engaged in detracking point out that the grouping process has been deeply embedded in their schools for generations. It has a tremendous hold in the public schools. It is unlikely that tracking will wither tomorrow or next year, despite

the seemingly overwhelming amount of evidence against its effectiveness or the most earnest efforts of those who seek to eliminate it. In order to protect the interests of everyone involved and the success of the detracking effort itself, a comprehensive strategic planning process — such as that proposed by Pfeiffer, Goodstein, and Nolan (1989) — is essential. Such a process should envision a clearly desirable future state for the organization of the schools, identify tactics required for success, and create an action plan. Such a plan should involve a variety of efforts over a period of several years.

The worst possible results can be expected if school leaders take unilateral, impulsive action to end tracking in their school or district. When this happens, practitioners familiar with such experiences report that parents and policy makers react angrily and noisily. Many middle school teachers will find such plans difficult to implement successfully and will feel frustrated, insulted, and discontented. Such efforts rarely lead to success; more often the program, the participants, and the leadership suffer.

In fact, experience indicates that long-term middle school program quality almost always is tied to systematic, authentic, and effective school-wide decision making, problem solving, and policy making (George and Alexander 1993). When school and classroom leaders share in the decisions that affect their professional lives, everything works better. Virtually all the research on organizational change suggests that successful innovation that is maintained over the long term is tied directly to high involvement of this sort (Kanter, Stein, and Jick 1992; Weisbord 1987).

Step 4: Extend the culture of detracking.

Include representation from all stakeholders. Educational change of any kind is always at least partially political. In the case of tracking and ability grouping in middle schools, it is very political. The attempt to alter current grouping arrangements will surely go awry, practitioners say, unless all those affected are involved to some extent.

This is particularly the case with two groups of middle school parents: those who believe that the current situation benefits their children and those who believe that it is inequitable. The first group must be persuaded that their children's educational experiences, their prospects for selective college admission, and their chances of a professional career will not be damaged. They must be helped to see that educational excellence will not suffer as a result of "social engineering." They must learn that the research suggests that high-ability, high-achieving students do well, academically, in virtually any setting.

144

Other parents, perhaps initially less informed, must learn how important class placements are for the success of their children. They must come to see how important peer-group influences are, especially for less successful learners. They must understand how important one teacher can be in the lives of their children. They must be willing to speak out against what they believe to be unjust and unfair practices. They must be encouraged to insist on equity in the assignment of students, teachers, and school resources.

School board members must become acquainted with the research. They must see that current grouping practices may not meet the tests of equity or effectiveness for all students. They must see that it can be politically safe to change.

Practitioners who have untracked successfully at the middle school level frequently used a task force or steering committee of educators, parents, community members, and representatives from the board. Such groups become informed, participate in the design of the alternative, and in doing so become committed to the implementation of alternative approaches.

Step 5: Conduct a local middle school self-study.

Practitioners say that research based on national studies alone is unlikely to convince the local professionals, parents, and policy makers who most need to be persuaded. The national research is necessary and especially good as a starting point, but it must be reinforced with a study of the grouping practices in the local schools. One such study, conducted by principal Harry Martin at Riverview Middle School on the east coast of Maryland, sought answers to the following 10 sets of questions:

1. How careful are we in the way we place students in ability-grouped classes? Do we rely on a single measure? Do we use student behavior as an important criterion? Are all parents informed about the placement of their children in sufficient time for them to explore the ramifications? Can we be confident that students are placed accurately and fairly?

2. What are the results of our identification and placement processes? Are the high-track classes populated primarily by students from higher-income home situations? Are minority children under-represented in high-track classes or over-represented in low-track classes?

3. What are the results in academic achievement? Can we say with confidence that the results are not skewed in terms of ethnic group or

family income? Are the ranges of higher academic achievement the almost exclusive province of majority culture, upper-middle-class children? Are the bottom levels of achievement predominantly populated by children from minority culture, lower-income families?

4. How flexible are our grouping strategies? How much mobility do our plans permit, from day to day and from year to year? Do students spend most of the day, most of the year, and most of their tenure in the school in one ability group?

5. How does the current situation affect students' perceptions of themselves? Do high-track students, for example, have an advantage in terms of self-concept? Might positive self-perceptions of high-track students be unjustifiably inflated, leading to an unreasonable sort of elitism? Do low-track students feel good about themselves and about school?

6. How do high-track and low-track students feel about school, and about each other? Is there a sense of community in the school, such that students all enjoy being there and being together? Do members of different ethnic and income groups evaluate school, and each other, positively? Is there a substantial amount of voluntary integration, in terms of seating in classes and elsewhere, choice of friends, etc.?

7. Is there a relationship between track placement and student behavior in school? For example, do most of the discipline referrals to the office involve lower-track students? How about suspensions? Do high-track students represent most of the participation in extracurricular activities of an academic nature?

8. How do teachers respond to the current arrangements? Does faculty support for maintaining ability grouping come primarily from teachers assigned to high-track classes? Are such assignments made fairly? That is, do all teachers share in the teaching of both high- and low-track groups? Given an opportunity, would most teachers honestly prefer to teach high-track classes?

9. Do teachers actually prepare different lessons for different ability groups, or do both groups get the same content with substantially different expectations for mastery? Do teachers actually use different instructional strategies with high- and low-track classes, or are both groups expected to learn the same way?

10. Does parental support of — and involvement in — school programs come from a broad spectrum of the school population, or is it primarily a middle-class, middle-income phenomenon?

If most of the answers to these questions result in a positive evaluation of the school organization as it is, there may be little need for the potentially upsetting changes that untracking might cause. However, if the results of the self-study call the current situation into question, the data are likely to be much more persuasive than the results of national studies.

Data often confirm the need to change. Such was the case in Ann Arbor, Michigan, where a study of the school system's ability grouping confirmed the task force's and the school board's worst fears about racial isolation: students "locked in" to placements early in their elementary school years, faulty identification and placement methods for initial grouping, behavior problems related to group placement, teacher preference for class assignments, and other concerns. The case against tracking was clear and convincing.

Step 6: Disseminate information before initiating change.

The results of both national and local research need to be widely publicized, and stakeholders need time to process the information. Practitioners assert that opposition to proposed changes from parents and board members can be substantially allayed by thorough information. Well-educated, upper-middle-class parents, despite their anxieties about their children's futures, can be important supporters of inclusive middle school models. Such parents tend to understand fairness and to be committed to it when they are helped to see that their own children's academic development will not suffer as a result of a parental commitment to equity.

One middle school principal evolved a strategy for frequent one-on-one sessions with parents and policy makers. First, he gave the concerned visitor a period "to ventilate" without interruption. Then he asked this question: Do your concerns come from intuition or knowledge? Inevitably, the answer was "intuition." Then he said: "I'm using knowledge. Here are some of the resources and information I've been consulting. Please take this material with you and read it carefully. Then let's talk again." According to this principal, there never was a need for a follow-up session.

Policy makers, responsible for all the children in the middle schools, must be helped to see the wisdom in John Dewey's belief that the community must want for all its children what the sagest and best parents aspire to for theirs. It is the responsibility of the change-oriented practitioner to see that board members and others have all the information they need for reasoned, balanced decisions.

Step 7: Consider implementing partial, pilot, or other step-by-step measures.

My experience in nearly 30 years of working with change in schools suggests that middle school educators rarely have at hand the resources and time to achieve the successful implementation of total, complex, comprehensive, and lasting changes in school programs or organization. I have learned, in at least some situations, that it is best to work for small victories that are permanent, rather than to make showy efforts that result in little real change. If educators in a school or district have the energy, resources, mindset, and time to accomplish whole-school change to complete heterogeneous grouping, I definitely support their efforts. If these conditions are not present, I believe in taking smaller steps that can lead to permanent improvements.

A number of middle school practitioners have suggested, for example, that virtually everything is implemented more readily when the changes are aimed at the lower grades in a middle school. In a 6-8 middle school, start in the sixth grade. Teachers with an elementary background, certification, and experience — often the sixth-grade teachers in a middle school — seem to be more able to envision and undertake the sort of instructional strategies that succeed in diverse classrooms. Teachers' success at the sixth-grade level may increase the likelihood that those working with seventh- and eighth-graders will be willing to investigate heterogeneous options.

Some practitioners use another strategy for partial realization of more diverse classrooms. Their approach is to say to their teachers, "Just do your best with the slow students." The principal in these situations appears to be saying to the teachers, "I know there's only so much you can do with the slower students. Do your best with them, but I won't expect you to accomplish miracles." Some readers may cringe in horror at such statements. But such statements might encourage some anxious teachers to agree to increasing the heterogeneity of their classes. So long as this temporary situation is followed by the kind of staff development that will permit the teacher to deal effectively with heterogeneity, it can be a sensible stop-gap measure.

In middle schools with established teams, several other possibilities present themselves. For example, moving from five or more groups per team to two groups — advanced and standard — is a fairly painless option. If teams retain one advanced section in mathematics and group all other students in regular sections (eliminating compensatory or remedial sections), I would call that real progress and a cause for celebration.

In some middle schools, the process has been to permit teams of teachers limited autonomy in making grouping decisions. For example, a school might require that students be grouped heterogeneously in social studies, science, physical education, and the arts but permit ability grouping in mathematics and language arts. Some teams might group for only reading, others for only math, while still others might choose not to group their students at all. In these circumstances, the students would be placed on teams where teachers were delivering instruction in the manner in which they believed they could do the very best job. Every parent would be told that his or her child was receiving instruction in the manner with which teachers felt most confident and capable. Teachers, then, are more likely to feel empowered to do their jobs with an increased sense of professional efficacy.

Joplin-Style Plans. Grouping students for specific skills across grades appears to make instructional groups more manageable in terms of the range of achievement, but mitigates the worst effects of traditional ability grouping. Several real-world examples are instructive.

For a decade (1972-1982), a 6-8 middle school in Florida engaged in what its teachers and principal defined as "multi-age grouping." In this setting, students became members of one of six interdisciplinary teams in the school, to which they belonged for three years, their entire middle school education. Each team consisted of five teachers (specialists in reading, language arts, science, mathematics, and social studies) and approximately 150 students, about 50 from each grade. Teams were mirror images of each other, heterogeneous in every possible way: age, race, sex, achievement, and neighborhood. Each team represented the characteristics of the school population as a whole.

Each spring, one-third of the team's students moved on to the ninth grade; each fall a new group of sixth-graders joined each team. Teachers and students knew each other and worked together in learning situations for three years, instead of the customary nine months. A wholly different sense of community developed.

Grouping strategies followed the Joplin Plan (named for the Missouri city where this approach was first used). Students were grouped by achievement in reading and math without regard for grade level. A math class might have 10 sixth-graders, 7 seventh-graders, and 5 eighth-graders, or some other combination. In this way, the range of ability levels that the teacher had to accommodate was narrower, permitting the teacher to use large-group, teacher-directed instruction and to spend less time in arranging the traditional three groups of low, medium, and high ability. Students were grouped and regrouped depending entirely on the progress they made in their classes.

Home-school connections became firm earlier and grew more positive as the years passed. Peer relationships were far more positive than the school demographics would have led one to expect. Time-on-task was easier to achieve in the fall of the year and to sustain throughout the spring.

The advantages of this arrangement were so clear to the faculty and administration that, when the school board made decisions (unrelated to multi-age grouping or the school in particular) that inadvertently rendered multi-age grouping impossible, the entire faculty protested. Faculty and administration implored the board to make a policy exception that would allow them to continue multi-age grouping, but they were unsuccessful. Consequently, the following year the school was organized into another version of the three-year team: student-teacher progression (STP), where grade-level teams stay together for three years. This STP organization remains in place and now is being adopted by numerous middle schools in several regions of the nation.

Currently, the Success for All program (Slavin et al. 1990) is attempting to establish a model for the reform of urban education that includes a substantial measure of Joplin-style school organization. Children in inner-city elementary schools are grouped for reading across grades one, two, and three. The students spend most of their day in grade-level heterogeneous classes, but in reading they are grouped by skill level, regardless of grade. Joplin-plan strategies develop a real sense of community through team and school-within-school operations and may offer much to middle schools.

Before- and After-School "Acceleration." A number of school programs are being redesigned to shift funding for remedial programs away from the formal school day to early morning, late afternoon, and Saturday sessions. Whether these changes will make a measurable difference is yet to be determined, but there is some precedent for feeling positive about them: The Japanese do it that way (George 1989).

Emphasizing effort rather than ability, the Japanese encourage those who are not being successful to try harder, to study more, to *gambaré* (endure with effort). In the Japanese schools, contrary to many Americans' beliefs, there is very little ability grouping before high school. Schools (grades 1-6 and 7-9) draw from adjoining neighborhoods, and classroom groups are almost entirely heterogeneous. Students who fall behind are encouraged to enroll in mostly private after-school remedial and acceleration programs, called *juku*. Many Japanese school children spend one or two hours, one or two afternoons each week at such private schools. American children might do the same, especially if the costs are borne by the school system.

Split-Level Grouping (Winchester Plan). A number of schools are organizing both to maintain and to minimize ability grouping in an

150

attempt to get the best of both educational worlds. Although I have encountered this plan in several districts, I first became aware of it in Winchester, Kentucky, a small, forward-looking school district.

At Conkwright Middle School, students and teachers are organized into grade-level teams of about 125 students. Students on a team are placed into one of five ability levels. Each of these groups is further subdivided into two groups of 12 or 13 students, yielding 10 ability groups, two each at five levels. This grouping arrangement makes it possible for teachers to be assigned students from all five levels, but never to have more than two ability levels in class at any one time. More important, perhaps, is the fact that students travel with a group of peers of the same approximate ability but never spend the whole day with any one ability group. All students mix with students of all ability groups throughout the day. (More information on the Winchester design may be found in George 1992.)

Repackaging the Curriculum. One wily school administrator reports solving the honors-math conundrum by requiring every student in the middle-level school to take regular grade-level mathematics. Honors mathematics is placed on the exploratory wheel and may be chosen by students at every grade level, every year. This way, students get two periods of math a day, not an unpopular option with parents.

More Rigorous Identification Procedures. Practitioners agree that virtually all procedures for the identification and placement of students into ability-grouped classes can profit from being closely examined and evaluated. A number of suggestions apply here. Because of the nature and vulnerability of standardized instruments, educators in many districts are now reluctant to place students in any program on the basis of only one such test or evaluation. In other schools, evaluators avoid placing students in low sections because of the classroom behavior they exhibit. In still others, educators take pains to explain the potential ramifications of placement to parents prior to finalizing the process.

Step 8: Make comprehensive staff development a priority.

Those who will be expected to implement changes in the way students are grouped in a middle school must be competent and confident. It is not enough to include teachers in the research, although it is essential to do so. Teachers also must be prepared to deal with a different mix of learners.

Practitioners suggest that there are several important components to successful staff development. Teachers must have an opportunity to think through the philosophical rationale that supports flexible grouping. They must have a chance to study the national and local research.

Teachers also must become acquainted with the skills for effective management and instruction in heterogeneous classes. Techniques for giving in-class assistance to less successful students and for challenging more successful students will need to be developed. Alternative models of grading, emphasizing individual progress and de-emphasizing the normal curve, must become part of the teacher's repertoire. Techniques for providing choice and diversity in homework and major assignments will be instituted.

Special education teachers can be a resource for staff development. These educators can provide training to general education teachers in making learning more concrete, in alternative assessment, and in classroom management.

Specific teaching methods that work well in inclusive middle school classrooms include:

- Cooperative learning. Many models of cooperative learning are popular with middle school teachers and their students. However, none is learned easily in one-shot workshops. School leaders who say, "We sent them to a workshop on cooperative learning," have not completed their responsibilities.
- Mastery learning. Two decades of research and practice support several models. The work of Guskey (1985) at the University of Kentucky is an example.
- Whole-language, thematic-curriculum, and workshop approaches to reading and writing instruction. These promising departures from rigid basal programs bring new measures of excitement to students involved in self-chosen reading and writing projects. Particularly impressive is the reading/writing workshop approach of Atwell (1987).
- Individualized instruction. Such time-honored approaches as learning centers and what used to be called "unipacs" may find new life in heterogeneous classrooms.
- Consultation and co-teaching approaches to collaboration between regular-classroom teachers and special educators. Participants must be willing, time for planning must be made available, and those involved must be trained in how to work together.
- Computerized instruction. Computers may contribute to some students' lack of access to important learning resources and inequitable learning experiences, especially if only one track of students is allowed to use them. But accessible computerized instruction can open a world of diverse experiences for all types of learners.

Step 9: Keep at it.

It seems that the move away from ability grouping has only begun, and the strategies that lead to success are just now emerging. Middle school educators have assumed the lead in an important school-change process fraught with frustration and difficulty. As the 21st century begins, when new models of inclusive schools and heterogeneous classrooms appear, they will do so fully and first in middle schools.

References

Atwell, N. *In the Middle: Writing, Reading, and Learning with Adolescents.* Portsmouth, N.H.: Heinemann, 1987.

George, P.S. *The Japanese Junior High School: A View from the Inside.* Columbus, Ohio: National Middle School Association, 1989.

George, P.S. *How to Untrack Your School.* Alexandria, Va.: Association for Supervision and Curriculum Development, 1992.

George, P.S., and Alexander, W.M. *The Exemplary Middle School.* 2nd ed. Fort Worth: Harcourt Brace Jovanovich, 1993.

Guskey, T.R. *Implementing Mastery Learning.* Belmont, Calif.: Wadsworth, 1985.

Kanter, R.M.; Stein, B.A.; and Jick, T.D. *The Challenge of Organizational Change: How Companies Experience It and Leaders Guide It.* New York: Free Press, 1992.

MacLeod, J. *Ain't No Makin' It: Leveled Aspirations in a Low-Income Neighborhood.* Boulder, Colo.: Westview, 1987.

Pfeiffer, J.W.; Goodstein, L.D.; and Nolan, T.M. *Shaping Strategic Planning: Frogs, Dragons, Bees, and Turkey Tails.* Chicago: Scott, Foresman, 1989.

Slavin, R.E.; Madden, N.A.; Karweit, N.L.; Livermon, B.J.; and Dolan, L. "Success for All: First-Year Outcomes of a Comprehensive Plan for Reforming Urban Education." *American Educational Research Journal* 27 (1990): 255-78.

Weisbord, M.R. *Productive Workplaces: Organizing and Managing for Dignity, Meaning, and Community.* San Francisco: Jossey-Bass, 1987.

IN THE MEANTIME:
USING A DIALECTICAL
APPROACH TO RAISE LEVELS
OF INTELLECTUAL
STIMULATION AND INQUIRY
IN LOW-TRACK CLASSES

BY BARBARA G. BLACKWELL

Perhaps the most compelling evidence against tracking comes from a study by Adam Gamoran and Mark Berends (1988). They conclude that tracking favors students in the high track, accounts for disparities in student achievement, produces a cycle of low expectations for low-track students, and creates poor morale among other teachers and students. In addition to this telling statement, there are many education theorists and social scientists (Coleman 1966; Merton 1948; Oakes ·1985; Rist 1970) who attest that academic excellence is more a social and economic phenomenon than one based on innate ability or potential for academic and social success. Yet, for the most part, our schools have done little to reconceptualize grouping patterns and rigid tracking systems, at least in actual practice.

Although they note inconclusive findings on the benefits of tracking, Good and Brophy (1994) report that teachers dislike teaching low-ability students, spend less time preparing for them, and schedule less interesting or less challenging activities for them. Such unsurprising findings show that the benefits of tracking do indeed accrue to the high-track students, while those identified as low-ability are relegated to education's back burners. Is it any wonder that many students in low-track classes have poor attitudes about teachers and schools, tend to have poor work habits, exhibit more acting out or withdrawn behaviors, demonstrate few approved and sanctioned leadership skills, and generally meet the self-fulfilling prophecies that are mapped out for them at an early age? If educators are serious about providing all our children with the intellectual and social tools needed for successful functioning in the 21st century, then stimulating educational experiences must be given not only to the talented and fortunate students, but to all our students.

In the meantime, we dare not wait for a clear break from entrenched tracking practices that have, for the most part, been advanced and developed by those in power who perpetuate existing social-class, economic-status, ethnic, and racial biases. Although new grouping patterns are emerging through cooperative-learning studies (Slavin 1987), tutoring models (cross-age and peer), and new assessments developed from multiple-intelligence studies, tracking remains the insidious norm, rather than the reluctant exception. When the quality of schooling is defined in terms of equity and excellence, the issue is even more volatile — as if both could not possibly exist at the same time and for all students. With devastating clarity, tracking versus heterogeneous grouping is a political and emotional issue as much as it is an educational one.

One recent maxim states, "All children can learn." Unfortunately, educators who profess to believe this truism still can become bogged down in the complexities of what it really means and how one can translate this ideal into action: the learning-teaching process that is compelling and takes into account the strengths and weaknesses of the learner, understanding that the limitations we all possess are tentative and can be overcome with time and effort. It is crucial that educators move beyond many traditional and unproductive school practices in an attempt to reach the alarming numbers of disenchanted students. Increasingly, slow, average, above-average, and gifted students are being turned off by the read-write-regurgitate syndrome that exists in far too many classrooms. Educators must value — and create — higher-level thinking experiences for all students and view education as a way to engage students beyond the ordinary. Restructuring the teaching-learning experience — especially in terms of "why" we teach, "what" we teach, "how" we teach, and perhaps most important, "who" the teacher is as an individual — needs our serious attention.

When one realizes that *education* means to uplift, to enrich, and to help individuals become noble and good and productive and effective, then a dialectical approach utilizing the borrowed sayings of Socrates, Confucius, Plato, Jesus, Buddha, Mohammed, Pestalozzi, Montessori, Dewey, and other great teachers may be helpful. Such an approach will allow those students an opportunity to see that there are many issues to be considered when learning "why" they must become self-motivated and uplift themselves and "how" that might occur in the classroom. Lower-tracked students need to explore such issues about humanity and be given strategies and techniques for coping with a sometimes-despotic majority that consciously or unconsciously relegates them to lives of powerlessness and ignorance.

Delivering coping skills is a crucial part of affirming students. Without confrontation or hostility, students can learn to extrapolate for themselves the values of truth, honesty, empathy, and compassion; a keen sense of justice for all individuals; the right use of power; and the ability to grow in self-respect, self-discipline, and self-responsibility — higher goals than maintaining a 4.0 average or making more than $200,000 a year. Let me quickly add that there is nothing inherently evil in a 4.0 average or making $200,000 a year. Rather, are these goals balanced with the noble and good?

Too often we concern ourselves only with academic achievement, thereby producing what might be called "intelligent idiots" who have fantastic paper credentials but are narrow-minded, manipulative, greedy, and selfish; who cannot get along with other people or form meaningful, honest relationships; who have no desire to work for the common good and no sense of justice except for themselves. These types of individuals use power inappropriately in their jobs and in life situations and seem to have little understanding of the concept of justice. They continue to do grave damage to the emotional and psychological well-being of those outside the realm of their own ethnic, class, economic, religious, or national group. If they are principals, teachers, or paraprofessionals, this damage can and does lead to academic and social failure for the students they serve.

Untracking schools will remove the stigmas of tracking and raise the levels of intellectual stimulation and inquiry. It heightens the moral and ethical consciousness of students who previously may not have been considered bright enough to discuss such weighty concerns.

Visual aids and simple props (similar to Pestalozzi's object lessons) can be used to set the stage for thought-provoking discussions that students can carry into everyday living. Adages, axioms, parables, fables, or short stories can stimulate discussion. Such informal, mini-dialectical lessons can take place at the beginning of the class session for 10 or 15 minutes. Some lessons might be continued for an entire week or longer, depending on the interests of the students and the activities pursued as a result of the discussion.

The intent of such lessons is to involve students in meaningful, relevant discussions of important, yet simple concepts that show the connections between learning and the real world. Further, they help students learn to cope with the "what is" while they strive for the "what can be" and become self-motivated and self-directed in terms of both academic and social maturity.

Rehabilitative and wholesome discussions about life and living can move students to higher levels of thinking and can help them become self-motivated to enlarge their views of teachers, schools, and academic and social achievement. Following are nine scenarios using maxims, adages, or stories taken from various disciplines. These scenarios show how such devices can excite learners and spur them to new levels of thinking.

Scenario 1. The Peanut Exercise

As students enter the class, a bowl of peanuts is on a table in the front of the room. The overhead projector beams the image of a large peanut on the screen. A colorful tablecloth can be used to draw even more attention to the bowl of peanuts and to add visual excitement.

Each student is handed a peanut from the bowl and asked to examine it for a minute or two and then to state some observed characteristics. Responses are recorded on the chalkboard by a volunteer student and might include: tan, curly tail, smells peanutty, smashed on one end. Then students are asked, "If I collect all the peanuts and return them to the bowl, would you be able to find your peanut?" Invariably, a more detailed analysis of the peanut immediately takes place. They are challenged and have a clearer sense of purpose about the task at hand. Brainstorming continues with more detailed descriptors forthcoming: shaped like a seal, three peanuts enclosed, a blemish on the end with the curly tail, a small hole approximately a half-inch from the curly-tail end of the peanut. The shape of the peanut may be traced on paper, estimates of length and width given, etc.

There are several directions in which a teacher can take this brief lesson. One is to discuss the sanctity of each individual. The teacher might discuss that each peanut in the room is different from any other peanut that has ever been grown or that ever will be grown. Students begin extrapolating from this example when asked to do so, and they add their own examples of unique phenomena: each grain of sand in the world, each leaf, raindrop, snowflake. Inevitably the subject of individual differences among human beings comes up. Ultimately, the discussion can lead to awareness and understanding of how we all need to respect and appreciate individual differences.

Scenario 2. "Behold the Only Thing Greater than Yourself"

In Alex Haley's book, *Roots* (1976), the father of Kunta Kinte lifts his infant son at birth and, with his face to the heavens, says, "Behold the only thing greater than yourself." Students are asked to share their thoughts about this statement. This exercise can be a way to explore with students the concept of "self" and how important it is to see one's self in positive ways. Attitudes are formed from our understanding and sense of self and lead us to believe or not believe in ourselves, our abilities, and our potential. Discussions about how other people around us help form our concept of self can lead students to understand, perhaps for the first time in an informal and safe environment, how other important people affect their self-concept. Students can see the need to discard negative images they and others have formed of them. Further discussions can lead to student-selected topics, such as the self-fulfilling prophecy and the concept of destiny control.

Scenario 3. Knowledge and Knowing

The teacher first shows a transparency with two classical sayings: "Know thyself" (inscription at the Delphi Oracle, from Plutarch) and "Knowledge is power" (Francis Bacon). The teacher then leads a discussion by asking questions: Who are you? What are you about as a person? What do you believe in? What positive character traits do you possess? Which characteristics do you attempt to develop consciously? How do you treat every person you meet? What do you think I mean when I say, "Your word is your bond"?

Asking students these types of questions and allowing time for meaningful interaction will provide them with the opportunity to grapple with issues and problems concerning honesty, empathy, compassion, friendliness, self-respect, self-discipline, self-responsibility, courage, patience, decorum, cooperation, convictions, and trustworthiness. Each student might be asked to explore one or two of the concepts presented and attempt to make meaningful changes in his or her own character development on a daily basis. Teachers can point out the importance of consciously and deliberately exploring who we are as individuals. We can enhance some of our better qualities and remove others that are self-defeating and self-limiting.

Scenario 4. The Clothesline Exercise

In this scenario, the teacher uses two projectors simultaneously to show these transparencies: 1) a humorous drawing of a doctor spanking a newborn baby's bottom, with the caption, "Do not fold, spindle, or mutilate," and 2) a statement, "The only thing necessary for the triumph of evil is for good men to do nothing," which Beck, writing in the preface to the 15th edition of Bartlett's *Familiar Quotations*, believes may be a 20th century paraphrase of Edmund Burke's view that "When bad men combine, the good must associate; else they will fall one by one, an unpitied sacrifice in a contemptible struggle."

The students explore the meaning of the two sayings and make connections between them. Then two students stretch a clothesline across the front of the room. The class deliberates on what this might signify. A large cloth is fastened at the waist of the student to the class's left with huge, clearly visible diaper pins; a baby bonnet is placed on this student's head. The student on the right dons a black robe or gown and holds up a cardboard scythe. At this point, the class again brainstorms about the symbolism of birth, the span of life, and death. Students discuss the significance of the scene and how it affects them.

The teacher may follow up with statements about how we have no say in where we were born, who our parents are, where we live, whether we come from a family that is poor or rich; educated or uneducated; black or white; Muslim, Jew, or Gentile; speak standard English or nonstandard English; live on an estate or in a trailer camp; or attend a school with excellent teachers, abundant resources, and high expectations or one that is in a high-crime neighborhood with a dilapidated building, outmoded books and equipment, and low expectations of staff and students.

The crux of the discussion is to lead students to see the importance of what part they do have some control over — the time between birth and death. This is an important concept of destiny control that is needed very much by students who feel fragmented and buffeted in their lives. They need to believe that they can take control over their lives in many important ways, including the pursuit of academic and social excellence.

In relation to the statement attributed to Burke, the class can discuss the apathy that exists in society's dealings with such social ills as poverty, homelessness, nepotism, failing schools, war, environmental issues, rising crime and violence, racism, sexism, classism, drug and alcohol abuse, teenage pregnancies, dropouts, illiteracy, injustice, biased media, employment discrimination, mental illness, delinquency, and vandalism. Although students may feel overwhelmed by the number and intensity of problems that are raised, the teacher can lead them to see that their individual thoughts and attitudes about each of those issues can be put into a more manageable perspective. For example, they can learn to take more responsibility for their own attitudes and actions. They can create a cognitive map of how they visualize their future. A community-service project may be initiated as a result of continued discussions of this sort.

Scenario 5. "We Use Only 10% of Our Potential"

An overhead transparency with the familiar statement, "We use only 10% of our potential," begins the discussion. Students are asked to define the word "potential." Small groups of students can explore the steps needed to change low aspirations into higher ones. Students might be asked to learn something totally new every month or two and report back to the class on that new learning experience. Small groups of students might decide to work on a project such as following the stock market, gardening, rowing or sculling, or playing chess, which they will pursue for a month or six weeks. Such a discussion might spur students to reach and flex and surpass former academic and social achievements.

Scenario 6. The Elephant Story

Students are shown a picture of an elephant with one of its back legs tied to a stake. This is another quick motivational story that will give students the opportunity to think about how they allow peer pressure and the low expectations of self and important others (parents, friends, family members, and teachers) to cloud their minds in terms of developing their full potentials. The story is this:

> A baby elephant was captured from its home in Africa to be used in a circus. The trainer tied her back legs with a rope and buried a stake in the ground to keep her from running away. The baby elephant struggled and tugged at the rope for a number of weeks in an attempt to escape. Finally, she gave up the struggle and adjusted to her captive state. A few years later, though the rope had been lengthened to allow for wider movement, the thickness of the rope and the nature of her captivity remained the same. What was different was that the elephant now weighed two tons. Obviously, the full-grown elephant could now give the rope a mighty tug and

escape the bonds that held her, except that for so long she had believed that she could not escape that she never attempted to escape again.

This story might lead to discussions about human enslavement (both physical and mental), brainwashing techniques, biased textbooks and media, and stereotyping. When we allow others to define who we are and what we can achieve, we give up our self-responsibility. Frequently, we can "buy into" the prophecy and lead fragmented, frustrated, unproductive, and unfulfilled lives because of the seeds planted in our minds by others. The teacher might assign *Pygmalion in the Classroom* (Rosenthal and Jacobson 1968), with a discussion to follow regarding the power of suggestion and positive and negative self-fulfilling prophecies. This small vignette may help students change their low aspirations.

Scenario 7. The Four-Minute Mile

In the early 1950s, Roger Bannister was the first man to break the four-minute mile. While viewing a transparency of a person breaking the tape in a race, the students are asked to describe what happened once the four-minute mile was broken. They will probably bring up the names of other athletes who ran the mile in under four minutes once Bannister's accomplishment was known. Students will discuss how, once a barrier is broken, others begin to realize that they can reach the same goal. Others can inspire us to even higher goals. Indeed, the potential is there for all of us to break barriers.

Scenario 8. Pebble in a Pond

Student are asked to discuss what Commoner (1971) refers to as "the first law of ecology," that "everything is connected to everything else" (p. 33). Then they write down their thoughts to share with other members of the class. The teacher might write on the board, "No man is an island," "The family of man," and related ideas. A student drops a pebble into a jar of water, which simulates "the pond," to obtain a ripple effect. Then the class discusses the concept that a pebble thrown into a quiet pond affects the entire pond and that, if one person fails to achieve in this world, it affects the quality of all our lives.

Students might be asked to respond to and elaborate on the effectiveness of the division of labor in a beehive or the behaviors of a colony of ants and their cooperative spirit. The teacher might discuss our responsibility as members of the human race to help every person succeed in life.

Scenario 9. The Power of Positive Thinking

Students can discuss the meaning of the title of the book by Norman Vincent Peale, *The Power of Positive Thinking* (1956). Our minds can and do affect how we live. Students might explore strategies for chasing away negative thoughts and replacing them with positive self-images.

The class might be asked to make connections between their stated thoughts and a bowl of lemons on a table in the front of the classroom. The teacher can write on the chalkboard, "If life deals you a lemon, make lemonade!" Then the dialogue can turn to how we can learn to transform negatives into positives and to change for the better those things over which we have no control.

Final Thoughts

Teachers' expectations and biases influence student achievement and success (Merton 1948; Oakes 1985). In numerous Pygmalion-type experiments, teachers have been told that various groups are "slow" and "accelerated." The clear-cut and predictable results (regardless of IQ scores, ethnic origin, previous success in school, or race) are that the groups labeled "accelerated" do well and the "slow" groups do not.

If our teaching style is closely aligned with the philosophical tradition of pragmatism and we truly believe in the importance of uplifting those in our charge, we will make sure that our students are involved in experiences that encourage them to interact with their environment, exploring its frailties and its virtues, particularly as they relate to the individual self-concepts of lower-track students. Just as pragmatic philosophy emphasizes the process of activities rather than simply the content, these approaches are intended to open up a way for students to act on, react to, and interact with issues of academic and social success couched in a moral and ethical construct.

Valuing and stimulating intellectual inquiry in our schools demands an active curriculum in a social, engaging, and safe environment. Such a climate allows for individual reflection and musings, self-disclosure, risk-taking, and collaboration. Inspirational and motivational strategies can help ground students in crucial character development, and open discussions can lead both students and teachers to higher levels of self-knowledge.

As Carl Rogers (1969) said, realness or authenticity is the attitude most basic to the learning-teaching relationship. The teacher-student relationship is perhaps second only to that of the parent-child relationship. No matter what their assigned academic levels, all students can

163

explore central values of truth and justice and what constitutes the good and noble life, at the same time putting forth a greater effort through a newly acquired sense of self.

Maslow (1968) pointed out that security is one of our basic needs. Perhaps students in lower tracks will be able to concentrate more on academic learning and achievement when they are provided with a warm, safe, and caring environment; when they have discussions about real concerns that surround them; and when they are armed with new ways of thinking about and dealing with problems relevant to their lives.

References

Coleman, J.S. *Equality of Educational Opportunity*. Washington, D.C.: U.S. Department of Health, Education, and Welfare, 1966.

Commoner, B. *The Closing Circle: Confronting the Environmental Crisis*. London: Jonathan Cape, 1971.

Gamoran, A., and Berends, M. "The Effects of Stratification in Secondary Schools: Synthesis of Survey and Ethnographic Research." *Review of Educational Research* 57, no. 4 (1988): 415-35.

Good, T., and Brophy, J. *Looking in Classrooms*. 6th ed. New York: HarperCollins, 1994.

Haley, A. *Roots*. Garden City, N.Y.: Doubleday, 1976.

Maslow, A.H. *Toward a Psychology of Being*. 2nd ed. New York: Van Nostrand Reinhold, 1968.

Merton, R. "The Self-Fulfilling Prophecy." *Antioch Review* 8, no. 2 (1948): 193-210.

Oakes, J. *Keeping Track: How Schools Structure Inequality*. New Haven, Conn.: Yale University Press, 1985.

Peale, N.V. *The Power of Positive Thinking*. New York: Prentice-Hall, 1956.

Rist, R. "Student Social Class and Teacher Expectations: The Self-Fulfilling Prophecy in Ghetto Education." *Harvard Educational Review* 40, no. 3 (1970): 411-51.

Rogers, C.R. *Freedom to Learn: A View of What Education Might Become*. Columbus, Ohio: Charles E. Merrill, 1969.

Rosenthal, R., and Jacobson, L. *Pygmalion in the Classroom: Teacher Expectation and Pupils' Intellectual Development*. New York: Holt, 1968.

Slavin, R.E. "Ability Grouping and Student Achievement in Elementary Schools: A Best-Evidence Synthesis." *Review of Educational Research* 57, no. 3 (1987): 293-336.

15

SYNTHESIS OF RESEARCH ON COOPERATIVE LEARNING*

BY ROBERT E. SLAVIN

There was once a time when it was taken for granted that a quiet class was a learning class, when principals walked down the hall expecting to be able to hear a pin drop. Today, however, many schools are using programs that foster the hum of voices in classrooms. These programs, called cooperative learning, encourage students to discuss, debate, disagree, and ultimately to teach one another.

Cooperative learning has been suggested as the solution for an astonishing array of education problems. It often is cited as a means of emphasizing thinking skills and increasing higher-order learning; as an alternative to ability grouping, remediation, or special education; as a means of improving race relations and acceptance of mainstreamed students; and as a way to prepare students for an increasingly collaborative work force. How many of these claims are justified? What effects do the various cooperative-learning methods have on student achievement and other outcomes? Which forms of cooperative learning are

---

*This chapter is an adapted version of an article that first appeared in *Educational Leadership* 48, no. 5 (1991): 71-77, 79-82. Copyright 1991 by the Association for Supervision and Curriculum Development, Alexandria, Va. Adapted by permission.

most effective, and what components must be in place for cooperative learning to work?

To answer these questions, I've synthesized in this chapter the findings of studies of cooperative learning in elementary and secondary schools that have compared cooperative learning to traditionally taught control groups studying the same objectives over a period of at least four weeks (and up to a full school year or more). Here I present a brief summary of the effects of cooperative learning on achievement and noncognitive outcomes. (For a more extensive review, see Slavin 1990.)

Cooperative-Learning Methods

There are many different forms of cooperative learning, but all of them involve having students work in small groups or teams to help one another learn academic material. Cooperative learning usually supplements the teacher's instruction by giving students an opportunity to discuss information or practice skills originally presented by the teacher. Sometimes cooperative methods require students to find or discover information on their own. Cooperative learning has been used — and investigated — in every imaginable subject in grades 2 through 12 and is used increasingly in college.

Small-scale laboratory research on cooperation dates back to the 1920s (see Deutsch 1949; Slavin 1977b); research on specific applications of cooperative learning to the classroom began in the early 1970s. At that time, four research groups, one in Israel and three in the United States, began independently to develop and study cooperative-learning methods in classroom settings.

Now researchers all over the world are studying practical applications of cooperative-learning principles, and many cooperative-learning methods have been evaluated in one or more experimental/control comparisons. The best evaluated of the cooperative models are described below (adapted from Slavin 1990). These include four Student Team Learning variations, Jigsaw, Learning Together, and Group Investigation.

Student Team Learning. Student Team Learning (STL) techniques were developed and researched at Johns Hopkins University. More than half of all experimental studies of practical cooperative-learning methods involve STL methods.

All cooperative-learning methods share the idea that students work together to learn and are responsible for one another's learning, as well as their own. STL methods, in addition to this idea, emphasize the use of team goals and team success, which can be achieved only if all mem-

166

bers of the team learn the objectives being taught. That is, in Student Team Learning the students' tasks are not to *do* something as a team but to *learn* something as a team.

Three concepts are central to all Student Team Learning methods: team rewards, individual accountability, and equal opportunities for success. Using STL techniques, teams earn certificates or other team rewards if they achieve above a designated criterion. The teams are not in competition to earn scarce rewards; all (or none) of the teams may achieve the criterion in a given week. Individual accountability means that the team's success depends on the individual learning of all team members. This focuses the activity of the team members on explaining concepts to one another and making sure that everyone on the team is ready for a quiz or other assessment that they will take without teammate help. Equal opportunities for success means that students contribute to their teams by improving over their own past performances. This ensures that high, average, and low achievers are equally challenged to do their best and that the contributions of all team members will be valued.

The findings of these exceptional studies indicate that team rewards and individual accountability are essential elements for producing basic-skills achievement (Slavin 1983*a*, 1983*b*, 1990). It is not enough simply to tell students to work together. They must have a reason to take one another's achievement seriously. Further, if students are rewarded for doing better than they have in the past, they will be more motivated to achieve than if they are rewarded based on their performance in comparison to others, because rewards for improvement make success neither too difficult nor too easy for students to achieve (Slavin 1980).

Four principal Student Team Learning methods have been intensively developed and researched. Two are general cooperative-learning methods adaptable to most subjects and grade levels: Student Teams-Achievement Divisions (STAD) and Teams-Games-Tournament (TGT). The remaining two are comprehensive curricula designed for use in particular subjects at particular grade levels: Team-Assisted Individualization (TAI) for mathematics in grades three through six and Cooperative Integrated Reading and Composition (CIRC) for reading and writing instruction in grades three through five.

In Student Teams-Achievement Divisions (Slavin 1978, 1986), students are assigned to four-member learning teams mixed in performance level, sex, and ethnicity. The teacher presents a lesson, and then students work within their teams to make sure that all team members have mastered the lesson. Finally, all students take individual quizzes on the material, at which time they may not help one another.

Students' quiz scores are compared to their own past averages, and points are awarded based on the degree to which students can meet or exceed their own earlier performances. These points then are summed to form team scores, and teams that meet certain criteria earn certificates or other rewards. The whole cycle of activities, from teacher presentation to team practice to quiz, usually takes three to five class periods.

STAD has been used in a wide variety of subjects, from mathematics to language arts and social studies. It has been used from grade two through college. STAD is most appropriate for teaching well-defined objectives with single right answers, such as mathematical computations and applications, language usage and mechanics, geography and map skills, and science facts and concepts.

Teams-Games-Tournament (DeVries and Slavin 1978; Slavin 1986) was the first of the Johns Hopkins cooperative-learning methods. It uses the same teacher presentations and teamwork as in STAD, but replaces the quizzes with weekly tournaments. In these, students compete with members of other teams to contribute points to their team scores. Students compete at three-person "tournament tables" against others with similar past records in mathematics. A "bumping" procedure changes table assignments to keep the competition fair. The winner at each tournament table brings the same number of points to his or her team, regardless of which table it is; this means that low achievers (competing with other low achievers) and high achievers (competing with other high achievers) have equal opportunities for success. As in STAD, high-performing teams earn certificates or other forms of team rewards. TGT is appropriate for the same types of objectives as STAD.

Team-Assisted Individualization (Slavin, Leavey, and Madden 1986) shares with STAD and TGT the use of four-member, mixed-ability learning teams and certificates for high-performing teams. But where STAD and TGT use a single pace of instruction for the class, TAI combines cooperative learning with individualized instruction. Also, where STAD and TGT apply to most subjects and grade levels, TAI is specifically designed to teach mathematics to students in grades three to six (or older students not ready for a full algebra course).

In TAI, students enter an individualized sequence according to a placement test and then proceed at their own rates. In general, team members work on different units. Teammates check each other's work against answer sheets and help one another with any problems. Final unit tests are taken without teammate help and are scored by student monitors. Each week teachers total the number of units completed by all team members and give certificates or other team rewards to teams that exceed a criterion score based on the number of final tests passed, with extra points for perfect papers and completed homework.

Because students take responsibility for checking each other's work and managing the flow of materials, the teacher can spend most of the class time presenting lessons to small groups of students drawn from the various teams who are working at the same point in the mathematics sequence. For example, the teacher might call up a decimals group, present a lesson, and then send the students back to their teams to work on problems. Then the teacher might call the fractions group, and so on.

The newest of the Student Team Learning methods is a comprehensive program for teaching reading and writing in the upper elementary grades called Cooperative Integrated Reading and Composition (Stevens et al. 1987). In CIRC, teachers use basal or literature-based readers and reading groups, much as in traditional reading programs. However, all students are assigned to teams composed of two pairs from two different reading groups. For example, a team might have two "Bluebirds" and two "Redbirds." While the teacher is working with one reading group, the paired students in the other groups are working on a series of cognitively engaging activities, including reading to one another, making predictions about how narrative stories will come out, summarizing stories to one another, writing responses to stories, and practicing spelling, decoding, and vocabulary. If the reading class is not divided into homogeneous reading groups, all students in the teams work with one another. Students work as a total team to master "main idea" and other comprehension skills. During language-arts periods, students write drafts, revise and edit one another's work, and prepare team books for "publication."

Jigsaw. Jigsaw was originally designed by Elliot Aronson and his colleagues (1978). In Aronson's Jigsaw method, students are assigned to six-member teams to work on academic material that has been broken into sections. For example, a biography might be divided into early life, first accomplishments, major setbacks, later life, and impact on history. Each team member reads his or her section. Next, members of different teams who have studied the same sections meet in "expert groups" to discuss their sections. Then the students return to their teams and take turns teaching their teammates about their sections. Since the only way students can learn sections other than their own is to listen carefully to their teammates, they are motivated to support and show interest in one another's work.

Slavin (1986) developed a modification of Jigsaw at Johns Hopkins University and then incorporated it in the Student Team Learning program. In this method, called Jigsaw II, students work in four- or five-member teams as in TGT and STAD. Instead of each student being assigned a particular section of text, all students read a common narrative, such as a book chapter, a short story, or a biography. However, each student receives a topic (such as "climate" in a unit on France) on which to become an expert. Students with the same topics meet in expert groups to discuss them, after which they return to their teams to teach what they have learned to their teammates. Then students take individual quizzes, which result in team scores based on the improvement-score system of STAD. Teams that meet preset standards earn certificates. Jigsaw primarily is used in social studies and other subjects where learning from text is important.

Learning Together. David Johnson and Roger Johnson at the University of Minnesota developed the Learning Together models of cooperative learning (Johnson and Johnson 1987). The methods they have researched involve students working on assignment sheets in four- or five-member heterogeneous groups. Each group hands in a single sheet and receives praise and rewards based on the group product. The Johnsons' methods emphasize team-building activities before students begin working together and regular discussions within groups about how well they are working together.

Group Investigation. Group Investigation, developed by Shlomo Sharan and Yael Sharan at the University of Tel-Aviv, is a general classroom organization plan in which students work in small groups using cooperative inquiry, group discussion, and cooperative planning and projects (Sharan and Sharan 1976). In this method students form their own two- to six-member groups. After choosing subtopics from a unit being studied by the entire class, the groups further break their subtopics into individual tasks and carry out the activities necessary to prepare group reports. Each group then makes a presentation or display to communicate its findings to the entire class.

Research on Cooperative Learning

Cooperative-learning methods are among the most extensively evaluated alternatives to traditional instruction. Outcome evaluations include:

- academic achievement,
- intergroup relations,

170

- mainstreaming,
- self-esteem,
- others.

Academic Achievement. More than 70 high-quality studies have evaluated various cooperative-learning methods over periods of at least four weeks in regular elementary and secondary schools; 67 of these have measured effects on student achievement (see Slavin 1990). All these studies compared the effects of cooperative learning to those of traditionally taught control groups on measures of the same objectives pursued in all classes. Teachers and classes were either randomly assigned to cooperative or control conditions or matched on pretest achievement level and other factors.

Overall, of 67 studies of the achievement effects of cooperative learning, 41 (61%) found significantly greater achievement in cooperative than in control classes. Twenty-five (37%) found no differences, and in only one study did the control group outperform the experimental group. However, the effects of cooperative learning vary considerably according to the particular methods used. As noted earlier, two elements must be present if cooperative learning is to be effective: group goals and individual accountability (Slavin 1983*a*, 1983*b*, 1990). That is, groups must be working to achieve some goal or to earn rewards or recognition, and the success of the group must depend on the individual learning of every group member.

In studies of methods such as STAD, TGT, TAI, and CIRC, effects on achievement have been consistently positive; 37 out of 44 such studies (84%) found significant positive achievement effects. In contrast, only 4 of 23 studies (17%) lacking group goals and individual accountability found positive effects on student achievement. Two of these positive effects were found in studies of Group Investigation in Israel (Sharan et al. 1984; Sharan and Shachar 1988). In Group Investigation, students in each group are responsible for one unique part of the group's overall task, ensuring individual accountability. Then the group's overall performance is evaluated. Even though there are no specific group rewards, the group evaluation probably serves the same purpose.

Why are group goals and individual accountability so important? To understand this, consider the alternatives. In some forms of cooperative learning, students work together to complete a single worksheet or to solve one problem together. In such methods, there is little reason for more able students to take time to explain what is going on to their less able group mates or to ask their opinions. When the group task is to *do* something, rather than to *learn* something, the participation of less able students may be seen as interference rather than help. It may be easier in this circumstance for students to give each other answers than to explain concepts or skills to one another.

In contrast, when the group's task is to ensure that every group member *learns* something, it is in the interests of every group member to spend time explaining concepts to his or her group mates. Studies of students' behaviors within cooperative groups consistently have found that the students who gain most from cooperative work are those who give and receive elaborated explanations (Webb 1985). Webb found that giving and receiving answers without explanations were *negatively* related to achievement gain. Group goals and individual accountability motivate students to give explanations and to take one another's learning seriously, instead of simply giving answers.

Cooperative-learning methods generally work equally well for all types of students. While occasional studies find particular advantages for high or low achievers, boys and girls, and so on, the great majority find equal benefits for all types of students. Sometimes teachers or parents worry that cooperative learning will hold back high achievers. The research provides absolutely no support for this claim; high achievers gain from cooperative learning (relative to high achievers in traditional classes) just as much as do low and average achievers (Slavin 1991).

Research on the achievement effects of cooperative learning has taken place more often in grades 3-9 than in 10-12. Studies at the high school level are about as positive as those at earlier grade levels, but there is a need for much more research at that level. Cooperative-learning methods have been equally successful in urban, rural, and suburban schools and with students of different ethnic groups, though a few studies have found particularly positive effects for black students (see Slavin and Oickle 1981).

Among the cooperative-learning methods, the Student Team Learning programs have been most extensively researched and most often found instructionally effective. Of 14 studies of STAD and closely related methods, 11 found significantly higher achievement for this method than for traditional instruction, and two found no differences. For example, Slavin and Karweit (1984) evaluated STAD over an entire school year in inner-city Philadelphia ninth-grade mathematics classes. Student performance on a standardized mathematics test increased significantly more than in either a mastery-learning group or a control group using the same materials. Substantial differences favoring STAD have been found in such diverse subjects as social studies (for example, Allen and

172

VanSickle 1984), language arts (Slavin and Karweit 1981), reading comprehension (Stevens et al. 1988), mathematics (Sherman and Thomas 1986), and science (Okebukola 1985). Nine of 11 studies of TGT found similar results (DeVries and Slavin 1978).

The largest effects of Student Team Learning methods have been found in studies of TAI. Five of six studies found substantially greater learning of mathematics computations in TAI than in control classes, while one study found no differences (see Slavin 1985*b*). Experimental-control differences still were substantial (though smaller) a year after the students were in TAI (Slavin and Karweit 1985). In mathematics concepts and applications, one of three studies (Slavin, Madden, and Leavey 1984) found significantly greater gains in TAI than control methods, while two found no significant differences (Slavin and Karweit 1985).

In comparison with traditional control groups, three experimental studies of CIRC have found substantial positive effects on scores from standardized tests of reading comprehension, reading vocabulary, language expression, language mechanics, and spelling (Madden et al. 1986; Stevens et al. 1987; Stevens et al. 1990). Significantly greater achievement on writing samples also was found favoring the CIRC students in the two studies that assessed writing.

Other than STL methods, the most consistently successful model for increasing student achievement is Group Investigation (Sharan and Sharan 1976). One study of this method (Sharan et al. 1984) found that it increased the learning of English as a foreign language, while Sharan and Shachar (1988) found positive effects of Group Investigation on the learning of history and geography. A third study of only three weeks' duration (Sharan et al. 1980) also found positive effects on social-studies achievement, particularly on higher-level concepts. The Learning Together methods (Johnson and Johnson 1987) have been found instructionally effective when they include the assignment of group grades based on the average of group members' individual quiz scores (for example, Humphreys et al. 1982; Yager et al. 1985). Studies of the original Jigsaw method have not generally supported this approach (for example, Moskowitz et al. 1983); but studies of Jigsaw II, which uses group goals and individual accountability, have shown positive effects (Mattingly and VanSickle 1990; Ziegler 1981).

Intergroup Relations. In the laboratory research on cooperation, one of the earliest and strongest findings was that people who cooperate learn to like one another (Slavin 1977*a*). Not surprisingly, the cooperative-learning classroom studies have found quite consistently that students express greater liking for their classmates in general as a result of participating in a cooperative-learning method (see Slavin 1983a, 1990). This is important in itself and even more important when the students have different ethnic backgrounds. After all, there is substantial evidence that, left alone, ethnic separateness in schools does not naturally diminish over time (Gerard and Miller 1975).

Social scientists have long advocated interethnic cooperation as a means of ensuring positive intergroup relations in desegregated settings. Contact Theory (Allport 1954), which in the United States is the dominant theory of intergroup relations, predicted that positive intergroup relations would arise from school desegregation if and only if students participated in cooperative, equal-status interaction sanctioned by the school. Research on cooperative-learning methods has borne out the predictions of Contact Theory. These techniques emphasize school-sanctioned, cooperative, equal-status interaction among students of different ethnic backgrounds (Slavin 1985a).

In most of the research on intergroup relations, students were asked to list their best friends at the beginning of the study and again at the end. The number of friendship choices students made outside their own ethnic groups was the measure of intergroup relations.

Positive effects on intergroup relations have been found for STAD, TGT, TAI, Jigsaw, Learning Together, and Group Investigation models (Slavin 1985b). Two of these studies, one on STAD (Slavin 1979) and one on Jigsaw II (Ziegler 1981), included follow-ups of intergroup friendships several months after the end of the studies. Both found that students who had been in cooperative-learning classes still named significantly more friends outside their own ethnic groups than did students who had been in control classes. Two studies of Group Investigation (Sharan et al. 1984; Sharan and Shachar 1988) found that students' improved attitudes and behaviors toward classmates of different ethnic backgrounds extended to classmates who had never been in the same groups, and a study of TAI (Oishi 1983) found positive effects of this method on cross-ethnic interactions outside as well as in class. The U.S. studies on cooperative learning and intergroup relations involved black, white, and (in a few cases) Mexican-American students. A study of Jigsaw II by Ziegler (1981) took place in Toronto, where the major ethnic groups were Anglo-Canadians and children of recent European immigrants. The Sharan (Sharan et al. 1984; Sharan and Shachar 1988) studies of Group Investigation took place in Israel and involved friendships between Jews of both European and Middle Eastern backgrounds.

Mainstreaming. Although ethnicity is a major barrier to friendship, it is not so large as the one between physically and mentally handicapped children and their normal-progress peers. Mainstreaming, an unprecedented opportunity for handicapped children to take their place in the school and society, has created enormous practical problems for classroom teachers; and it often leads to social rejection of the handicapped children. Because cooperative-learning methods have been successful in improving relationships across the ethnicity barrier — which somewhat resembles the barrier between mainstreamed and normal-progress students — these methods also have been applied to increase the acceptance of the mainstreamed student.

The research on cooperative learning and mainstreaming has focused on the academically handicapped child. In one study, STAD was used to attempt to integrate students performing two years or more below the level of their peers into the social structure of the classroom. The use of STAD significantly reduced the degree to which the normal-progress students rejected their mainstreamed classmates and increased the academic achievement and self-esteem of all students, mainstreamed as well as normal-progress (Madden and Slavin 1983). Similar effects have been found for TAI (Slavin, Leavey, and Madden 1984), and other research using cooperative teams has also shown significant improvements in relationships between mainstreamed academically handicapped students and their normal-progress peers (Ballard et al. 1977; Cooper et al. 1980).

In addition, one study in a self-contained school for emotionally disturbed adolescents found that the use of TGT increased positive interactions and friendships among students (Slavin 1977b). Five months after the study ended, these positive interactions still were found more often in the former TGT classes than in the control classes. In a study in a similar setting, Janke (1978) found that the emotionally disturbed students were more on-task, were better behaved, and had better attendance in TGT classes than in control classes.

Self-Esteem. One of the most important aspects of a child's personality is his or her self-esteem. Several researchers working on cooperative-learning techniques have found that these methods do increase students' self-esteem. These improvements in self-esteem have been found for TGT and STAD (Slavin 1990), for Jigsaw (Blaney et al. 1977), and for the three methods combined (Slavin and Karweit 1981). Improvements in student self-concepts also have been found for TAI (Slavin, Leavey, and Madden 1984).

Other Outcomes. In addition to efforts on achievement, positive intergroup relations, greater acceptance of mainstreamed students, and self-esteem, effects of cooperative learning have been found on a variety of other important educational outcomes. These include liking school, development of peer norms in favor of doing well academically, feelings of individual control over the student's own fate in school, and cooperativeness and altruism (see Slavin 1983*a*, 1990). TGT (DeVries and Slavin 1978; Janke 1978) and STAD (Slavin 1978) have been found to have positive effects on students' time on task. One study found that lower-socioeconomic-status students at risk of becoming delinquent who worked in cooperative groups in sixth grade had better attendance, fewer contacts with the police, and higher behavioral ratings by teachers in grades 7-11 than did control students (Hartley 1976). Another study implemented forms of cooperative learning beginning in kindergarten and continuing through the fourth grade (Solomon et al. 1990). This study found that the students who had been taught cooperatively were significantly higher than control students on measures of supportive, friendly, and prosocial behavior; were better at resolving conflicts; and expressed more support for democratic values.

Useful Strategies

Returning to the questions at the beginning of this chapter, we now see the usefulness of cooperative-learning strategies for improving such diverse outcomes as student achievement at a variety of grade levels and in many subjects, intergroup relations, relationships between mainstreamed and normal-progress students, and student self-esteem. Further, their widespread and growing use demonstrates that cooperative learning is an outstanding example of the use of education research to create programs that have improved the educational experiences of thousands of students and will continue to affect thousands more.

References

Allen, W.H., and VanSickle, R.L. "Learning Teams and Low Achievers." *Social Education* 48, no. 1 (1984): 60-64.

Allport, G. *The Nature of Prejudice*. Cambridge, Mass.: Addison-Wesley, 1954.

Aronson, E.; Blaney, N.; Stephan, C.; Sikes, J.; and Snapp, M. *The Jigsaw Classroom*. Beverly Hills, Calif.: Sage, 1978.

Ballard, M.; Corman, L.; Gottlieb, J.; and Kaufman, M.J. "Improving the Social Status of Mainstreamed Retarded Children." *Journal of Educational Psychology* 69, no. 5 (1977): 605-11.

Blaney, N.T.; Stephan, C.; Rosenfield, D.; Aronson, E.; and Sikes, J. "Interdependence in the Classroom: A Field Study." *Journal of Educational Psychology* 69, no. 2 (1977): 121-28.

Cooper, L.; Johnson, D.W.; Johnson, R.; and Wilderson, F. "Effects of Cooperative, Competitive, and Individualistic Experiences on Interpersonal Attraction Among Heterogeneous Peers." *Journal of Social Psychology* 111, no. 2 (1980): 243-52.

Deutsch, M. "A Theory of Cooperation and Competition." *Human Relations* 2, no. 2 (1949): 129-52.

DeVries, D.L., and Slavin, R.E. "Team-Games-Tournament (TGT): Review of Ten Classroom Experiments." *Journal of Research and Development in Education* 12, no. 1 (1978): 28-38.

Gerard, H.B., and Miller, N. *School Desegregation: A Long-Range Study.* New York: Plenum, 1975.

Hartley, W. *Prevention Outcomes of Small-Group Education with School Children: An Epidemiologic Follow-up of the Kansas City School Behavior Project.* Kansas City: University of Kansas Medical Center, 1976.

Humphreys, B.; Johnson, R.T.; and Johnson, D.W. "Effects of Cooperative, Competitive, and Individualistic Learning on Students' Achievement in Science Class." *Journal of Research in Science Teaching* 19, no. 5 (1982): 351-56.

Janke, R. "The Teams-Games-Tournament (TGT) Method and Behavioral Adjustment and Academic Achievement of Emotionally Impaired Adolescents." Paper presented at the annual meeting of the American Educational Research Association, Toronto, April 1978.

Johnson, D.W., and Johnson, R.T. *Learning Together and Alone.* 2nd ed. Englewood Cliffs, N.J.: Prentice-Hall, 1987.

Madden, N.A., and Slavin, R.E. "Effects of Cooperative Learning and Social Acceptance of Mainstreamed Academically Handicapped Students." *Journal of Special Education* 17, no. 2 (1983): 171-82.

Madden, N.A.; Stevens, R.J.; and Slavin, R.E. *A Comprehensive Cooperative Learning Approach to Elementary Reading and Writing: Effects on Student Achievement.* Center for Research on Elementary and Middle Schools Report No. 2. Baltimore: Johns Hopkins University, Center for Research on Elementary and Middle Schools, 1986.

Mattingly, R.M., and VanSickle, R.L. *Jigsaw II in Secondary Social Studies: An Experiment.* Athens: University of Georgia, 1990.

Moskowitz, J.M.; Malvin, J.H.; Schaeffer, G.A.; and Schaps, E. "Evaluation of a Cooperative Learning Strategy." *American Educational Research Journal* 20, no. 4 (1983): 687-96.

Oishi, S.S. "Effects of Team-Assisted Individualization in Mathematics on Cross-Race and Cross-Sex Interactions of Elementary School Children." Doctoral dissertation, University of Maryland, 1983. *Dissertation Abstracts International* 44, 3622A.

Okebukola, P.A. "The Relative Effectiveness of Cooperative and Competitive Interaction Techniques in Strengthening Students' Performance in Science Classes." *Science Education* 69, no. 4 (1985): 501-509.

Sharan, S., and Shachar, C. *Language and Learning in the Cooperative Classroom*. New York: Springer, 1988.

Sharan, S., and Sharan, Y. *Small-Group Teaching*. Englewood Cliffs, N.J.: Educational Technology Publications, 1976.

Sharan, S.; Hertz-Lazarowitz, R.; and Ackerman, Z. "Academic Achievement of Elementary School Children in Small-Group Versus Whole-Class Instruction." *Journal of Experimental Education* 48, no. 2 (1980): 125-29.

Sharan, S.; Kussell, P.; Hertz-Lazarowitz, R.; Bejarano, Y.; Raviv, S.; and Sharan, Y. *Cooperative Learning in the Classroom: Research in Desegregated Schools*. Hillsdale, N.J.: Lawrence Erlbaum Associates, 1984.

Sherman, L.W., and Thomas, M. "Mathematics Achievement in Cooperative Versus Individualistic Goal-Structured High School Classrooms." *Journal of Educational Research* 79, no. 3 (1986): 169-72.

Slavin, R.E. "Classroom Reward Structure: An Analytical and Practical Review." *Review of Educational Research* 47, no. 4 (1977): 633-50. a

Slavin, R.E. "A Student Team Approach to Teaching Adolescents with Special Emotional and Behavioral Needs." *Psychology in the Schools* 14, no. 1 (1977): 77-84. b

Slavin, R.E. "Student Teams and Achievement Divisions." *Journal of Research and Development in Education* 12, no. 1 (1978): 39-49.

Slavin, R.E. "Effects of Biracial Learning Teams on Cross-Racial Friendships." *Journal of Educational Psychology* 71, no. 3 (1979): 381-87.

Slavin, R.E. "Effects of Individual Learning Expectations on Student Achievement." *Journal of Educational Psychology* 72, no. 4 (1980): 520-24.

Slavin, R.E. *Cooperative Learning*. New York: Longman, 1983. a

Slavin, R.E. "When Does Cooperative Learning Increase Student Achievement?" *Psychological Bulletin* 94, no. 3 (1983): 429-45. b

Slavin, R.E. "Cooperative Learning: Applying Contact Theory in Desegregated Schools." *Journal of Social Issues* 41, no. 3 (1985): 45-62. a

Slavin, R.E. "Team-Assisted Individualization: A Cooperative Learning Solution for Adaptive Instruction in Mathematics." In *Adapting Instruction to Individual Differences*, edited by M.C. Wang and H.J. Walberg. Berkeley, Calif.: McCutchan, 1985. b

Slavin, R.E. *Using Student Team Learning*. 3rd ed. Baltimore: Johns Hopkins University, Center for Research on Elementary and Middle Schools, 1986.

Slavin, R.E. *Cooperative Learning: Theory, Research, and Practice*. Englewood Cliffs, N.J.: Prentice-Hall, 1990.

Slavin, R.E. "Are Cooperative Learning and 'Untracking' Harmful to the Gifted?" *Educational Leadership* 48, no. 6 (1991): 68-71.

Slavin, R.E., and Karweit, N.L. "Cognitive and Affective Outcomes of an Intensive Student Team Learning Experience." *Journal of Experimental Education* 50, no. 1 (1981): 29-35.

Slavin, R.E., and Karweit, N.L. "Mastery Learning and Student Teams: A Factorial Experiment in Urban General Mathematics Classes." *American Educational Research Journal* 21, no. 4 (1984): 725-36.

Slavin, R.E., and Karweit, N.L. "Effects of Whole-Class, Ability Grouped, and Individualized Instruction on Mathematics Achievement." *American Educational Research Journal* 22, no. 3 (1985): 351-67.

Slavin, R.E., Leavey, M.B., and Madden, N.A. "Combining Cooperative Learning and Individualized Instruction: Effects on Student Mathematics Achievement, Attitudes, and Behaviors." *Elementary School Journal* 84, no. 4 (1984): 409-22.

Slavin, R.E.; Leavey, M.B.; and Madden, N.A. *T-A-I Mathematics: Team Accelerated Instruction*. Watertown, Mass.: Mastery Educational Corporation, 1986.

Slavin, R.E.; Madden, N.A.; and Leavey, M. "Effects of Team-Assisted Individualization on the Mathematics Achievement of Academically Handicapped and Nonhandicapped Students." *Journal of Educational Psychology* 76, no. 5 (1984): 813-19.

Slavin, R.E., and Oickle, E. "Effects of Cooperative Learning Teams on Student Achievement and Race Relations: Treatment by Race Interactions." *Sociology of Education* 54, no. 3 (1981): 174-80.

Solomon, D.; Watson, M.; Schaps, E.; Battistich, V.; and Solomon, J. "Cooperative Learning as Part of a Comprehensive Classroom Program Designed to Promote Prosocial Development." In *Cooperative Learning: Theory and Research*, edited by S. Sharan. New York: Praeger, 1990.

Stevens, R.J.; Madden, N.A.; Slavin, R.E.; and Farnish, A.M. "Cooperative Integrated Reading and Composition: Two Field Experiments." *Reading Research Quarterly* 22, no. 4 (1987): 433-54.

Stevens, R.J.; Slavin, R.E.; and Farnish, A.M. "A Cooperative Learning Approach to Elementary Reading and Writing Instruction: Long-Term Effects." Paper presented at the annual meeting of the American Educational Research Association, Boston, April 1990.

Stevens, R.J.; Slavin, R.E.; Farnish, A.M.; and Madden, N.A. "The Effects of Cooperative Learning and Direct Instruction in Reading Comprehension Strategies on Main Idea Identification." Paper presented at the annual meeting of the American Educational Research Association, New Orleans, April 1988.

Webb, N. "Student Interaction and Learning in Small Groups: A Research Summary." In *Learning to Cooperate, Cooperating to Learn*, edited by R. Slavin, S. Sharan, S. Kagan, R. Hertz-Lazarowitz, C. Webb, and R. Schmuck. New York: Plenum, 1985.

Yager, S.; Johnson, D.W.; and Johnson, R.T. "Oral Discussion, Group-to-Individual Transfer, and Achievement in Cooperative Learning Groups." *Journal of Educational Psychology* 77, no. 1 (1985): 60-66.

Ziegler, S. "The Effectiveness of Cooperative Learning Teams for Increasing Cross-Ethnic Friendship: Additional Evidence." *Human Organization* 40, no. 3 (1981): 264-68.

179

16

INCORPORATING COOPERATION: ITS EFFECTS ON INSTRUCTION

BY HARBISON POOL, CHERRY C. BREWTON,
STEPHEN J. JENKINS, AND BRYAN W. GRIFFIN

Educators who serve in schools that make a deliberate choice to untrack generally have compelling reasons for their decision. They usually hope, for example, to improve their students' 1) academic performance; 2) attitudes toward themselves and their peers with different racial, achievement, ability, and socioeconomic characteristics or backgrounds; and 3) classroom, playground, and cafeteria behavior. Clearly, untracking has potential in each of these areas (George 1992; Oakes 1985; Wheelock 1992; Williams et al. 1993). A nontracked school is one that has between-class heterogeneous grouping. Common sense suggests that such a place is an appropriate setting for the practice of cooperative learning.

The Kernel of an Idea

In spring 1992, we were attending an educator-citizen study session sponsored by our local board of education on the possible assets and liabilities of nontracking. For most of the 1991-92 school year, the board and community had been grappling with whether one of their elementary schools should be untracked. (This case study is presented in some detail by Page and Page in Chapter 24.) This controversial and divisive issue prompted further questions. For example, what can be done to enhance the chance that untracking, if attempted, will be effective and productive — that is, if it will make the schools better for all students?

In the course of our brainstorming, we recognized the contribution that cooperative learning (CL) could make. After all, most CL models involve students of various achievement and ability levels in small groups (Davidson 1980; Johnson, Johnson, and Holubec 1986; Slavin 1983). As we discussed the possible connection between untracking and cooperative learning, we asked ourselves: Is there a set of circumstances to test CL? Can we then conclude that if CL works in those circumstances, it probably will work everywhere else?

We decided that the greatest challenge probably would be in the middle grades and perhaps in the field of science. Most of the research with which we were familiar had been conducted at the elementary level and concerned students' self-esteem and their performance in social studies, reading/language arts, and arithmetic computation. However, it seemed to us that what we saw as the main principles of cooperative learning (sharing, heterogeneous grouping, helping, discussion, "two heads are better than one") should be natural allies of — and certainly compatible with — the belief system of contemporary science teaching (inquiry, discovery, the use of hands-on materials, laboratory work) and the middle school concept (early adolescent socialization, broad content treatment, thematic and problem-solving units, interdisciplinary teaching teams).

We further speculated that the use of cooperative learning would, at least initially, be made even more challenging when it was attempted by traditional teachers with little or no background in this methodology. Its likelihood of successful implementation would be additionally circumscribed, we suspected, if it were being tried with students who also had no previous exposure to cooperative learning, who had spent most of their earlier schooling in tracked classrooms, or who lived in impoverished and disadvantaged home situations.

We resolved to take a look at the use of cooperative learning in middle-grades, departmentalized science classes. After several people suggested it, we also decided to examine same-level mathematics classes. We would compare traditionally taught classes and comparable classes in which cooperative-learning approaches were employed.

Theorists, Researchers, and Practitioners:
Ideas, Findings, and Experiences

Considerable professional literature promotes the use of CL in mathematics (for example, Andrini 1989; Artzt and Newman 1990; David-

182

son 1990) and in science (for example, Hannigan 1990; Jones and Steinbrink 1989; Luallen and Leonard 1990). The new curriculum and evaluation standards of the National Council of Teachers of Mathematics (1989) support the use of cooperative learning in math instruction. In many cases, such strategies as problem-solving (Duren and Cherrington 1992) and laboratory instruction (Tobin 1990) should use cooperative learning.

Cooperative learning is recognized as particularly worthwhile in raising the self-concept, peer status, and achievement of mentally handicapped students (Ballard et al. 1977), bilingual and minority children and youth (Cohen and DeAvila 1983; Preston 1991), and other at-risk students. CL approaches also have been successful with gifted students, both for social interaction and intellectual growth (Joyce 1991; Slavin 1991a). Augustine, Gruber, and Hanson (1990) found that cooperative assignments seldom negatively affect even the brightest students' individual performance, while all learn truly valuable lessons in such important life skills as management of conflict within a group.

Cooperative learning does not refer to a single technique; there are a number of methods and perspectives from which to choose (Hilke 1990). Brandt (1991-1992) contrasts cooperative learning with the traditional classroom in which one student is pitted against another and, as he puts it, "heaven help the hindmost" (p. 127). In most forms of CL, he states, groups of three to five mixed-ability students work together to some purposeful end. One of the strengths of cooperative learning, Brandt declares, "is that it is an effective method for teaching even the most traditional subjects" (p. 127). Also, he says, in cooperative learning students, not teachers, do the active intellectual work. Sachse (1989) remarks that the teacher also has a critical role, both as the most vital resource in creating the blueprint for learning and in monitoring the execution of the design.

Cohen observes that, while there are many advantages when "students serve as resources for one another in collaborative groups" (1990, p. 135), certain requirements must be met for cooperative learning to work: 1) the development and implementation of unique group-type assignments and materials, 2) the know-how to solve problems of status that arise in small-group arrangements, and 3) good organizational support for teachers undertaking CL methods. Strother (1990) cautions that, though only limited training may be necessary for many CL models, more preparation and help are probably needed for consistently high-quality implementation on a broad scale.

An Exploratory Investigation

We conducted research in six public schools in three southeastern Georgia school systems to see, in part, what effects, if any, middle-level mathematics and science teachers would experience when they introduced cooperative-learning approaches into their classes. Participating teachers were asked to match two classes according to subject matter (math or science), grade level, and grouping approach (heterogeneous or ability-tracked). They randomly decided, by flipping a coin, which class in each two-class set would experience CL strategies and which class would receive only standard (traditional) instruction with no cooperative learning for the first six-week grading period of the 1992-93 school term. In each instance, the CL class was designated as the "experimental group," the traditional (TR) class as the "control group."

There were 29 matched classes: 19 in science, 10 in math. All teachers who took part in the study attended two workshops at their own school, both conducted before the beginning of the school year. In the first workshop, we reviewed a number of printed materials with participating teachers, including: 1) a sheet titled, "Basic Elements of Cooperative Learning," adapted from Johnson, Johnson, and Holubec (1986); 2) an article, "Synthesis of Research on Cooperative Learning," by Slavin (1991b; an adapted version of this article appears as Chapter 15 of this book); 3) an "Overview of Selected Structures," a page-length figure in an article by Kagan (1989-1990, p. 14); and 4) the instrument we constructed for teachers to use in reporting the results of their efforts.

In the second workshop, the workshop leader and teachers: 1) discussed the various CL instructional techniques they planned to use with their experimental groups, 2) shared specific ways to use CL strategies in mathematics and science instruction, 3) drew a clear distinction between CL and TR methodologies to avoid contamination of either group, and 4) reviewed the instrument. The amount of previous training was not a precondition for teachers' participation in this study. However, all but one teacher had taken part in at least one prior CL inservice course.

At the end of the six-week study period, participating teachers were asked to complete a six-page, 21-item instrument. Nine items sought biographical and demographic information about the teachers, their students, and their schools. Two items asked about the subjects and units being studied, and one item asked about how the classes were organized (heterogeneous or homogeneous grouping).

One item questioned which aspects of each of the five elements of cooperative learning (Johnson, Johnson, and Holubec 1986) were incorporated into their CL classes. The five elements — positive interdependence, face-to-face interaction, individual accountability, interpersonal and small-group skills, and group processing — were defined and broken into 17 subelements. One question listed a number of CL models and techniques, as well as approaches that can be used in forming student CL teams. Respondents were asked to check all of the subelements they employed in their CL classes.

Several items inquired about the differences, if any, noted between the experimental and control groups. We wanted to know how students responded to cooperative learning. Did instruction, classroom climate, student attitudes, student discipline, and student performance improve, decline, or remain the same when cooperative-learning strategies were introduced? Were students more or less on task? Did teaching seem more or less fulfilling?

The final question concerned the extent to which supervisory and administrative personnel were supportive of teachers' efforts to use cooperative learning. Did the level of support make a difference in teachers' attitudes and their level of success in using a new methodology?

The number of paired classes per school ranged from three to eight. About half of the cases were in urban settings, nearly a third were rural, and the remaining one-sixth were suburban. In the 19 class sets where the majority of students came from a single socioeconomic group, the dominant group was the middle class or below, with the modal level being lower-middle. Most of the mixed-SES class sets contained students from a combination of lower and lower-middle classes. Two schools reported having some students from upper-middle and upper socioeconomic backgrounds.

The racial makeup of participating students varied from one school that was mostly white to one in which about 75% of students were black. Three of the schools also had a small percentage of Asian and Hispanic students. Overall, about 52% of the students in these six schools were white and approximately 48% were minorities, mostly African-American.

The teachers in this study ranged in age from comparatively young to middle-aged, with an almost even distribution across the three intermediate categories (between 26 and 50 years of age). Teaching experience varied from two years in the profession to more than 20 years. A substantial majority were white, about a third were black, and only two teacher respondents were Asian-Americans.

Of the 29 pairs of classes, about one-third studied mathematics and two-thirds studied science. Nearly one-third of the classes were at grade six or below. (In one rural school, fourth and fifth grades were departmentalized and considered middle grades.) Almost half were at grade seven, and one-fifth were at grade eight. Approximately four out of five pairs were heterogeneously organized (nontracked), with the remaining fifth homogeneously structured (tracked). Of the six tracked pairs in the study, the breakdown was as follows: one each in which both classes were of high, average, or low ability; one in which the students in the class receiving cooperative-learning instruction had average ability, while those students in classes where only traditional methodology was used were of low ability; one where the CL class was classified as average, the TR class as high; and one in which the CL group was average and the TR group was high-average.

The teachers in the experimental groups took seriously the need to incorporate the five essential elements of cooperative learning. More than two-thirds of the respondents used 15 of the 17 subelements identified in the questionnaire. All but two teachers employed at least one subelement under each of the five elements; two incorporated all the subelements in their CL classes. One subelement, "materials and information were shared among group members," was checked by all but one teacher. The least frequently exercised subelement, "groups receive feedback from student observers on how well their groups are working," was used in 10 CL classes (34.5%).

The most popular cooperative-learning methods used by these teachers were Student Team Learning (used in 18 CL classes), Learning Together (17), Partners (15), and Group Investigation and Think-Pair-Share (12 each). Jigsaw Teaching was tried in eight CL classes. Student Teams-Achievement Divisions, Teams-Games-Tournaments, and Team-Assisted Individualization each were used in seven classes. Additional models were named by two teachers.

More than two-thirds of the respondents (20) used a single approach in forming their student CL teams: six heterogeneous teams, 13 random teams, and one student self-selection. Seven teachers used two of these methods, one used all three approaches, and one left this item blank. Overall, 13 teachers used heterogeneous teams, 19 used random teams, and five used student self-selection.

Respondents were asked to compare cooperative learning with traditional instruction. Six areas of comparison were pursued: 1) teacher attitude, 2) classroom climate, 3) student behavior, 4) student attitude, 5) the extent to which students stayed on task, and 6) student achievement.

On average, teachers found cooperative learning to be a better approach than the traditional method in all six of the areas in which comparisons were made. The difference was most pronounced on the variables of student attitude toward cooperative learning, general class-room climate, and teacher attitude toward cooperative learning.

More than 40% of the respondents rated CL highly in all areas of comparison. Another 27.6% (eight respondents) rated CL highly on most comparisons; seven rated CL positively on five of the six items. Six of these eight teachers marked "about the same" in response to a question that asked, "How did student behavior in the CL class com-pare with that in the TR class?" The other two respondents indicated "no appreciable difference between the two classes in student achieve-ment." If these two categories are combined, 69% of the teachers per-ceived cooperative-learning instruction to be generally superior in the areas examined in this study.

Only nine teachers marked any items that did not favor cooperative learning; three marked one item favoring the TR class, and four rated two items in this way. Two respondents favored the TR class on four of the six items of comparison. One of these two participants was the only teacher in this study who made no responses favoring CL.

Following are representative comments from the teachers who strongly favored CL classes:

- There was more input from students and more interest.
- The students brought up many more ideas or ways of solving problems with the group.
- Students knew what to do and started on assignments before the teacher became involved. Each wanted the group to be effective.
- The students showed confidence in their learning.
- The environment in the classroom seemed to have more energy, excitement, and life when working in the CL class.
- The students were so busy interacting in group work and helping each other, there was no time for behavior problems.
- The behavior seemed better because the students knew they were responsible for specific information in the CL class. The TR stu-dents were all doing the same thing and not responsible for giv-ing their information to others, which resulted in lack of concen-tration in some students and "playing" around.
- They were always on task because they never had to wait on the instructor. If part of the subject was incomplete, they finished it up before the teacher came forward.
- Assignments that were completed in [the] cooperative-learning class received much higher grades. The groups were definitely

working together because the grades among group members did not vary much.

- CL students related to the material assigned and would often tell me about past learning experiences and personal experiences. I think the CL groups allowed the "talk" time students needed to begin the first step in the learning cycle — relating prior knowledge to new knowledge.

Of the teachers who marked at least one of the six comparative items favoring their work with the control (traditional) group, comments following the negative responses about the CL classes may provide some clues as to why teachers answered in this way:

- I don't think the students got the meat of the lessons as I would teach it, but they did get enough to pass the test.
- More frustrating, more behavior problems.
- Students are too immature to work in groups.
- Seventh-graders at this time in [the] year need to develop better organizational skills.
- My students, who are extremely bright, seemed frustrated with the groups. They felt as though everyone was cheating off them.
- Some problems with overall noise level with so much movement.
- Many students cannot handle the freedom to talk and interact — will not stay in seat and confine communication to [their own] group.
- Stayed on task a few minutes; then tend to be "on and off" remainder of each class.

What the Findings Mean

Cooperative learning is judged by the teachers who took part in this study to be at least somewhat more effective than traditional instruction across a wide variety of situations. Indeed, the effectiveness of cooperative learning could be said to be, as a statistician might put it, "robust" to different circumstances. If the findings of this study can be generalized to other school environments, levels, subject matters, and populations, one could say that cooperative learning is likely to have at least a measure of success within a variety of conditions.

Participating teachers' encounters with cooperative learning in urban, suburban, and rural schools were essentially the same. The typical teacher, regardless of location, found cooperative learning to be more professionally fulfilling than conventional teaching. CL was judged praiseworthy by a broad range of teachers who taught students from very diverse backgrounds in a wide variety of schools.

The classroom climate in the CL class also was more positive: Students liked CL and felt better about instruction when CL was used, and CL students were more likely to be on task. In addition, students exposed to cooperative learning for the limited six-week period of this study learned at a somewhat higher level and exhibited moderately better classroom behavior.

Lessons to Be Learned

When we began this enterprise, the idea of cooperative learning appealed to us. What we knew of it and had read about it made sense to us. But we wondered what its limitations were. Were there situations and settings in which CL would not work? Were there students who would not respond to cooperative approaches?

We pursued possible answers to these and other questions under what seemed to us to be fairly demanding conditions: with early adolescent students in the middle grades in what usually are considered "nonsocial" subjects — mathematics and science — at the beginning of the school year and with students and teachers who, for the most part, were previously unfamiliar with CL methodology. We provided only two short teacher workshops. And most of the respondents were working primarily with students who were considered "at-risk."

A review of our data and the professional literature associated with CL leads us to the general conclusion that cooperative learning has the potential to make a positive difference in virtually any subject at the elementary, middle, and secondary levels. We are convinced that there are few, if any, students who cannot benefit from cooperative learning in some form.

Most, though not all, people believe there is still a place for competition in schools — both in the classroom and on the playground. Some cooperative-learning structures incorporate group competition. Individualistic learning also has its place. But many areas of study lend themselves to the use of cooperative techniques in which all students can work together and all can be "winners."

What can we learn from the comments made by teachers in this study who did not favor CL classes? A few observations seem to have merit:

1. Students in these classrooms appear to be less organized and less disciplined; as one respondent put it, they are unable to "handle the freedom" afforded by the CL class.

189

2. Some precocious students may find the lack of individual competition with its commensurate rewards for high performance to be upsetting.
3. Students must be taught to function in a CL class.

Our experiences and those reported by the participants in this study prompt us to offer several recommendations that, we believe, will enhance the potential for cooperative learning:

- Teachers should have positive expectations.
- Teacher inservice programs should be as in-depth as possible.
- Students should receive training, and there should be transitions to more complex CL structures.
- Teachers should recognize that some extra work on their part will be involved, especially when they first start using CL.
- Teachers should welcome "productive noise" and learn how to calm down students (or how to have them calm themselves down) before the excitement level becomes unacceptable.

Almost all middle school mathematics and science students like CL approaches and activities. Clearly, teachers planning to undertake cooperative learning for the first time start with something going for them: Students are predisposed in a distinctly positive direction.

In our study, all respondents believed that their principals supported their work with new instructional approaches. This kind of support may be a reason — perhaps a major one — that most participants experienced success with their CL classes. We maintain that strong, affirmative leadership that actively promotes promising new curricular programs, instructional practices, and organizational strategies is extremely important, sometimes critical, to moving away from the status quo.

As students grow more acclimated to this new way of working (and teachers become more experienced with and skilled at using CL), more definitive, positive results will occur in terms of student achievement and behavior.

All teachers should get involved, try out some of the existing CL methods, and perhaps even invent some new ones. Teachers can improve the state of the art. There is much that still needs to be investigated: How should groups be formed? How can their progress best be monitored? How can group members be influenced to contribute to a group goal? Every teacher should be trying to discover what will meet the needs of each particular group of students.

We do not assert that cooperative learning is the only good way to teach or that it should be used exclusively by any teacher. But it is exciting and fun for both teachers and their students. We contend that cooperative learning will have a prominent place in the repertoire of every teacher who is willing to try new ways to optimize students' growth and development. Finally, as we stated at the beginning of this chapter, we see a clear and vital link between cooperative learning and nontracking. We believe that cooperative learning can probably contribute more to this purpose than any other known set of instructional models or approaches.

References

Andrini, B. *Cooperative Learning and Math: A Multi-Structural Approach.* San Juan Capistrano, Calif.: Resources for Teachers, 1989.

Artzt, A.F., and Newman, C.M. *How to Use Cooperative Learning in the Mathematics Class.* Reston, Va.: National Council of Teachers of Mathematics, 1990.

Augustine, D.K.; Gruber, K.D.; and Hanson, L.R. "Cooperation Works!" *Educational Leadership* 47, no. 4 (1990): 4-7.

Ballard, M.; Corman, L.; Gottlieb, J.; and Kaufman, M.J. "Improving the Status of Mainstreamed Retarded Children." *Journal of Educational Psychology* 69, no. 5 (1977): 605-11.

Brandt, A. "Teaming with Possibilities." *Parenting* 12, no. 11 (1991-1992): 124-25, 127-28, 130.

Cohen, E.G. "Continuing to Cooperate: Prerequisites for Persistence." *Phi Delta Kappan* 72, no. 2 (1990): 134-36, 138.

Cohen, E.G., and DeAvila, E. *Learning to Think in Math and Science: Improving Local Education for Minority Children.* Final Report to the Walter S. Johnson Foundation. Stanford, Calif.: Stanford University Programs for Complex Instruction, 1983.

Davidson, N. "Small-Group Learning and Teaching in Mathematics: An Introduction for Nonmathematicians." In *Cooperation in Education*, edited by S. Sharan, P. Hare, C.D. Webb, and R. Hertz-Lazarowitz. Provo, Utah: Brigham Young University Press, 1980.

Davidson, N., ed. *Cooperative Learning in Mathematics: A Handbook for Teachers.* Menlo Park, Calif.: Addison-Wesley, 1990.

Duren, P.E., and Cherrington, A. "The Effects of Cooperative Group Work Versus Independent Practice on the Learning of Some Problem-Solving Strategies." *School Science and Mathematics* 92, no. 2 (1992): 80-83.

George, P. *How to Untrack Your School.* Alexandria, Va.: Association for Supervision and Curriculum Development, 1992.

Hannigan, M.R. "Cooperative Learning in Elementary School Science." *Educational Leadership* 47, no. 4 (1990): 25.

Hilke, E.V. *Cooperative Learning.* Fastback 299. Bloomington, Ind.: Phi Delta Kappa Educational Foundation, 1990.

Johnson, D.W.; Johnson, R.T.; and Holubec, E.J. *Cooperation in the Class-room*. Rev. ed. Edina, Minn.: Interaction, 1986.

Jones, R.M., and Steinbrink, J.E. "Using Cooperative Groups in Science Teaching." *School Science and Mathematics* 89, no. 7 (1989): 541-51.

Joyce, B. "Common Misconceptions About Cooperative Learning and Gifted Students." *Educational Leadership* 48, no. 6 (1991): 72-74.

Kagan, S. "The Structural Approach to Cooperative Learning." *Educational Leadership* 47, no. 4 (1989-1990): 12-15.

Luallen, J., and Leonard, D. "Using What We Are Learning About Learning, Talking Less and Listening More: A Means of Helping Students Make Sense of Science." Paper presented at the annual meeting of the National Association for Research in Science Teaching, Lake Geneva, Wis., February 1990. ERIC Document Reproduction Service No. ED 342 622.

National Council of Teachers of Mathematics, Commission on Standards for School Mathematics. *Curriculum and Evaluation Standards for School Mathematics*. Reston, Va., 1989.

Oakes, J. *Keeping Track: How Schools Structure Inequality*. New Haven, Conn.: Yale University Press, 1985.

Preston, V. "Mathematics and Science Curricula in Elementary and Secondary Education for American Indian and Alaska Native Students." In *Indian Nations at Risk Task Force Commissioned Papers*, edited by United States Office of Education, Office of Educational Research and Improvement. Washington, D.C.: Indian Nations at Risk Task Force, U.S. Department of Education, 1991. ERIC Document Reproduction Service No. ED 343 767.

Sachse, T.P. "Making Science Happen." *Educational Leadership* 47, no. 3 (1989): 18-21.

Slavin, R.E. *Cooperative Learning*. New York: Longman, 1983.

Slavin, R.E. "Are Cooperative Learning and 'Untracking' Harmful to the Gifted?" *Educational Leadership* 48, no. 6 (1991): 68-71. a

Slavin, R.E. "Synthesis of Research on Cooperative Learning." *Educational Leadership* 48, no. 5 (1991): 71-77, 79-82. b

Strother, D.B. "Cooperative Learning: Fad or Foundation for Learning?" *Phi Delta Kappan* 72, no. 2 (1990): 158-62.

Tobin, K. "Research on Science Laboratory Activities: In Pursuit of Better Questions and Answers to Improve Learning." *School Science and Mathematics* 90, no. 5 (1990): 403-18.

Wheelock, A. *Crossing the Tracks: How "Untracking" Can Save America's Schools*. New York: New Press, 1992.

Williams, F.D.; Hart, B.C.; and Michel, G.J. *Academics, Race, Class, and Tracking in Rural Georgia Schools: Background Paper for the Musgrove Conference*. St. Simons Island, Ga.: Sapelo Island Research Foundation and Boggs Rural Life Center, 1993.

IMPROVING ALL STUDENTS' ACHIEVEMENT: TEACHING COGNITIVE AND METACOGNITIVE THINKING STRATEGIES

BY ROBERT W. WARKENTIN AND
DOROTHY A. BATTLE

Student achievement is a major concern of educators who advocate heterogeneous grouping of students. In this regard, educators have sought ways to combine improvements in the quality of student learning and achievement with equality in opportunity for learning (Jones 1986; Oakes 1992). One instructional approach that has proven particularly useful in increasing both the quality and equality of learning is instruction in cognitive and metacognitive thinking strategies.

The goal of this instructional approach is to provide students with tools for productive thinking and learning. Such tools enable students to take control over their own learning. Cognitive-strategy instruction provides students with techniques to improve their ability to comprehend, remember, and organize information. Metacognitive-strategy instruction provides techniques to improve students' ability to plan, monitor, regulate, and evaluate their own learning and thinking. The use of these strategies has been shown to enable all students — both lower- and higher-ability, younger as well as older — to become more efficient and effective learners (Brown et al. 1983).

Although learning and thinking strategies have been shown to enhance all students' achievement, their instruction in the classroom has been associated more with gifted and high-ability students (Jones

1986). In contrast, teachers working with less academically able students have tended to focus more on basic-skills training, emphasizing such lower-level strategies as drill, rote memorization, and repetition. In addition, for these students, academic-content information often is presented in a fragmented, disjointed manner or in a watered-down curriculum (Oakes 1992). By emphasizing drill, practice, and attention to facts and details, students not only are less likely to develop higher-level thinking operations, but they also are less likely to construct the kind of conceptual understandings of information that are needed to solve problems and to think critically and creatively.

The long-term consequence of providing qualitatively different instructional activities and curricula to students of different ability levels has been to create a cumulative deficit or ability gap among students across the years of schooling. Lower-achieving students fall further behind in academic performance. The harm of this practice is that by not providing lower-ability students with cognitive and metacognitive instruction, teachers have deprived these students of the kinds of learning opportunities that hold the most promise for reversing inequality in academic access and opportunity.

As we move "beyond tracking," we need to enlarge our vision of instruction to include teaching higher-level thinking skills to all students, especially to those most in need of them. This new vision would have as its primary aim helping all students become self-directed, self-initiated learners and thinkers.

Good Learners Compared to Poor Learners

Research comparing higher-achieving students to lower-achieving students consistently has found that higher-achieving students, or good learners, learn strategically (Brown et al. 1983). For example, not only do good learners apply more strategies while learning, but the strategies they use are qualitatively superior and more precise than those used by poorer learners (Bransford and Stein 1984). In addition, good learners constantly assess their understanding (Pressley et al. 1989). They examine their thinking to determine whether they understand adequately. Self-assessment is an ongoing process.

In contrast, poor learners are deficient in strategy knowledge (Brown, Campione, and Day 1981). They possess less strategy knowledge, apply strategies less often, and use strategies that are less elaborate and therefore less helpful (Pressley et al. 1989).

If less able learners lack specific strategy knowledge and skills and if using these specific strategies is responsible for learning, then providing strategy instruction to less able learners should improve their performance. Such reasoning has formed the basis for strategy-training research (Brown et al. 1983). Over the past decade many strategy-training studies have been performed using students from all ability levels. The results have been consistent and positive (Weinstein, Goetz, and Alexander 1988; Weinstein and Mayer 1986).

For example, one study used the reciprocal-teaching method to foster students' cognitive and metacognitive strategies for reading comprehension (Palincsar and Brown 1984). This instructional method teaches students to use strategies in an interactive-dialogue procedure wherein the teacher first provides explicit modeling and guidance on relevant strategies, then relinquishes control to students as they improve in their ability to use strategies.

In this study, fifth-grade students who were diagnosed as "academically deficient" were given instruction in such higher-level thinking skills as summarizing main points, formulating questions, making predictions, and clarifying. The researchers reasoned that using these strategies would increase students' ability to monitor, regulate, and evaluate their learning; and since these skills underlie reading comprehension, the students' reading performance would also improve. Thus strategy instruction was aimed at the cognitive and metacognitive processes or operations responsible for reading. The results supported the researchers' hypothesis. Before strategy training, the students' rate of correct responses on the criterion test was about 20%. After training, the students' performance jumped to 80% correct. In addition, the students transferred their learning skills to other academic areas (Palincsar and Brown 1984).

Such results are encouraging because they indicate that strategic activities are responsible for academic achievement and that students who lack these strategies can be taught to use them effectively. However, these findings bring up other related problems. For example, research also shows that strategy skills can be difficult to acquire and that many students, especially younger students, do not tend to use them spontaneously. Evidence also indicates that such skills develop slowly over the years, and that strategic activity does not "just happen." Experience also seems to play a crucial role. However, even though students do not tend to acquire and maintain such skills on their own, research does indicate that students benefit from specific strategy instruction and practice. Thus the evidence suggests that it is necessary for teachers to provide both explicit training and a variety of opportunities for students to practice higher-level thinking and learning strategies.

Why Do Students Fail to Use Strategies?

If strategic learning accounts for academic achievement, why don't all students act strategically? Why do only some students acquire and use strategies effectively? Research indicates four possible reasons for students' lack of strategic activity (Goetz et al. 1992).

First, students may not recognize or identify that a problem exists. For example, poor readers often are unaware that they are not comprehending or that there is an inconsistency in a text passage (Baker 1985). As a consequence, they fail to employ a fix-up strategy. The problem is especially evident with young students and when the information to be learned is novel or complex. This failure to recognize a problem may result from students' lack of relevant experience or knowledge in a specific content area. Thus the use of a strategy may require at least some amount of content knowledge.

Second, students may not possess enough strategy knowledge. In this case, even if students recognize that they are not understanding, they may not possess the strategy knowledge that is helpful to correct the problem. Thus multiple strategies should be deliberately taught to students.

Third, students may not apply a strategy appropriately. Just possessing strategy knowledge is not enough. Possessing a number of different strategies does not mean that a student can apply the most effective or efficient strategy to solve a particular problem. Students often fail to select the most appropriate strategy because they have not adequately identified the nature of the problem.

Fourth, students may lack commitment to use a strategy. Students may choose not to expend the effort if they believe that strategic activity does not "pay off" with success or achievement. For example, if a teacher just marks off whether an assignment is turned in and does not assess the quality of the response, students may copy answers from the text just to get the assignment done, rather than trying to construct their own answers by paraphrasing the information. Students need good reasons to use higher-level thinking strategies.

Guidelines for Fostering Learning and Thinking Strategies

Following are guidelines for teachers to promote and foster learning and thinking strategies:

1. Use students' background knowledge to increase their ability to use strategies. Research indicates that it is beneficial to give students a foundation of background knowledge to enhance their ability to use strategies, especially when the information is novel, complex, or abstract (Mayer 1983). For example, advance organizers, analogies, and conceptual models can act as a scaffold for students to compare and evaluate new information with what they already know. The provision of conceptual frameworks can enhance students' ability to monitor their comprehension and memory.

2. Provide modeling and training in how, when, where, and why strategies should be used. Teachers should explicitly teach a variety of cognitive and metacognitive strategies to students. Teachers should model thinking processes.

3. Provide opportunities for students to practice strategies in several contexts and tasks. Providing many opportunities to practice is necessary for students to become proficient strategy users. Moreover, providing students with opportunities to use strategies in multiple settings, in multiple tasks, and across different subject areas increases the likelihood that students will transfer their strategy knowledge to new situations.

4. Give students good reasons for using strategies. Teachers should reward students when they employ effective strategies in the classroom. Students are more likely to engage in demanding strategies — such as strategies for integrating, organizing, and making charts and graphs — if they know such activities will receive recognition.

5. Make strategy training a curriculum objective. Strategy instruction should not be thought of as a one-shot, all-or-none event. Strategy instruction involves reteaching, elaboration, and extension. For example, reteaching may include teaching target strategies as recurring themes over the school year. Elaboration may involve having students generate their own examples of how and why a strategy is useful. Extension may entail having students apply a strategy learned in one content area to a different content area.

Teacher-Student Interactions that Promote Thinking

Teacher-student interaction may be one of the best tools for integrating cognitive-strategy and thinking-skills instruction into everyday classroom practices. Raths, Wassermann, Jonas, and Rothstein (1986) provide an excellent model. They suggest an organizational framework for various kinds of thinking and learning processes used in academic learning. We have adapted their organizational scheme to emphasize a developmental sequence wherein less complex thinking operations form the foundation for more complex operations. Their 15 thinking operations include:

Elementary Level

Observing: Watching, noting, or perceiving through the senses.

Comparing: Observing differences and similarities in fact or in contemplation.

Classifying: Putting into a group or groups on the basis of similarities or differences.

Interpreting: Determining the meaning of facts or situations from which conclusions can be drawn.

Summarizing: Stating in brief or condensed form the substance of what has been presented.

Middle School Level

Criticizing: Making judgments, analyzing, and evaluating.

Looking for assumptions: Recognizing and identifying based on incomplete evidence.

Imagining: Visualizing or building mental images, feeling intuitively, reaching beyond real boundaries.

Collecting and organizing data: Gathering and placing information in a logical order.

Hypothesizing: Forming tentative explanations based on the available information.

Secondary Level

Applying facts and principles in new situations: Seeing relationships, noticing what belongs together in a new context, discriminating what is relevant from what is irrelevant.

Decision making: Emphasizing the values that impinge on problematic situations.

Designing projects or investigations: Involving many different activities, taking longer to complete, offering a rich potential for engaging in many thinking operations.

Coding one's own paper: Identifying specific patterns in the student's papers— that is, all or nothing, either-or, qualifying words and phrases, value statements, attributions.

Coding other papers: Directing students to look for the extreme statements in other students' papers.

This model for teaching thinking skills emerged out of an interactional analysis of the teaching process conducted by Raths and his associates (1986). According to their view, teacher-student interactions may either enhance or restrict students' creative thinking. For example, they propose that students' higher-level thinking skills are fostered through teacher prompts and open-ended questions that support and encourage students to process data and generate ideas. Teacher interactions that facilitate thinking encourage students to be more responsible for their own ideas and to be more independent and self-directed thinkers.

However, such interactions also increase the level of "risk" for students. Teacher prompts that call for creative, critical reasoning add tension by requiring students to rely on their own thinking and reasoning capabilities. Many students are unaccustomed to this. Students seldom are asked to provide genuinely creative, thoughtful responses and may avoid giving creative, independent responses because they fear failure.

In contrast, teacher interactions that restrict or "bring closure to" students' thinking call on students merely to recall facts or to retrieve data in order to get the correct answer. Such interactions increase students' dependency on others for learning and tend to impede the development of skills needed for creative, independent thought.

Raths and his associates (1986) present three categories of teacher responses that can facilitate and promote student thinking: 1) *Reflective responses* ask students to look at their ideas on a surface level and to make them theirs; such responses are at the very base of teaching for thinking interactions. 2) *Responses calling for analysis* are those that demand of students more in-depth exploration. 3) *Challenging responses* require students to venture into truly uncharted waters. Since analytical and challenging thinking may put students at greater cognitive risk and cause increased tension, teachers should be judicious and sensitive in asking for these responses.

Wassermann (1987) suggests some different ways in which teachers might respond to the same student statement.

> Pupil: It seems to me that we ought to reconsider the expenditure of funds for NASA projects, considering the terrible accident that occurred with the Challenger.
> Teacher A: Obviously, Melvin, you do not have all the data. If you did, you could not make such a statement.
> Teacher B: Good thinking, Melvin.
> Teacher C: You might wish to reconsider your own statement, Melvin. Can you think of other scientific investigations that were allowed to continue even when there was danger?
> Teacher D: It might be a good idea, you say, to have the public rethink the space shuttle program and perhaps cut back on its funding.
> Teacher E: You are saying that such a terrible accident ought to make us reconsider the funding for the space program. If a project fails, we ought to cut off the funds.

Teacher F: Because of the accident, we should perhaps cut back on the funding for the space program. What do you see as some potential consequences of such an action?

Teacher A shuts off discussion (and thinking) by putting down the student's idea. Teacher B rewards the student and, in doing so, terminates the interaction. Teacher C allows the student more opportunity to think, but, by directing the student toward a preferred response, limits that thinking to a very narrow compass. Teacher D asks the student to reflect on his answer. Teacher E asks the student to analyze the statement in light of its implicit assumption, while Teacher F asks the student to examine the dimensions of the statement and challenges the student's thinking. (pp. 464-65)

The responses of teachers D, E, and F vary in the level of cognitive risk placed on students. Such responses challenge students to construct answers that go beyond the factual data, to transform the data, to apply more background knowledge, to extend the information into new areas, to make broader conclusions, or to identify important implications. These teacher's responses encourage the student to provide different levels of self-directed, self-initiated answers. The effect of these interactions is to increase the students' capability to think more critically and independently.

As these examples show, it is important to remember that teachers should carefully plan the level of their questions (the level of cognitive risk and tension involved) to ensure that students experience success in coping with these demands. Since each student copes with different levels of cognitive tension, teachers must individualize their responses and then carefully analyze the adequacy of each student's response.

Applications in Elementary, Middle, and Secondary Classrooms

There are no explicit instructional strategies for teaching thinking in the classroom (Sternberg 1987). We advocate working with the entire class to enhance all students' achievement (Willis 1992). When using this approach, certain procedures should be followed. Raths and his associates (1986) advise:

1. Introduce the thinking operation.
2. Select an activity for the thinking operation.
3. The activity should be an appropriate one that furthers conceptual development.
4. The activity should be oral or require written responses.

5. When using manipulatives, be sure that all students get a chance to observe or handle materials.
6. Adequate time is necessary for studying and reflecting on an activity.
7. Allow sufficient time for writing and sharing responses.
8. Allow students to give feedback on the activity to improve teaching for thinking.

In working with the entire class, all curricular areas might be used. However, if teachers feel uncomfortable teaching thinking through all areas, they might select an area that would give them the best opportunity to engage their students in higher-order thinking. Raths and his associates recommend, "Use at least one thinking activity per day in the curriculum area of your choice" (p. 39). Once teachers become comfortable, they can add other subjects until thinking is infused in all content areas.

When selecting thinking activities for their students, teachers should follow certain guidelines (Raths et al. 1986):

1. The activity should be within the students' ability levels.
2. The activity should take into account the realm of students' experience.
3. The activity should relate to curriculum being studied.
4. The activity should relate to students' goals.

One way to embark on a thinking program would be to create a weekly plan of activities that includes several content areas. A general thinking activity might be emphasized every Monday to begin the challenge of a new week. The thinking activities then might be based on various content areas throughout the week. Many can be interdisciplinary.

Raths and his associates state:

> We emphasize that the approach you choose should be one that is educationally viable for you — and one that allows you the degree of freedom you need to grow and learn with your students about the delightful, intriguing, and challenging facets of teaching for thinking. (1986, pp. 39-40)

References

Baker, L. "How Do We Know When We Don't Understand? Standards for Evaluating Text Comprehension." In *Metacognition, Cognition, and Human Performance*, vol. 1, edited by D.L. Forrest-Pressley, G.E. MacKinnon, and T.G. Waller. Orlando, Fla.: Academic Press, 1985.

Bransford, J.D., and Stein, B.S. *The IDEAL Problem Solver*. New York: Freeman, 1984.

Brown, A.L.; Bransford, J.D.; Ferrara, R.A.; and Campione, J. "Learning, Remembering and Understanding." In *Handbook of Child Psychology: Cognitive Development*, vol. 3, edited by J. Flavell and E. Markman. New York: John Wiley and Sons, 1983.

Brown, A.L.; Campione, J.C.; and Day, J.D. "Learning to Learn: On Training Students to Learn from Text." *Educational Researcher* 10, no. 2 (1981): 14-21.

Goetz, E.T.; Alexander, P.A.; and Ash, M.J. *Educational Psychology: A Classroom Perspective*. New York: Macmillan, 1992.

Jones, B.F. "Quality and Equality Through Cognitive Instruction." *Educational Leadership* 43, no. 7 (1986): 4-11.

Mayer, R. *Thinking, Problem Solving, and Cognition*. San Francisco: Freeman, 1983.

Oakes, J. "Can Tracking Research Inform Practice? Technical, Normative, and Political Considerations." *Educational Researcher* 21, no. 4 (1992): 12-21.

Palincsar, A.S., and Brown, A.L. "Reciprocal Teaching of Comprehension-Fostering and Comprehension-Monitoring Activities." *Cognition and Instruction* 1, no. 2 (1984): 117-75.

Pressley, M.; Goodchild, F.; Fleet, J.; Zajchowski, R.; and Evans, E.D. "The Challenges of Classroom Strategy Instruction." *Elementary School Journal* 89, no. 3 (1989): 301-42.

Raths, L.E.; Wassermann, S.; Jonas, A.; and Rothstein, A. *Teaching for Thinking: Theory, Strategies, and Activities for the Classroom*. 2nd ed. New York: Teachers College Press, 1986.

Sternberg, R. "Teaching Critical Thinking: Eight Easy Ways to Fail Before You Begin." *Phi Delta Kappan* 68, no. 6 (1987): 456-59.

Wassermann, S. "Teaching for Thinking: Louis E. Raths Revisited." *Phi Delta Kappan* 68, no. 6 (1987): 460-66.

Weinstein, C.E.; Goetz, E.T.; and Alexander, P.A., eds. *Learning and Study Strategies: Issues in Assessment, Instruction, and Evaluation*. San Diego: Academic Press, 1988.

Weinstein, C.E., and Mayer, R.E. "The Teaching of Learning Strategies." In *Handbook of Research on Teaching*, 3rd ed., edited by M.C. Wittrock. New York: Macmillan, 1986.

Willis, S. "Teaching Thinking: Educators Shift Emphasis from Recall to Reasoning." *ASCD Curriculum Update* (June 1992): 1-8.

18

INTEGRATING DIVERSE LEARNING STYLES

BY DAN W. REA

Adapting to individual differences in learning is important to teachers who are attempting to reach all their students. Traditionally, teachers have adapted to individual differences by using ability grouping. Unfortunately, ability grouping has many negative side effects, especially for low-ability groups (Gamoran and Berends 1987). An alternative way to adapt to individual differences is to identify and teach to students' learning styles.

Learning styles are the multiple ways and conditions under which knowledge can be processed (Keefe 1988). Research demonstrates that teaching to students' preferred learning styles improves achievement and motivation (Dunn, Beaudry, and Klavas 1989). Unlike ability groups, learning styles are not subject to the normative comparisons of more intelligent versus less intelligent or more desirable versus less desirable. Some learning styles are not better or smarter than others. Students' preferred learning styles are an individual expression of how they best learn. Adapting to individual differences with learning styles capitalizes on students' strengths and shows respect for their differences.

Although adapting to individual differences with learning styles avoids the pitfalls of ability grouping, it presents its own challenges. The major challenge is how to integrate diverse learning styles in the classroom. This chapter examines the management and developmental aspects of this challenge. Then, based on a literature review, it presents the "three M" practices for meeting this challenge: Matching, Mismatching, and Mixing learning styles to create integrated diversity.

The management aspect of this challenge is concerned with how teachers can integrate diverse styles in their classes. Teachers initially exposed to learning styles often remark, "Learning styles are wonderful, but how can I manage to teach everyone in so many different ways?" Researchers Doyle and Rutherford (1984) also have been skeptical of the value of learning-styles programs because of the overly complex demands placed on the teaching process.

The developmental aspect of this challenge is concerned with how to integrate diverse learning styles for each student. Students are capable of learning by different learning styles but usually prefer one style that is their strength. Although students have preferences, it is developmentally important for them to strengthen and balance all their learning styles. A narrow focus on preferences is maladaptive and can lead to a rigid overspecialization. They can become what Gregorc (1986) calls "pointy heads," who are highly developed in their preferences but underdeveloped in everything else. The goal is to develop well-rounded flexibility (Hunt 1979; Joyce 1984; Sternberg 1990).

The currently popular practice of formally "identifying" students' learning-style preferences and then "matching" teaching styles with preferences (Dunn and Dunn 1979) is not adequate to the challenge of integrated diversity. In fact, this practice by itself is counterproductive. A narrow focus on this practice generates a management problem for teachers and a developmental handicap for students. It creates a management problem by formally identifying an unmanageable number of learning styles. For instance, with the widely used Learning Style Inventory, teachers must manage classes of 30 or more students while simultaneously attending to 21 formally identified preferences for each individual (Dunn, Dunn, and Price 1985).

Also, this practice fails to account for the students' developmental need to expand their learning-style repertoires (Hunt 1979; Joyce 1984). It is based on the assumption that learning styles are unchanging and unmodifiable (Keefe 1988). If this were the case, it would be unreasonable to expect teachers to adapt their style preferences to the different style preferences of their students. The students' development is handicapped by this practice because of its lopsided emphasis on strengthening preferences. It ignores the students' need to develop a balanced flexibility of both preferred and nonpreferred styles. If a student were taught to walk according to this practice, he or she would be hobbling around on one preferred foot.

Matching has an essential role to play when balanced by two other practices. When matching is balanced with the mismatching and mixing of learning styles, then integrated diversity can be achieved. The balanced practices of Matching, Mismatching, and Mixing are called the "three M" practices. The three M's provide teachers with practical tools for accommodating students' learning-style needs.

Matching

The practice of matching most frequently mentioned in the literature states that when the instructional mode is congruent with the preferred learning style, learners' achievement, attitudes, and behavior are enhanced (Dunn, Beaudry, and Klavas 1989). This practice is especially useful in reaching underachievers because it allows teachers to build on students' strengths. For example, given the research that low-achieving readers tend to prefer adult direction, structured learning conditions, and tactile/kinesthetic modalities, teachers are well-advised to design learning conditions that build on these needs and strengths, rather than using the traditional phonetic method (Price, Dunn, and Sanders 1981).

A practical way to implement matching that reduces the complexities of management is to design multiple learning-style approaches to a common learning objective (Gregorc and Ward 1977). With multiple approaches, the teacher identifies three or four frequently used learning styles and prepares instructional modes for each to enable all students to achieve a common objective. For instance, to accommodate multiple perceptual modalities, teachers can design kinesthetic, auditory, and visual learning centers for the same objective. Students are assigned to learning centers according to their preferred modalities. In the visual center they can view a filmstrip. In the audio center they can listen to an audio tape. In the kinesthetic center they can do a construction project. Teachers move among the learning centers to offer assistance.

To provide for multiple social preferences, teachers can allow students to work alone, in pairs, in small groups, or with the teacher. The limitations of the matching practice for teachers depends on how much they can reasonably accommodate. Too demanding an accommodation to learning-style diversity can result in overload and ineffective teaching (Doyle and Rutherford 1984). For students, too much matching can eventually lead to boredom and rigidity. Even students with strongly preferred learning styles do not want or need to use them exclusively (Gregorc 1984).

Mismatching

The practice of mismatching refers to intentional training in a nonpreferred learning style. This training strengthens the nonpreferences by gradually and moderately adjusting the learning-style challenge (Hunt 1979; Joyce 1984). For example, Hunt found that when teachers teach at a slightly more abstract level on the abstract-concrete continuum, they can challenge concrete-thinking students to think more abstractly (Hunt 1971). Similarly, Meichenbaum (1986) discovered that when teachers model reflective self-talk strategies and gradually train students to take over these strategies, the students become more reflective problem solvers.

While matching encourages students to specialize in their preferred learning style, mismatching challenges students to expand beyond their preferred style to develop their nonpreferred styles. This is useful in helping students who are overspecialized in one learning style to develop a more wholesome balance. For example, students with a preference for visual learning also can benefit from learning kinesthetic skills, such as the manipulation of a computer keyboard. This kinesthetic training may feel awkward and uncomfortable in the beginning; however, with a gradual adjustment of the challenge level of the training, they eventually develop more skill and confidence. The goal of mismatching is not to eliminate or replace the students' preferred learning styles but to challenge them to strengthen their nonpreferred styles for a more complete balance.

For a social application of mismatching, consider how high achievers with a preference for working alone can benefit from working in cooperative groups. Such work encourages them to develop their social skills to a higher level. Also, it strengthens their intellectual skills in a new way by giving them the opportunity to teach what they know. Initially, they may resist, because they have received most of their positive reinforcement for working ahead rather than with the group. To overcome this resistance, teachers need to reward their social cooperation just as they have rewarded their academic acceleration.

For students who prefer to learn in cooperative groups, it is important for them not to become overly dependent on others. This dependency may retard their development of self-reliance, just as the high achievers' social development may be impeded by working alone. Mismatching may produce some intellectual disequilibrium and emotional discomfort; but when appropriately managed, this creative tension paves the way to fuller development (Joyce 1984).

It is important to caution that purposeful mismatching should be done with care. Both classroom practice and research have found that negative effects may result when students and teachers are required to experience prolonged periods of mismatch. Frustration, failure, and burnout have been attributed to this condition (Strother 1988). On the other hand, if the nonpreferred styles are not challenged, then the expansion of development is arrested and a wholesome balance cannot be achieved.

Mixing

Mixing involves exposure to a variety of instructional modes that can help students develop adaptability and flexibility in the use of different learning styles (Barbe and Milone 1980; Friedman and Alley 1984). "Style flex" is essential in a complex technological society that places increasing demands on multiple learning styles. The efficient use of computers, VCRs, microwave ovens, telephone answering machines, and digital watches requires the flexible use of various learning styles.

While mismatching helps overspecialized individuals and matching helps underachievers, mixing is most beneficial in sustaining motivation during large-group instruction (Brophy 1987). With this approach, teachers use a deliberate mix of instructional modes designed to appeal to all the main learning styles. Ideally, all these learning styles are intentionally matched at some point during the instructional process. A mixed approach is more than the traditional combination of lectures, discussions, and worksheets.

To assess the extent to which their teaching modes are representative of all learning styles, teachers can design a checklist of the main learning styles in their class and periodically self-check. For instance, some teachers' learning-styles checklists might include the perceptual modalities of visual, auditory, and kinesthetic learning and the social preferences of large groups, small groups, and individual learning. With a self-assessment, they might find they are using too many lectures and too much large-group instruction. Their students might need more visual and kinesthetic learning in small groups and individually.

Some mixing sequences are more effective than others, depending on the learners. Motivation and learning are enhanced by allowing students to learn an objective initially by using their preferred learning styles and then, after they are involved, by switching to different instructional modes to stimulate and reinforce their learning (Letteri 1988). For example, with a group of kinesthetic learners, a teacher could first have them learn an objective in a kinesthetic learning center. For enrichment and reinforcement, they would review the same objective in visual and auditory centers.

A limitation of the mixing practice is that a hodgepodge of learning activities can appear disjointed to students and lead to confusion and impatience. It is important to orchestrate the activities through appropriate pacing and smooth transitions (Kounin 1970). Mixing should not be applied with a checklist mentality but should enable teachers to facilitate the motivational flow of their classes.

The three M's provide teachers with practical options for meeting learning-style needs. No practice should be used to the total exclusion of the others. Each fulfills a special function that balances the others. Matching encourages students to specialize in their strengths and is very helpful in reaching underachievers. Mismatching challenges students to become more fully developed in their nonpreferred learning styles and is useful in helping the overspecialized student become well-rounded. Mixing stimulates students to be flexible and adaptable and helps to sustain motivation during large-group instruction.

A developmental approach to implementing the three M's begins with the application of mixing. This is a logical place to start, since most teachers already are teaching large, heterogeneous groups. This practice helps them to vary their instruction, thereby more fully taking into account the diverse learning styles of their students. Next, teachers can begin to use matching. With this practice, teachers strengthen their students' preferred learning styles by providing multiple approaches to the same learning objectives. Finally, teachers can use mismatching to design challenging activities that expand their students' learning-style repertoires. With this developmental approach, each practice builds on the preceding one, adding more instructional options for teachers and providing more learning flexibility for students.

In conclusion, the teaching goal is not to maximize the application of any one practice but to coordinate and balance their interaction. Too much mixing can lead to confusion and impulsiveness. Too much matching can lead to boredom and rigidity. Too much mismatching can lead to frustration and stress. The developmental application of the three M's is responsive to the needs of both teachers and students. This developmental strategy leads to a practical and wholesome accommodation of learning-style needs.

References

Barbe, W.B., and Milone, Fr. M. "Modality." *Instructor* 89, no. 6 (1980): 45-47.

Brophy, J. "Synthesis of Research on Strategies for Motivating Students to Learn." *Educational Leadership* 45, no. 2 (1987): 40-48.

Doyle, W., and Rutherford, B. "Classroom Research on Matching Learning and Teaching Styles." *Theory Into Practice* 23, no. 1 (1984): 20-25.

Dunn, R.S.; Beaudry, J.S.; and Klavas, A. "Survey of Research on Learning Styles." *Educational Leadership* 46, no. 6 (1989): 50-58.

Dunn, R.S., and Dunn, K.J. "Learning Styles/Teaching Styles: Should They. . . Can They. . . Be Matched?" *Educational Leadership* 36, no. 4 (1979): 238-44.

Dunn, R.S.; Dunn, K.J.; and Price, G.E. *Learning Style Inventory*. Lawrence, Kans.: Price Systems, 1985.

Friedman, P., and Alley, R. "Learning/Teaching Styles: Applying the Principles." *Theory Into Practice* 23, no. 1 (1984): 77-81.

Gamoran, A., and Berends, M. "The Effects of Stratification in Secondary Schools: Synthesis of Survey and Ethnographic Research." *Review of Educational Research* 5, no. 4 (1987): 415-35.

Gregorc, A.F. "Style as a Symptom: A Phenomenological Perspective." *Theory Into Practice* 23, no. 1 (1984): 51-55.

Gregorc, A.F. *Inside Styles: Beyond Basics*. Maynard, Mass.: Gabriel Systems, 1986.

Gregorc, A.F., and Ward, H.B. "A New Definition for Individual: Implications for Learning and Teaching." *NASSP Bulletin* 61, no. 406 (1977): 20-23.

Hunt, D.E. *Matching Models in Education: The Coordination of Teaching Methods with Student Characteristics*. Toronto: Ontario Institute for Studies in Education, 1971.

Hunt, D.E. "Learning Style and Student Needs: An Introduction to Conceptual Level." In *Student Learning Styles: Diagnosing and Prescribing Programs*, edited by J.W. Keefe. Reston, Va.: National Association of Secondary School Principals, 1979.

Joyce, B.R. "Dynamic Disequilibrium: The Intelligence of Growth." *Theory Into Practice* 23, no. 1 (1984): 26-34.

Keefe, J.W. "Development of the NASSP Learning Style Profile." In *Profiling and Utilizing Learning Style*, edited by J.W. Keefe. Reston, Va.: National Association of Secondary School Principals, 1988.

Kounin, J.S. *Discipline and Group Management in the Classroom*. New York: Holt, Rinehart and Winston, 1970.

Letteri, C.A. "The NASSP Learning Style Profile and Cognitive Processing." In *Profiling and Utilizing Learning Style*, edited by J.W. Keefe. Reston, Va.: National Association of Secondary School Principals, 1988.

Meichenbaum, D. "Cognitive Behavior Modification." In *Helping People Change: A Textbook of Methods*, edited by F. Kanfer and A. Goldstein. New York: Pergamon, 1986.

Price, G.; Dunn, R.; and Sanders, W. "Reading Achievement and Learning Style Characteristics." *The Clearing House* 54, no. 5 (1981): 223-26.

Sternberg, R. "Thinking Styles: Keys to Understanding Student Performance." *Phi Delta Kappan* 71, no. 5 (1990): 366-71.

Strother, D.B. "On Mixing and Matching of Teaching and Learning Styles." *Practical Applications of Research* 3, no. 2 (1988): 1-4.

SECTION IV

Untracking in the
Real World

19

REINTEGRATING SCHOOLS FOR SUCCESS: UNTRACKING ACROSS THE UNITED STATES

BY ANNE WHEELOCK

In any discussion of school reform and alternatives to tracking, the question most often asked is, What does an untracked school look like? Yet, as simple as this question seems, the answer is elusive. As schools depart from long-held forms of tracking and rigid ability grouping and respond to evolving education theory and knowledge, their practices reflect various understandings of how learning takes place. As these schools devise new traditions, norms, relationships, and classroom strategies that fit their circumstances, they become more different than similar.

Successful untracking is truly an exercise in school restructuring. As Donald LeMay, principal of Valley Junior High School in Carlsbad, California, a successfully untracked school, states, "The elimination of tracking and by implication the categorizing of students is the only meaningful way to 'restructure' schools for success."*

By extension then, untracking involves much more than regrouping students. In fact, simply blending students accustomed to learning in distinct classrooms may court a backlash of complaints from more ad-

---

*Quotations and examples of heterogeneously grouped schools in this chapter that are not otherwise identified first appeared in the author's book, *Crossing the Tracks*, published in 1992.]

vantaged students who suddenly find themselves in classes with others whom they believe have less interest in learning than they do (Cobb 1993; Welsh 1993).

In the most general sense, untracking involves reforming all classroom practices and rethinking all school routines to support the learning of diverse students in multiple-ability classrooms. This restructuring addresses three themes. First, untracking schools eliminates the segregation and isolation of students from each other by regrouping students into heterogeneous classes. Second, untracked schools extend the high expectations often reserved for the most facile learners to all students. Third, these schools ensure that all students have equal access to the valued, meaningful curriculum and instruction that will open doors to them in future years.

Beyond these themes, schools that set out to offer a challenging and nurturing educational environment to all students share certain characteristics. Certain conditions further enhance the possibility that schools' change efforts will successfully improve education for all students.

Beliefs About Learning Reflect High Expectations for All Students

Untracking is not an end in itself but a means to an end, and that end is improved learning for all students. While schools formulate the expected outcomes for students in different ways, the common threads that tie them together are the convictions that 1) all children have the capacity to learn at high levels and 2) schools are society's responsible institutions for developing this learning.

For example, at one untracked school, Wellesley Middle School in Wellesley, Massachusetts, teachers have adopted a set of core beliefs about learning that guide all their decisions about teaching (Saphier and D'Auria 1993). These core beliefs are:

1. All students are capable of high achievement, not just our fastest and most confident learners.
2. Consistent effort leads to success.
3. You are not supposed to understand everything the first time around.
4. Mistakes help one to learn.

Within the context of these beliefs, tracking at Wellesley Middle School was seen as undermining learning and a practice that should be rejected. Principal John D'Auria says:

214

If tracking would help us accomplish our goals at this school, then we would use it. But we believe in producing active learners, critical thinkers, and risk takers; and tracking our students by ability quite simply doesn't allow us to achieve our goals.

These beliefs about learning not only form a rationale for untracking but also shape decisions about all aspects of school improvement ranging from staff development to curriculum reforms. In addition, they serve as a broader platform for explaining changes in student grouping, curriculum, and instruction to parents, school board members, and new teachers. D'Auria emphasizes:

Heterogeneous groupings will fail without the core beliefs. It is not enough to institute a policy change on any level without a basic understanding of what you want to do, why you want to do it, and what you need to accomplish your goals.

Other principals agree that the success of untracking depends on teachers who honestly believe that all students can learn and who are prepared to engage in practices that facilitate all students' meeting that expectation. J.T. Crawford, principal of Crete-Monee Junior High in Crete, Illinois, notes, "Everyone in the school has to be committed to the philosophy of high expectations, and you have to infuse every part of the school with that philosophy."

Expected Outcomes Are Clearly Defined

In untracked schools, teachers in heterogeneous classes translate high expectations into clearly defined expected outcomes for all students. For example, at Pioneer Valley Regional School in Northfield, Massachusetts, a 7-12 school that has had heterogeneous grouping since 1985, the English Department as a whole identified the skills and knowledge that students would master in their classes. Teacher Amy Mann explains:

This skills list includes such expectations as, "Students will demonstrate critical and analytical reading and writing skills," that are specific regarding outcomes but don't confine teachers. Within the curriculum unit, then, teachers can decide what kinds of assignments or projects will meet expected standards. Teachers also define grading criteria so that we can say, "This is the kind of work you have to do for an 'A,' or this kind of work reflects a 'B' standard."

Mann further explains that, within this context, it is up to individual teachers to develop learning activities that allow students choices of how they will master material. For example, she asks pairs of students to choose from a list of paired authors — Emerson and Thoreau, Dickinson and Lowell, Pound and Eliot, and so on — and assume their identities. The two student then write a series of letters to each other on topics that require extensive reading, biographical research, and analysis of the authors' works. Although she might negotiate modified expectations for students with disabilities, all students are expected to demonstrate understanding of the subject.

The emphasis on outcomes in untracking schools parallels a variety of "outcome-based" planning models, including the well-known Outcomes-Driven Developmental Model (ODDM) developed in Johnson City, New York, which some schools have adopted as a key planning tool. Brenda Lyons, Director of Secondary Education and Communications for Edmond Public Schools in Oklahoma, explains:

> The entire philosophy and teaching techniques associated with outcomes-based education are extensive and detailed. However, the main idea is that all students can succeed when given enough time. If a mastery-learning model is followed with correctives given for students who do not master the material and enrichment provided for those who do, then students of all levels can be taught in the same classroom.

As a result, tracking can be eliminated. Indeed, in some untracked schools, outcomes establish criteria not only for performance on specific assignments but also for graduation. At Central Park East Secondary Schools, for example, students must earn their diplomas by presenting a series of portfolios that meet established criteria and defending their work to a committee of educators and other adults from the community. While most students accomplish this required task in their four-year high school program, some students choose to complete requirements in five years. Regardless of the time students need, a high level of effort and performance is consistent for all.

Using Coaching to Meet High Expectations in Heterogeneous Classes

If schools adopt the belief that all students can learn at high levels, they also acknowledge that some students may need more time and attention than others. Almost without exception, untracking schools have rejected "pull-out" approaches, whether under the guise of compensatory or special education. Instead, they make extra help available in regular classes, rearrange schedules to allow additional time for students who need extra help, or implement other kinds of academic support strategies. In some schools that employ homogeneous groups for specific skill development, regrouping is designed to help students succeed in heterogeneous classes.

The logistics of offering students extra help often involves restructuring the school schedule. For example, many middle schools have restructured into an eight- or even nine-period daily schedule. Thus at Castle High School in Honolulu, ninth- and tenth-grade students are grouped in heterogeneous classes for all core subjects, and those who need extra help are slotted into small homogeneous groups during one of two elective periods or enrolled in a double period in a particular subject. Added periods during the day also allow for preteaching to provide weaker students with a "jump start" in some subjects or particular units. For example, at Willard Junior High School in Berkeley, California, students scoring below the 30th percentile on state tests and eligible for Chapter 1 support receive preteaching in which they are introduced to curriculum units a week or two before the units are introduced in their heterogeneous classes.

Some schools make extra help available in many settings. Coaching may involve cross-age tutoring, matching students with parent volunteers, or after-school tutoring by teachers. At Louis Armstrong Middle School in Queens, New York, any student who needs extra help is invited to a voluntary before-school tutoring program. Classes officially begin at 8:40 a.m., but the library opens at 8:00 a.m. for extra help. At Holyoke Magnet Middle School in Holyoke, Massachusetts, teachers offer students a lunchtime "Math Club" where they can snack with their teachers while discussing their academic problems. Teacher Marsha Bailey says:

> Everyone has the same invitation, so there's no labeling or stigma. I tell students, "The definition of a fine and admirable student is one who takes the initiative, who reaches out for what he or she needs and wants. That's what grown-ups do."

In other schools, the progress of the weakest students is monitored on a more formal basis. For example, at the Prescott Middle School in Baton Rouge, Louisiana, students in danger of failing meet on a regular basis with school counselors, their parents, and their teachers to develop plans for strengthening study habits and building personal confidence. Likewise, at Valley Junior High School, students experiencing academic difficulty are closely monitored and provided with extra support services coordinated through a Student Study Team.

Common to all these schools is the understanding that learning requires practicing skills regardless of student-performance levels. Students achieving above grade level may receive coaching in creative writing, while others may focus on specific classroom homework assignments. Making extra help available to all reduces the labeling of students and strengthens the chances that all students will succeed in heterogeneous classes.

Instructional Approaches Address Multiple Abilities

Effective learning in classrooms of diverse learning styles begins with the belief that intelligence is multi-dimensional and that schools can cultivate the intelligences of every child through a variety of learning strategies in heterogeneous classes. Moreover, in planning for diverse student groups, increasing numbers of teachers in untracked schools are guided by the belief that instructional approaches characterized as "good for the gifted" also are effective for average and lower-achieving students. These approaches include Socratic seminars, thematic curricula, experiential activities, and flexible groupwork. Learning incorporates rich materials, such as novels, original texts, films and videos, audio tapes, technology, art, and photography that appeal to divergent interests.

Following are brief descriptions of a few of these approaches:

Socratic Seminars. In classrooms that emphasize learning for understanding, Socratic seminars offer fertile ground for rich learning for all students. For example, at the Chattanooga School for the Arts and Sciences in Tennessee, a Paideia school where all students participate in a single-track liberal arts curriculum in grades K-12, one 80-minute period a week is allotted to Socratic seminars where students in heterogeneous groups, each led by a teacher, discuss an original text or piece of art (Wheelock 1994). They explore the meaning of works ranging from a chapter on the rain forest written by Harvard entomologist Edward O. Wilson to an etching created by M.C. Escher. As the teacher's questioning pushes them to articulate how they understand and interpret what they have read or seen, students develop their own perspectives on these works and come to appreciate the complexity of intellectual and artistic expression.

In some cases, untracking schools make use of commercial curricula available for discussion. Thus, in a seminar format, young adolescent students in "Philosophy for Children" classes at Livermore Falls Middle School in Maine read stories that raise philosophical questions related to loyalty, truth, and justice. In this school, this commercially available curriculum that often is adopted by classes for students labeled "gifted and talented" is incorporated into the heterogeneously grouped reading/study-skills classes.

Indeed, many educators who practice Socratic questioning have concluded that seminar approaches produce richer discussion in heterogeneous classes than in ability-grouped settings. Matthew Lipman, developer of the Philosophy for Children program, notes, "I don't think that ordinary children are incapable of thinking about complex matters. . . . [Philosophy for Children] works even better with mixed-ability groups than with homogeneous groups." Others note that students who are the least accustomed to seeking the "one right answer" are the most likely to prod those students who are most certain of their position. Combining these students enriches the learning dialogue for all (Cushman 1992*a*, *b*). Socratic seminars invite all students to participate in an exploration of ideas, experiences, and analysis of a common text to enrich understanding for all.

Thematic Curricula and Hands-On Projects. When a curriculum is organized around ideas, students of multiple abilities can engage in learning at various entry points. Themes may include topics as general as "Ships," "Pacific Northwest," or "Democracy," as they do at Islander Middle School in Mercer Island, Washington. They may address topics that link social issues to personal choices. For example, at the West Windsor-Plainsboro Middle School in New Jersey, curriculum developer Kay Goerss reports that a thematic interdisciplinary curriculum for heterogeneously grouped seventh-graders is organized around such social issues as family interaction, the environment, and problems of segregation and integration. Each topic provides one month of study, with students working cooperatively in teams to produce detailed magazines on each topic. Goerss explains:

> The magazines pull all the subject areas together. Students have to use math skills to produce charts, tables, and graphs to illustrate their topics. They use research in social studies and science to gather and organize information, and their literature selections — the school uses reading workshop, writing-across-the-curriculum, and whole-language approaches — include readings on [the topics]. It's different from year to year, since it all grows from the kids deciding what social concerns they're going to look at.

At West Windsor-Plainsboro, week-long schoolwide projects also promote interdisciplinary, social-concerns activities that touch on all parts of the school's curriculum. For example, just prior to the winter holidays, a week-long schoolwide focus on cultural diversity extends to physical education classes where students learn games from around the world. The use of cross-cultural topics adds further meaning for an ethnically diverse group of students who can see themselves and their lives reflected in their learning.

Increasingly, commercial curriculum developers are designing packaged thematic curricula. One popular thematic curriculum for the middle grades is "Voyage of the *Mimi*," which is especially oriented to multiple-ability classrooms. The National Science Foundation has awarded a number of grants for the development of thematic curricula, such as the Human Biology Middle Grades Life Sciences Project of Stanford University. This interdisciplinary thematic curriculum is oriented specifically to students of varied backgrounds and abilities and addresses adolescents' social, behavioral, and health problems through language arts, math, home economics, and health activities, including lab work, writing, role plays, debates, and groupwork.

Differentiated Instruction. Successful heterogeneous classrooms also rest on the tenet that "good teaching" must employ a variety of individualized instruction techniques. At Tate's Creek Middle School in Lexington, Kentucky, teachers Dorie Combs, Elizabeth Barrett, and Julia Robbins have identified methods that allow them to work successfully with a seventh-grade cluster that blends students described as "gifted," "general-advanced," "basic," and "learning disabled." These methods include personalized learning. For instance, students may complete identical language arts assignments (for example, "describe the sequence of events leading up to the conclusion" or "describe how the traits of the main character affect your book's plot") though they may be working on a common theme from different texts at different difficulty levels.

These teachers also engage students in personalized teacher-student correspondence, Socratic questioning at varying degrees of difficulty, direct teaching of study skills and note-taking strategies, and the use of learning centers. Students in their classes also may choose extension assignments from "mailboxes" containing materials of varying levels of challenge.

By combining these approaches with cooperative learning, untracked schools are able to accommodate diverse learners in multiple-ability classrooms without slowing academic progress. In these classes, teachers and students share leadership appropriately, with teachers describing the tasks, observing, intervening, and teaching social skills directly. Activities emphasize task accomplishment and maintenance of skills. While students share responsibility for each other's learning, with the most effective learning evolving from positive interdependence among students, students are individually accountable for their performance. Finally, groups are given opportunities to reflect on their effectiveness (Slavin 1990).

As a strategy for classrooms with diverse students, cooperative learning takes a number of forms. One in particular benefits classrooms with ethnic and language variations. Developed by Elizabeth Cohen, Beatriz Arias, and other researchers at Stanford University, this form of cooperative learning, called Complex Instruction, focuses on improving the achievement of children whose ethnicity, language background, perceived academic or reading ability, popularity, or length of time in the United States makes them vulnerable to reduced academic expectations. In Complex Instruction classrooms, students are clustered in small, heterogeneous work groups. Tasks are presented in relevant languages and pictographs — with reading, writing, and computation embedded in each assignment — and are focused on solving problems that are inherently interesting and conceptually demanding and that require various media, modes, and kinds of intelligence.

In Complex Instruction classrooms, teachers explicitly instruct students in the process of learning and working in groups, even before they begin their learning-station assignments. Rotating students' assigned roles, including the role of facilitator, promotes significant student interaction and high achievement gains.

Finally, Complex Instruction teachers employ two specific techniques called "status treatments," explicit teachings about ability that teachers convey to all students working in small groups. The first, "multiple-ability treatment," communicates to students that successful completion of assigned tasks requires many different skills, not just reading and writing. Teachers specifically identify all the skills necessary to complete a task, then announce to the class: "No one person is going to be good at all these abilities, but everyone will be good at at least one."

The second, "assigning of competence to low-status students," requires teachers to observe low-status students for demonstrations of competence and to remark on this ability within hearing distance of other students, explaining what the student did and why this specific skill is valuable in the adult world. Using these techniques to equalize and increase student interaction in diverse classrooms, teachers have realized significant achievement gains for low-status students (Cohen 1986).

In untracked schools, these and other innovative teaching strategies reflect the belief expressed by John Lounsbury of Georgia College that "increasingly, it is becoming obvious that one's ability to learn outweighs in importance any particular discrete bodies of knowledge that one has learned." Thus teachers in such schools are less purveyors of answers than directors of learning, so that students learn to pose questions, tolerate ambiguities, and interpret meaning — in the process becoming lifelong learners.

Norms and Routines that Value Effort and Inclusiveness

Schools that untrack do not rely solely on changes in classroom techniques for success. Many also challenge norms and assumptions that shape the culture of the school by shifting away from routines that isolate groups of students from each other and result in the exclusion of some students from challenging and nurturing learning opportunities. For example, these schools review course catalogues to ensure that course labels do not suggest "levels" that might persuade students to opt out of challenging classes. Others introduce routines to strengthen a caring school climate through the use of heterogeneously grouped, classroom-based guidance and teacher advisory programs that implement a "Community of Friends" curriculum.

In addition, many untracked schools implement a "no-cut" policy in extracurricular activities. Rather than exclude certain students on the basis of low academic performance, these schools treat extracurricular activities as learning opportunities and expand access to as many students as possible. At the McCullough Middle School in Dallas, Texas, the elimination of a selective group of cheerleaders in favor of a pep squad open to all eighth-grade girls makes for greater participation and stronger school spirit. At the Jericho Middle School in Jericho, New York, all students, including students with disabilities, who want to play varsity sports or join cheerleading activities can sign a contract to attend practice and share "playing time" equally with their teammates. Similarly, if the school play has fewer parts than students interested in acting, the school stages several productions to allow everyone interested to participate. Not surprisingly, schools with such policies report that student participation in after-school activities greatly increases.

Finally, a number of schools work at changing aspects of school life to ensure that the same high-achieving students are not repeatedly favored with the benefits of the school's limited resources. They seek ways in which all students can benefit from scarce resources, both tangible and intangible. For example, at the Shutesbury School in Massachusetts, teacher Ron Berger reports that sixth-graders themselves decide how such resources as donated tickets to special events will be distributed equitably. Free tickets to the symphony, field trips to museums or a local television station, opportunities to work with mentors from local industries or universities, and other enrichment experiences are not treated as rewards that recognize the achievement of only a few students.

Counseling Expands Opportunities Through Advocacy

Untracked schools extend norms of inclusiveness to one of the most traditional roles, that of the school guidance counselor. Rather than act as gatekeepers and sorters of students for differential learning opportunities, guidance counselors in untracked schools advocate for all students to have access to challenging and meaningful learning (Hart and Jacobi 1992). Underlying their work is a commitment to providing all students with opportunities to describe and develop their aspirations, identify their goals and interests, learn about occupational fields (not specific jobs) that are compatible with those interests, investigate those fields, and tie those fields to study decisions. This approach ensures that students will not unwittingly be closed out of future opportunities.

In schools that promote inclusive norms, guidance counselors work as leaders and curriculum developers to expand students' access to knowledge. For example, under the leadership of counselors at the Crete-Monee Junior High School, teachers are assigned to small groups of students to implement the school's "Pathways to Success: Individualized Educational and Career Plan." This two-year curriculum for seventh- and eighth-graders provides tools to direct students' thinking through future education plans in the context of their own aspirations, goals, and dreams. It requires students to take responsibility for reflecting on all dimensions of their expectations, interests, and values. Along with phasing out the school's lower-track classes, this program has contributed to a doubling of the enrollment of the school's graduating eighth-graders in the college-preparatory track in the district's high school.

Conclusion

Schools that offer equal access to knowledge to all students and engage all students in opportunities often reserved only for "high-track" groups clearly are doing more than simply regrouping students.

Educators in these schools understand that, though "life" may deem some people more suitable for some roles than others, it is not for schools to serve that function. In these schools, teachers truly believe that human intelligence is multifaceted and that they can develop the intelligence of all students by reforming teaching and learning to match that view. These are schools that envision themselves as authentic and inclusive communities of learners and that work daily to make that vision a reality.

References

Cobb, N. "Southie in Black and White: Two Students from South Boston High Talk About Their Hopes, Their Fears, and Their Lives." *Boston Globe*, 18 May 1993, p. 29.

Cohen, E. *Designing Groupwork: Strategies for Heterogeneous Classrooms*. New York: Teachers College Press, 1986.

Cushman, K. "Conversation in Classrooms: Who Are Seminars For?" *Harvard Education Letter* 8, no. 2 (1992): 1-4. a

Cushman, K. "Essential Schools' 'Universal Goals': How Can Heterogeneous Grouping Help?" *Horace* 8, no. 5 (1992): 1-8. b

Hart, P.J., and Jacobi, M. *From Gatekeeper to Advocate: Transforming the Role of the School Counselor*. New York: College Entrance Examination Board, 1992.

Saphier, J., and D'Auria, J. *How to Bring Vision to School Improvement Through Core Outcomes, Commitments, and Beliefs*. Carlisle, Mass.: Research for Better Teaching, 1993.

Slavin, R.E. *Cooperative Learning: Theory, Research, and Practice*. Englewood Cliffs, N.J.: Prentice-Hall, 1990.

Welsh, P. "Staying on Tracks: Can We Teach Honors Kids and Hard Cases Together?" *Washington Post*, 7 March 1993, p. C1.

Wheelock, A. *Crossing the Tracks: How "Untracking" Can Save America's Schools*. New York: New Press, 1992.

Wheelock, A. "Chattanooga's Paideia Schools: A Single Track for All — And It's Working." *Journal of Negro Education* 63, no. 1 (1994): 77-92.

CREATING A NONTRADITIONAL SCHOOL IN A TRADITIONAL COMMUNITY

BY NANCY B. NORTON AND CHARLOTTE A. JONES

As society has changed in the past twenty years, many so-called traditional ways of living and working in America have become almost extinct. In the past, many children came home from school to a two-parent home where they would be greeted with cookies and milk. Today many children use their own keys to open the door to an empty house or apartment and to wait for a single parent to come home from work.

In addition, drug use, AIDS, teen pregnancy, violence, unemployment, and divorce cause problems that children must face as they grow into adulthood. Frymier and his associates (1992) stated, "Growing up is a risky business for some youngsters — very risky — and the schools are not to blame" (p. v).

While schools are not to blame for the failures of society, they are responsible for preparing students to be successful and productive citizens. Many "traditional" school practices will not work with today's children. Schlechty (1990) argued that it is not enough to reform school practices; schools must be changed in radical ways. They must be restructured.

A traditional approach to meeting the needs of all students has been tracking. Frymier and his associates (1992) explained that the "explicit intention" of this practice was to provide special instruction, materials, and attention to each group in a concentrated manner so that lower students could catch up with their peers. However, the "implicit intention was to separate the slower students so that other more able students would not be held back" (p. 70). From their review of the research, Frymier and his associates concluded that "separating students according to risk is no more effective and no more appropriate than separating students according to intelligence, race, sex, or probably even age" (p. 70).

Black (1993) states that one successful alternative to tracking is multi-age grouping, where students stay with the same teacher for more than one year and move developmentally through the curriculum. In a review of 64 research studies, Pavan (1992) concludes that "students in nongraded settings do as well as or better than students in traditional self-contained classes in terms of both academic achievement and mental health" (p. 25).

Katz, Evangelou, and Hartman (1990) believe that multi-age grouping is appropriate for young children because it resembles traditional family and neighborhood groupings that provide avenues for education and socialization. Young children often are deprived of this contact. The authors add that research seems to indicate that social development is enhanced by multi-age experiences. They propose that the curriculum in a multi-age setting is more developmentally appropriate for children. In its report, the American Association of School Administrators (Davis 1992) adds that parent-teacher communication is improved and educational opportunities for all children are enhanced. Slavin (1992) contends that, while the nongraded organizational plan contributes to instructional success, "curriculum and instructional methods used within a nongraded framework are as important as the school organization plan in determining the ultimate effects" (p. 24).

AASA's report on *The Nongraded Primary* (Davis 1992) set forth several principles to consider when developing such a program:

1. Children learn as total persons through physical, social, emotional, and intellectual means.
2. While all children grow through similar stages, they grow in different styles and at different rates.
3. Self-esteem affects every learning act.
4. Children learn best through active interaction.
5. An integrated curriculum with a wide variety of activities promotes optimal learning in young children.
6. In order to learn, children must interact with their environment. They cannot be given knowledge.

7. Children learn through communication with others.
8. Children learn communication through expression with others in a variety of methods.
9. Children learn math skills through exploring, discovering, and solving real-life problems.
10. Children learn best in a flexible, yet organized, classroom.

The concept of nongraded primary schools is not new. The multiplicity of challenges confronting today's students has created a new period of interest in such organizational structures.

Dynamics of Change: A Case Study

In any implementation of change, several practices should be followed. Gaustad (in Davis 1992) asserts that 1) there must be advanced planning and study by teachers and parents; 2) implementation must be flexible, evaluated, and adjusted as needed; 3) teachers need practical training in the unique aspects of nongraded classrooms; 4) teachers need ongoing planning time in preparing for students; and 5) teachers and parents need to be constantly informed about and involved in decisions related to the education of their children. Following is a case study of one school's program for providing an exciting, challenging, and appropriate education to meet the needs of young children.

Metter Primary School is located in rural south Georgia with approximately 520 students. It is one of three schools in a 1,550-student district. About 61% of the students receive free or reduced-price lunches. The school is 58% white, 38% African-American, and 4% Hispanic. In 1987, per capita income for the county was $11,193, with 29% of the population below the poverty level; and 59% of persons 25 or older did not have a high school education (Bachtel 1990).

The nongraded, continuous-progress program at Metter Primary School was initiated by a new principal, Ronnie Sikes, in 1987. From the beginning, when heterogeneous grouping was instituted, teachers and staff believed that change was not only inevitable but necessary. Professional growth through attendance at conferences, professional reading, and inservice was encouraged, as was taking risks with new and innovative practices in the classroom. Whole language, hands-on math activities, and other developmentally appropriate practices began to take the place of traditional paper-and-pencil approaches.

The catalyst for the program was a speech given by the Georgia superintendent of schools at a conference in the summer of 1990, in which he proposed a nongraded, continuous-progress program in the primary grades for the state's elementary schools. Thus, with approval from the central office and the support of teachers and administrators, a proposal for an innovative grant to provide funding for the program was submitted. The grant was awarded in December 1990, and the PACE (Promoting Achievement in Child-Centered Education) project began in August 1991 at Metter.

During the planning phase before implementation, several committees were formed to address the major areas. These committees included public relations, staff development, curriculum, and assessment. Their functions were to design strategies in these areas that would facilitate implementation.

Public Relations. In a report on the nongraded-primary program, Davis states that "perhaps the greatest challenge in moving to the non-graded school is explaining its benefits to parents" (1992, p. 14). Shortly after receiving the grant, the staff began to prepare a public relations campaign. Gaining knowledge from professional reading, seminars, visits to other schools, conferences, and workshops helped the staff in providing background information to the public. A faculty meeting was held in which brainstorming generated anticipated questions from the community. Teachers were organized into groups of six. Each group was given several of the questions and asked to respond. Using an overhead projector, responses were written and discussed by the total group. Teachers were given a copy of questions and suggested answers. This method helped teachers with responses to parents' questions and provided uniformity in faculty understanding.

A community meeting was held in which the program was explained. About 200 parents and other citizens attended. After a brief meeting of the entire group, parents were divided into four groups and went to classrooms for a detailed orientation and question-and-answer session led by teams of teachers. Parents also were given handouts containing journal articles and a question-and-answer sheet about the PACE program. The administrators believed that small groups allowed for more exchange of information and prevented the problem of a few dissenters causing major objections.

Other public relations activities took place during the planning phase. Teachers wrote newspaper articles for local and regional newspapers. Administrators and teachers made presentations to civic and social organizations, including Lions, Rotary, Kiwanis, Chamber of Commerce, NAACP, and the DAR.

Staff Development. The staff-development committee made — and continues to make — decisions about purchasing teacher resource materials, visiting other programs, training teachers, and attending conferences. In order to facilitate site-based decisions, the committee recognized the need to improve communication skills. Training was conducted on such topics as communication styles and conflict resolution. In addition, all staff members were given the opportunity to visit a nongraded program in Oxford, North Carolina, to see an existing program in action. From the beginning, staff members were provided professional literature to enhance preparation for the program.

During the summer prior to implementation, all staff members were involved in three weeks of intense staff development. Practitioners from North Carolina, Florida, Alaska, and Massachusetts and consultants from Georgia Southern University worked with teachers to design developmentally appropriate, multi-age classrooms. Topics included designing interdisciplinary thematic units, learning centers, whole language, portfolio assessment, self-esteem, and using math manipulatives.

Staff development is ongoing. Teachers and other staff members continue to receive inservice training as needs arise. They are encouraged to attend conferences and workshops so that they can stay informed about current trends and practices. In addition, current literature is made available through subscriptions to professional journals.

Curriculum. The staff at Metter Primary generally believes that, while all children go through the same stages of development, they grow at different rates. The developmentally appropriate curriculum, based on a learning continuum designed by the teachers at Metter Primary, was adapted from one used in British Columbia. It contains but is not limited to Georgia's Quality Core Curriculum objectives. In order to discourage failure and boredom, there are no imposed time limits or learning ceilings in the continuum. Instruction is provided through interdisciplinary, thematic units designed by the teachers. These units are rotated among the teaching pods.

Recognizing that children learn best when exposed to a wide variety of materials that address numerous learning styles and stages of development, the teachers use many research-based instructional strategies. Whole-language instruction in reading has been implemented for several years. Basals are used only as resources, along with classroom book sets, "big books," and other materials for language development. Math manipulatives allow young children to use higher-order thinking skills when solving problems, rather than depending on only pencil-and-paper computation. Such programs as Marietta Math, Box It-Bag It, and Calendar Math promote inquiry-based learning and offer real-life activities. Computer-assisted instruction in reading, writing, and math provides activities that relate to units being taught.

Field trips are an integral part of instruction. Students are exposed to learning environments beyond the classroom by going on trips in Metter, Candler County, Statesboro, and Savannah, Georgia, and occasionally to Jacksonville, Florida. Trips are planned around thematic units. For example, students studying the solar system would travel to the Savannah Science Museum and visit the planetarium. Interdisciplinary units about the farm and farm animals may include a field trip to the local peanut plant, dairy, or goat farm.

Field trips and resource people bring the real world to the child and make learning meaningful. It becomes more significant for children to read and write stories and solve math problems based on real-life experiences. Many visitors to Metter Primary School are involved in classrooms to share their expertise about such topics as karate (during a unit on Japan) or deer and other animals in winter.

Assessment. Metter Primary School uses student portfolios that include samples from various stages of writing, journals, and student surveys to demonstrate student progress to parents. Teachers write narratives three times annually on "continuous-progress review forms" and share student work in conferences with parents. Parents and teachers select conference times that are convenient for both. Informal assessments of reading and math are ongoing. When students move from one team to another or from Metter Primary School to Metter Middle School, informal reading inventories and math checklists are completed to determine performance levels.

State-mandated assessments are done at the required grade levels. At the end of the first year of school, the Georgia Kindergarten Assessment Program is completed. This developmentally appropriate assessment reports a student's readiness for traditional first grade. Fourth-year students are required to take a norm-referenced test in reading and math and a curriculum-based assessment designed for Georgia students. Based on samples of a child's work, teachers are asked to determine a process-writing level for all fourth-year students.

The formal objectives of PACE are: 1) to create a nurturing learning environment to ensure maximum opportunities for academic success at the primary level, 2) to create a nurturing learning environment to ensure maximum opportunities for developing positive self-esteem and socialization at the primary level, and 3) to create a shared decision-making structure for faculty, staff, administrators, and students to ensure a cohesive, unified approach to the development of a nurturing learning environment (Jones 1991).

First- and second-year (traditional kindergarten and first-grade) students are grouped heterogeneously in 12 classrooms. An average class consists of approximately 10 first-year and 10 second-year students. Third- and fourth-year (traditional second- and third-grade) students are grouped heterogeneously in 13 classrooms. To help promote an atmosphere of stability, understanding, belonging, security, and confidence — characteristics that nurture a child's total development — students remain with the same teacher for two years. All but three classrooms have teacher assistants. Funding for teacher assistants is provided through existing local, state, and federal programs. Instruction offered by resource, compensatory, and special-education teachers is accomplished within the regular classroom whenever possible, enabling students to be served based on their social, emotional, and instructional needs and not their label.

Teachers are grouped in pods as cooperative teaching units to plan instruction, to discuss special student needs, and to support each other in professional endeavors. Teachers in pods containing five- and six-year-olds make up the Cub team, and teachers in pods containing seven- and eight-year-olds make up the Tiger team. Pods meet once a week to discuss curriculum and to coordinate activities. Pod leaders bring problems and ideas to the leadership team for action. Support teachers from special education, media, Chapter I, and other areas comprise a third team.

To facilitate decision making, a leadership team consists of the principal and the assistant principal; one representative, selected annually by consensus, from each teaching team; the pod leaders; a representative from the support team; and a teacher-assistant representative. Information from and feedback to the leadership team are disseminated by team members.

Leadership team meetings are held every other week. Decisions made by the team include the allocation of funds, the planning of school-wide activities and special events, certain student issues, and matters regarding curriculum and instruction.

Assessment of the program has been ongoing. In December 1992 and in February 1993, a project evaluator not associated with the school conducted interviews with teachers. Teachers indicated some stress and discomfort with multi-age grouping. They expressed concern about adequately reaching students with such a wide range of abilities. However, they were generally pleased with the program. They felt the major advantages were that students were able to help each other, that self-esteem was enhanced, and that there were few discipline problems. It was a general feeling that multi-age grouping fosters the nurturing atmosphere conducive to optimal learning.

An organizational-health inventory, administered in April 1991 and again in April 1992, revealed that the overall school-health score was significantly higher in 1992. The results seemed to indicate that strong leadership, friendly and productive working relationships, and control over the educational program contributed to continued growth of the school and success of the project.

Parent involvement was enhanced through portfolio conferences. In a survey completed at the end of the first year, parents overwhelmingly favored the portfolio conference over the traditional report card. They felt that the process created a bond with the teacher and that they had a clearer picture of their children's progress.

Teachers reported that learning strategies, such as whole language and real-life math activities, provided expanded and enriched opportunities for all students, academically, socially, and emotionally. However, they also indicated that it was very time-consuming to develop and implement new units, centers, and a continuous-progress approach. They anticipated that, as materials accumulate and teachers become more comfortable with the process, the stress will be lessened.

Guidelines in the innovation grant for the PACE project specified that an evaluation was to be completed at the end of the second year for state validation. This was accomplished in August 1993. A case-study design, using quantitative and qualitative techniques for data collection and analysis, was employed (Metter Primary School PACE Project Evaluation Committee 1993).

The Metter plan specified three major objectives:

1. To create a nurturing environment to ensure maximum opportunities for academic skills at the primary level.
2. To create a nurturing environment to ensure maximum opportunities for positive self-esteem and socialization at the primary level.
3. To create a shared decision-making structure for faculty, staff, administrators, and students to ensure a cohesive, unified approach to the development of a nurturing learning environment.

Each objective was met. Items from students' portfolios, Iowa Tests of Basic Skills (ITBS), and teacher rankings of student ability were used to measure Objective 1. End-of-year (1992-93) Informal Reading Inventories (IRI) were completed with all students. Teachers also estimated the academic ranking of all students. The reading inventories, teacher rankings, and ITBS scores for all fourth-year students were correlated to determine the strength of the relationships between standardized and nonstandardized indicators of student performance. Statistically significant correlations (p ≤ .05) were found between the IRI and ITBS reading and math scores and between teacher rankings and IRI scores. The congruence among these measures supports the argument that PACE teachers have a clear assessment of their students' academic abilities.

Nearly two-thirds of the parents completed an August 1993 survey. Parents continued to prefer portfolios to report cards, citing informative parent-teacher conferences, well-organized information, and their ability to gain a better understanding of their children's academic (and other) development.

Parent questionnaires, teacher interviews, and teacher questionnaires were used to assess the second objective. Most parents found positive effects resulting from their children's working with older and younger children. Children were more willing to help and share, relationships were enhanced, and higher self-esteem was noted. Teachers also observed greater self-confidence.

As a result of the endeavor to generate a structure for shared decision making (Objective 3), teachers indicated that they had more opportunities for professional growth and the sharing of ideas. They also were pleased with the freedom to be innovative and to participate in important school decisions. Several comments reflected a renewed sense of enthusiasm and enjoyment in teaching.

Some parents are still worried about adequate academic progress and discipline in the new program, and some teachers continue to find time a major concern. However, most evidence indicates that this bold new plan — an innovative, nongraded primary school in a traditional, rural, Southern community — is working and is working well.

Conclusion

The process of restructuring is a difficult one. A metamorphosis of the magnitude attempted here is not without a price — hard work, some stress and discomfort, a substantial commitment. But real change is taking place, and the PACE project final evaluation report (Metter Primary School PACE Project Evaluation Committee 1993) shows the power of the determination of a few courageous educators willing to venture forth on behalf of their students.

Lives have been affected, and a genuine effort to improve and enhance instruction for the children at Metter Primary School is under way. Overall, the results of this "experiment" have been decidedly positive. And the future of children who have had the good fortune to be students in Metter's new nongraded program promises to be brighter by virtue of that experience.

References

Bachtel, D., ed. *The Georgia County Guide*. Athens: University of Georgia, 1990.

Black, S. "Derailing Tracking." *The Executive Educator* 15, no. 1 (1993): 27-30.

Davis, R. *The Nongraded Primary: Making Schools Fit Children*. Arlington, Va.: American Association of School Administrators, 1992.

Frymier, J.; Barber, L.; Carriedo, R.; Denton, W.; Gansneder, B.; Johnson-Lewis, S.; and Robertson, N. *Growing Up Is Risky Business, and the Schools Are Not to Blame*. Bloomington, Ind.: Phi Delta Kappa, 1992.

Jones, C.A., ed. *PACE Developmental Project Plan*. Metter, Ga.: Candler County School System, Metter Primary School, 1991.

Katz, L.G.; Evangelou, D.; and Hartman, J.A. *The Case for Mixed-Age Grouping in Early Education*. Washington, D.C.: National Association for the Education of Young Children, 1990.

Metter Primary School PACE Project Evaluation Committee. *Final Evaluation Report of the Metter Primary School PACE Project*. Metter, Ga.: Candler County School System, 1993.

Pavan, B.N. "The Benefits of Nongraded Schools." *Educational Leadership* 50, no. 2 (1992): 22-25.

Schlechty, P.C. *Schools for the 21st Century: Leadership Imperatives for Educational Reform*. San Francisco: Jossey-Bass, 1990.

Slavin, R.E. "The Nongraded Elementary School: Great Potential, but Keep It Simple." *Educational Leadership* 50, no. 2 (1992): 24.

UNGROUPING OUR WAY: A TEACHER'S STORY

BY DAPHRENE KATHRYN SHEPPARD

Though the schools in our county still used modified ability group-ing in the 1991-92 school year, the practice was being re-evaluated. My school, Marvin Pittman Laboratory School, which serves students in kindergarten through eighth grade, never had any kind of grouping except in the eighth grade, where conventional wisdom dictated that we were preparing students for high school with its implicit academic "tracks."

Social studies teacher Sharon Edenfield and I, the language arts teacher, began discussing the possibility of ungrouping in our eighth-grade block of teaching time. We realized that as long as Challenge (advanced) classes for ninth-grade math required Algebra I in the eighth grade, there could be no revision of the current grouping policy in the math/science block. However, we felt that this single constraint ought not to dictate what we believed to be the best practice in our sub-ject areas. Therefore, we approached our principal and assistant princi-pal with our new plan for eighth-grade language arts and social studies. They were receptive.

In this chapter, I describe what we have implemented. This is not intended as a prescription. Rather, it is an outline of our initial plan to un-group that may provide ideas for others. We are already re-evaluating it and adjusting our practice. But the plan is a mix of ideas and strategies that we believe to be best practice.

There were a number of things that Sharon and I discussed before we began the planning that formed the basis of our task. First and foremost, we were and are firmly committed to the idea that arbitrary separation of students is largely indefensible. We believe that there are all kinds of intelligence, and that children benefit from exposure to variety.

Second, we think of our ungrouping as a "leveling up" to high expectations for all students. All students may need help in a subject at times, and all students benefit from enrichment. We also are committed to blurring distinctions between narrowly departmentalized instruction and the development of interdisciplinary instruction. We believe that choice and variety are extremely important elements for students. We might not be able to revolutionize our curriculum overnight; but if we commit to training lifelong learners, then we must begin to provide both scope and depth of ideas and assignments.

In both social studies and language arts classes, we emphasized a variety of writing activities and opportunities for oral expression. Emphasis on oral and written discourse rather than on traditional question-and-answer or exercise formats certainly is not new. But a visit to almost any American public school will convince one that classroom communications are undervalued and underused. We have tried to make it central to most of our activities and assessments.

Though we already used cooperative groups, we also tried to incorporate more group activities than we had used previously. Sometimes they were based on interest, occasionally on ability; but most often we aimed at mixed-ability groups.

One simple, yet valuable, activity was designed for mixed-ability groups. Students were given a question of topical interest, such as: Should the ownership of handguns be controlled? Students had to come up with pros and cons to the question in a cooperative fashion. Then they decided who would present which side of the question, with each member writing a response in his or her journal and presenting it to the class. Because the whole group was responsible for both pros and cons, students were introduced to opinions of their peers and challenged to think beyond their own beliefs. Not only did lively discussions abound, but all students were better able to express a clear position in written and oral forms.

The textbook our school system adopted for language arts uses an integrated approach. Each unit focuses on a form of writing, a grammar topic, and a literary selection based on the writing theme. I use that format in my planning. We begin a unit with a grammar pretest. Those who achieve 90% correct or above are given an alternative assignment based on the unit theme. Following are some of the alternative activities that I have used:

Unit I: Personal Writing
1. Research a historical period of your choice. Then write at least two journal entries as if you lived during that period. Use library resources to find more information.
2. Find out about these diary writers; they all are mentioned in Unit 1 of the textbook in sentences and exercises: Lorraine Hansberry, Louisa May Alcott, Mary Chesnut, Sarah Kemble Knight, William Byrd, Lewis and Clark, Mollie Doirsdy, Abigail Adams, Michel-Guillaume de Crevecoeur.
3. Read Longfellow's *The Courtship of Miles Standish.* (Our literature selection dealt with this time and place in history.)
4. See if you can find Mary Chesnut's *Civil War* and summarize at least four entries.

Unit II: Writing to Inform
1. Read "The Millennium of Discovery" in the Fall 1992 Special Issue of *Time* magazine, pp. 16-21.
   a. Define *millennium, reformation*, and five other words unfamiliar to you.
   b. Describe Europe before the year 1000.
   c. What circumstances paved the way for the Age of Exploration?
   d. How did colonization affect Native Americans?
2. Read about *Kon-Tiki* and do a short report on Thor Heyerdahl.
3. Read Columbus' letter about his discovery. Write a summary. Be sure to include the basics: who, what, when, where, and why.

Interestingly enough, those who do the alternative work are not just the gifted students. About one-third to one-half are "average" students.

We use our block of time (8:40-11:05 a.m.) with our 43 students flexibly and cooperatively. Usually we meet in two distinct classes that are scheduled back to back; but we have met in large groups for presentations, videos, and speakers. We plan cooperatively, such as using vocabulary from social studies (and other subject areas) in language arts.

Another example of curriculum integration is our study of the Georgia Charter. In social studies, students explored the Charter's implications for the young colony. In language arts, they deciphered the document's antiquated spellings, lack of punctuation, and style. At another time, students researched topics about the American Revolution in social studies and wrote and edited the papers in language arts. In addition, we planned and executed two interdisciplinary units with math and science teachers. We hope that these efforts emphasized the interrelatedness of all knowledge.

Following are examples of the objectives we devised for each discipline in our interdisciplinary unit on elections:

Language arts activities:
1. Explain how a candidate's image is created and projected.
2. List and describe media used in a campaign.
3. Define, use, and differentiate among different kinds of propaganda.
4. Explain features of and interpret political cartoons.
5. Defend in an essay form the choice of the most important issue in the campaign.

Social studies activities:
1. List and describe constitutional provisions for the election of the president.
2. Compare and contrast elections of the early 1800s with those of today and assess the role of political parties.
3. Define and explain the role of caucuses, primaries, and conventions.
4. Defend the addition of the 25th Amendment.
5. Describe the concept of impeachment, using Andrew Johnson and Richard Nixon as examples.
6. Identify proposed amendments to the Georgia Constitution.
7. Describe at least two other issues on the ballot in other states.
8. Identify candidates in presidential races as well as senators and representatives. Compare national and state positions.

Mathematics activities:
1. Describe the way in which the electoral college elects the president.
2. Evaluate the electoral-college system.
3. Color code a U.S. map based on the popular/electoral vote on the night of the election.
4. Describe how a candidate who receives fewer popular votes than another candidate can be elected.

Science activities:
1. Discuss issues in the campaign.
2. Research issues related to science (the environment, health insurance, AIDS research, abortion, etc.).
3. Defend your position on a chosen issue.
4. State the position of the presidential candidates on these issues.

Within our block of time, I also teach exploratory Spanish; and Sharon teaches Current Events as separate but related to the eighth-grade social studies curriculum, which requires Georgia History. She has access to CNN news for schools and its curriculum guides and uses these materials as the basis of her course.

Sharon decided to use a contract for the Current Events class. Contracts are an excellent way to allow students to be responsible for their own learning, as well as to individualize expectations and outcomes. The following illustrates options available in the student contract:

Option A. Due each Friday
- Four CNN newsroom summaries.
- Three outside summaries taken from newspapers, magazines, and news programs.
- One research paper at least one page in length.

Option B. Due each Friday
- Four CNN newsroom summaries.
- Two outside summaries taken from newspapers, magazines, and news programs.
- One- to two-page research paper.

Option C. Due each Friday
- Four CNN newsroom summaries.

Allowing students choices, a variety of ways to learn and exhibit mastery, is central to any effort to engage fully all students in the learning process. If there is appropriate variety, allowing for different abilities and learning styles, then true individualization can occur. Activities should be open-ended enough to allow students to bring their gifts to an assignment and to encourage them to expand their understandings. In the alternative assignments, as well as in the whole-group activities, I allow students to pick and choose among the assignments offered. Following are activities that reflect choices offered to the whole group.

Activities for Columbus Unit
1. Writing activities. Choose two:
   a. Prepare a recruiting poster.
   b. Write a poem.
   c. Write a news article about the voyage.
   d. Write a letter as if you were Columbus.
   e. Tell Columbus about America today.
   f. Write an obituary for Columbus.
   g. Write a journal entry as if Columbus realized he had not found Asia.
   h. Describe how Native Americans felt when they saw Europeans.
   i. Describe the Caribbean through a European sailor's eyes.
   j. Write entries in Columbus' ship's log.
2. Performance activities. Choose one:
   a. Write and perform a "rap."
   b. Debate whether the earth is flat or round.
   c. Interview Columbus.
   d. Debate whether the discovery of America was good or bad.

Activities for Election Unit
1. Describe the image being projected in your picture of the candidate.
2. You are a consultant. Describe ways you would improve your candidate's image.
3. Give examples of kinds of propaganda used in real election ads.
4. Write and illustrate (or describe) a distorted ad, using at least one propaganda technique.
5. Interpret symbols, caricatures, and messages in political cartoons.
6. Write an essay explaining what you think is the most important issue of the campaign.

When I "tested" on the novel, *Sweetly Sings the Donkey*, I provided five choices the students could prepare at home:

1. Write a ballad/song about Lily's life. You may want to pattern it after one you know.
2. As the story progresses, the Snow family faces many difficulties. Discuss how each of the following affects the Snows' ability to function as a family:
   a. Danny's withdrawal.
   b. Judson's denial.

    c. Martha's fear.

3. Lily says her father believes there are no impossibles, only "possibles." Yet she is the fighter who makes the dream come true. What qualities does Lily have and how does she use them to make her dream a reality?
4. Write and answer your own question.
5. Make a collage using visual images to show events, objects, and characters in Lily's life. Write a short paragraph explaining them.

Questions 1, 2, and 3 were adapted from story cards in the Silver Burdett and Ginn classroom library accompanying our language arts series, *World of Language*. In my opinion, the ballads for number 1 were excellent and included poems to the tune of "On the Road Again" and "Sweet Betsy from Pike." Currently, I am teaching the process of writing a research paper. Topics were chosen by the students and range from "Cheetahs" to "Teen Pregnancy" and "Modern Farming" to "Malcolm X."

Our ungrouping was far more than a rejection of tracking; it represented a gradual and systematic effort to incorporate in our instruction things we always had believed and new techniques we had begun using. We hoped to help students want to learn and become responsible for their choices and how they performed. In the process, we have become learners and experimenters as well.

EDUCATING ALL OUR STUDENTS: SUCCESS IN SERVING AT-RISK YOUTH

BY EDWARD B. STRAUSER AND JOHN J. HOBE

There is no doubt that our public education system is insufficiently responsive to the needs of our society. The word "insufficiently" was chosen deliberately. We have many fine teachers and programs in this country, producing intellectually strong high school graduates. Unfortunately, we have far too many low-quality or, at best, mediocre programs, producing low-quality or mediocre graduates, if the students graduate at all.

Changing an ingrained system of educating students is exceedingly difficult. At one time, tracking seemed to be the way to go. Intuitively, the arguments for tracking make sense. Separate the high achievers so they need not be burdened by the slow learners; separate the low achievers so they can receive specific individual attention. Readers of *Beyond Tracking* should be convinced that what intuitively appeared to make sense just did not meet the expectations of the real world. In fact, many students suffered and still suffer needlessly because of tracking.

This chapter is intended to assist districts to switch to a heterogeneous grouping system by offering an alternative approach to helping at least some at-risk children succeed. It describes a specific program and effective teaching strategies. In 1985, a program headed by Lyle Jensen was initiated in western New York. The program responded so well to the needs of at-risk students that the National Middle School Association awarded Jensen and the program an NMSA President's Award in November 1988.

Jensen and Strauser (1988) describe this program as having several components, the most nontraditional of which is work experience. Specifically, the program is structured so that students alternate between a full week away from school at a job site and a full week at school. The job-site mentor is expected to show his or her academically at-risk apprentice how and why basic skills are necessary. Even an auto wrecking-yard mechanic has to be able to search the computer banks for cross-reference numbers, calculate sales taxes, read the manuals for the most efficient way of removing a part, communicate coherently with customers, and so on. The mentor also is asked to share behind-the-scenes information about wage and Social Security calculations, Workman's Compensation book work, and general inventory.

The school makes an effort to teach the traditional curriculum during the alternate weeks, using examples that are appropriate for a worksite. For example, they write business letters in ninth- and tenth-grade language arts and teach about invoices, taxes, and computer skills in ninth- and tenth-grade math.

This type of education is not for the average middle school or junior high school student. Program youths have repeated one or more grades. As a group, these young people have a negative reputation. They are the students away from whom parents try to steer their own children. They are not special education candidates. They have reading and math equivalents ranging from fourth grade to post-high school on standardized tests, as one might find in any typical ninth-grade class. Yet for one reason or another, they have dropped behind their chronological peers. They were put in the low track, and they have stayed there. Thus their school system must be willing to use its legal powers to "push" these 14- to 17-year-old middle school youth into a ninth-grade setting, even though they have completed only seventh or, in some cases, sixth grade.

A question often is asked: How can one expect a youngster who has just repeated sixth grade for the third time to succeed in a high school setting. This is where the psychology of the program comes in. All the program youth are in the same boat. Negative reputations do not set them apart. Self-esteem training is infused into every component of the two-year plan. The students are expected to succeed. In fact, the success rate for completion is better than 80%. When students realize why academics are important, which they discover on the worksite, then they respond to the expectations. Program teachers are chosen for their sensitivity to the needs of this type of student. And an effort is made to use effective teaching practices, such as those identified by Reid (1983), Rosenshine (1986), and others as essential to preventing student failure. These practices include:

Provide the number of practices necessary for students to learn. One way to accomplish this is to elicit rapid, overt responses from students during instruction and as they practice. The group response offers security and motivation to students during instruction. If a student responds incorrectly, the teacher reteaches the whole group without pointing out the student or error.

Allow as much time as students need in order to learn. This can be done in part by squeezing out students' "lapse" (free) time. The teacher provides and monitors practice time during the school day and carefully monitors students' responses during instruction. He or she teaches less responsive students to use their time in the same way as the students who are learning well. And the teacher believes aptitude to be the level of students' responsiveness rather than how they score on a test. Hence, student aptitude is an alterable characteristic and a function of teaching effectiveness.

Increase each student's response rates. Specifically, teachers try to help students to do more in less time. They pay special attention to those who are the slowest. They realize this necessity for the less responsive student to become more like the more responsive student.

Believe that students can learn. Teachers expect high accuracy levels and use fluency (rate as measured in time) as another criterion competency measure for all students. Teachers demonstrate their belief in their students' learning ability by allowing each student to move through the curriculum at his or her own best pace. No student waits for another.

Model for students ("I show you"). Then students show the teacher what they have learned with the teacher's help ("you show me"). Finally, the teacher concludes by asking students to demonstrate the objective from pure recall without the teacher's help. The teacher is able to reteach during the "I show you" and "You show me" lesson portions, promoting student success. This allows students to err less as they learn.

Teach so students make few mistakes. The teacher is able to diagnose and prescribe instantly when the student responds incorrectly or not at all. When the response does not clearly reflect mastery of the objective, a new prescription is written. The prescription's worth is judged by the student's subsequent response following prescription delivery.

Pay attention to what the students do well. And he or she reteaches if the students respond incorrectly or not at all. The teacher wants the students' learning consequences to be rewarding. So his or her teaching leads the students to "being right." Then this "being right" becomes the students' rewarding consequence.

Correlate instructional activities so students respond in different ways. For example, he or she may teach students to read, find, and understand similes in a newspaper. Then students learn to include similes in their prose. Finally, they may discuss simile interpretation among themselves.

These teaching practices affect students' achievement and attitudes. Teachers can experience the success of teaching all their students, including those at risk, to high accuracy and fluency criteria. Coupled with the direct application to work experiences, a formula for success apparently has been found. These students have experienced success and will be able to graduate from high school and obtain meaningful employment.

The people with the most influence over potential change include politicians, school superintendents, civic leaders, and corporate CEOs. These are successful people who have done well within the present system. It is probable that most of these influential members of the community were in the top track of an age-graded, lockstep system with low, middle, and high tracks. It is understandable that they might be reluctant to change a system that, from their point of view, is successful. However, the nation cannot continue to tolerate a system that fails to graduate one out of four students. Breaking the tracking system, breaking or at least bending the age-grade coupling, and providing alternatives for the most difficult cases all show that we are capable of doing better. We must take advantage of every proven opportunity to help at-risk youths to become truly productive, functioning members of society.

References

Jensen, L., and Strauser, E.B. "Middle-Level Alternative Education: A Preventive Means for Dealing with High School Dropout Problems." *Transescence* 16, no. 1 (1988): 23-29.

Reid, E.R. *Teaching Scheduling and Record Keeping.* Salt Lake City: Cove, 1983.

Rosenshine, B.V. "Synthesis of Research on Explicit Teaching." *Educational Leadership* 43, no. 7 (1986): 60-69.

TECHNOLOGY EDUCATION: A NEW APPLICATION OF THE PRINCIPLES OF UNTRACKING AT THE SECONDARY LEVEL

BY N. CREIGHTON ALEXANDER*

Many school administrators over the years have believed — and many still hold the view — that students who lack academic skills are better served in an environment where they use more psychomotor skills. Such administrators see "shop" as the place where such students achieve success, because shop classes, in their view, involve few thinking skills. Thus shop is a solution for problem students who need to be separated from the academic track. The "shop track" was another way to justify ability grouping and to retain funding for it.

Recent research and reform reports indicate that changing demographics, today's culture, and the impact of technology all point to a need to take a new look at what should be taught in American secondary schools. If the United States is to survive as a nation, improve its economic status, and compete in the global arena, education must meet the demands of the forces affecting the future. To this end, today's young people must be educated in a different way. Formal secondary schooling must be reshaped to provide integration of basic skills, higher-

---

*The author wishes to express his appreciation of the late Dr. Sharon C. Abbott, associate professor of Business Education at Georgia Southern University, whose work inspired this chapter.

order thinking skills, and problem-solving skills for every student at every level.

Obviously, we must meet the needs not only of America's elite, but also of the "forgotten half," which may really be closer to 70% (see Parnell 1985). We must not allow many members of this group to be relegated to a quagmire of unemployment, disillusionment, welfare, despair, and further social stratification. Basic economics dictates that formal secondary education must be reshaped to address present-day technological demands and the consequent needs of a new workforce.

In many locations what used to be industrial arts education is being replaced by a new field known as "technology education." New philosophy, curricula, and facilities based on the study of technology are emerging. Technology education is creating a more broadly accepted image for nonacademic education. It also is generating excitement among students, parents, teachers, and administrators in secondary education that is unmatched in recent years.

Technology education is here in the state of Georgia, and it is this state's program that I will describe in this chapter as an example of how this fresh approach to nonacademic education is progressing. Technology education is making an impact in middle schools, high schools, and postsecondary institutions. Following are a few examples:

- In the 1989-90 school year, 15 programs were redesigned from industrial arts to technology education in curriculum and facilities (Georgia Department of Education 1989-1990).
- At its September 1990 meeting, the State Board of Education adopted new rules for technology education criteria and certification standards and mandated the name change from "industrial arts" to "technology education," effective 1 July 1991.
- By the end of the 1993-94 school year, 140 Georgia middle school and 60 high school technology education programs are expected to be in place (Barker 1993).
- The teacher-education program at Georgia Southern University was converted from industrial arts to technology education in the academic year 1990-1991, thus becoming the first (and only one to date) to be fully accredited by NCATE, the Southern Association of Colleges and Schools, and the Georgia State Department of Education (Alexander 1991).

Program Philosophy

Technology education acquaints students with the origin and development of technology and industry and reflects the technological advances of our culture. The curriculum is changing constantly because technology constantly changes. Technology education develops attitudes that will help students adjust to the complexities of modern life, both technical and social. And technology education provides insight into our industrial environment by having students study and experience technology and its techniques (Olson 1973).

In a classroom laboratory, students explore technology through processes, tools, and materials, and by applying English, science, and mathematics in solving everyday technological problems. Technology education provides concrete activities designed to promote self-expression and self-evaluation. At a level and a pace that allow for a range of individual differences, technology education offers the thrill of personal creativity in transforming raw materials into finished products (Alexander 1970, 1991).

The technology education program in Georgia at the secondary level serves young men and women in grades 6 through 12 (Georgia Department of Education 1988). The program allows students to identify and develop their own interests and basic competencies for use in our technological society. This is accomplished through planned instruction with specifically designated tools, materials, equipment, and facilities. The students are exposed to cognitive content, psychomotor experiences in manipulating tools and materials, and affective development of group social skills, such as cooperation, responsibility, leadership, dependability, desirable habits and attitudes, respect for others and community property, and self-actualization.

The technology education program is undergirded by the philosophical tenet that secondary school students learn by doing (Dewey 1916/ 1966). People remember about 10% of what they hear, 20% of what they see, 40% of what they discuss, and 90% of what they do. Abstract concepts and symbols have meaning only as substitutes for concrete realities derived from a tangible experience base.

Adolescents are motivated by manipulative activities that allow them to exercise a degree of creative control over their environment. The technology laboratory is a place where cognitive activities are enhanced through the application of scientific, mathematical, communication, and problem-solving skills (Dyrenfurth and Kozals 1991).

Curriculum and Facilities Redesign

The move from industrial arts to technology education in Georgia's secondary schools is reflected in both curriculum changes and facility alterations. "Explorations in Technology" at the middle school creates a new image for such programs. Students begin to learn about basic technology by exploring manufacturing, construction, communication, and energy/power (Snyder and Hales 1981). The state has adopted a modular learning structure for hands-on experiences, implementing this structure through a high-technology curriculum and redesigned facilities.

The traditional program began to give way to the new explorations in the technology program during the 1989-90 school year. Matching funds for program conversion were provided by appropriations from the Georgia State Legislature. Workshops were designed to assist teachers in the curriculum and laboratory change from the traditional program to the new technology program.

This process literally has transformed programs all across Georgia, as Bachler (1992) puts it, from "wood chips to computer chips." "Shop" has been remolded into a laboratory that contains 12 or more modules, or learning stations, which is required by the state to receive a matching grant. All new programs in the state have more than the minimum, a large number having as many as 18 modules, each containing a different technology activity. Nearly every module contains a computer and other equipment, instructional packets, textbooks, videos, computer software, notebooks, and various prototypes to assist with hands-on activities.

Classroom management in the new technology program is different by design. The program is organized to place greater responsibility on the individual student to manage his or her own activity, behavior, grade, and use of laboratory time. This aspect of the program is monitored mainly through the use of individual notebooks that all students are required to maintain on a daily basis.

The program places two students in each module for a period of 10 days to two weeks, followed by a rotation to a new module with a change in partners. This process enables students to learn to work with various classmates. In this setting, students are required to follow daily instructions provided by the teacher in a notebook specifically designed for each module. These notebooks outline such activities as reading and interpreting instructions, completing computations, writing answers and solutions to problems, and performing some form of hands-on activity. If the partners are unable to answer a question or solve a problem themselves, they may secure the attention of the teacher by using a call-light system that is installed in each module. Students are required to stay in the module, which helps teachers manage the classroom and provides a better learning environment for the students.

Many of the modules allow the students to design, produce, and construct some form of a prototype to illustrate their proficiency in a phase of technology. Students are introduced to such concepts as mass-production in whole-class settings. For example, they may learn as a class about the way a corporation is operated, divisions of labor and management, and other subjects.

The Explorations in Technology curriculum in middle schools and similar programs in high schools include content information and laboratory designs for 12 to 18 modules (Georgia Department of Education 1989-90). Following are a few of the modules with a brief description of their activities:

Research and Design: Students research ideas for a race car. Then they design and build a CO_2 dragster and see how fast it will run on a computerized race track.

Applied Technology: Students explore pneumatics and mechanisms. The module provides a variety of hands-on activities.

Space and Flight: This module gives students the opportunity to experience the thrill of using flight simulation on a computer and to build a rocket and a Delta Dart airplane.

Robotics: Students learn how to program a robot. They then use their program to operate a robot. They also get to work on several computer programs and watch a few videos.

Automotive Systems: In this module students learn about several parts of the automobile, including the internal combustion engine. Students disassemble and reassemble a small gas engine.

Publishing and Printing: Students use desktop publishing and screen-printing principles to develop an article for their school newspaper and to print a T-shirt.

Structural Engineering: In this module students design and build a bridge or tower. A structural analyzer is used to test the student-made structures.

Computer Numerical Control (CNC): Students learn how to program, control, and operate a CNC lathe or milling machine to produce a part.

Electronics: In this module students build and experiment with various electronic-control devices and mechanical applications.

Electricity: Students learn the basic principles of electricity.

Computer-Aided Drafting: Students learn how to design a part using the computer after learning drafting fundamentals.

T.V. Broadcast Production: Students work on a broadcast team and learn how to operate the video, audio, and mixing equipment so that they can produce a videotape of a newscast.

Lasers and Fiber Optics: Students study the latest in communications technology by learning to use a laser and fiber-optic voice transmission equipment.

Radio Communications: Students first learn about communications in general and radio in particular. They write news and sports reports, make commercials, and choose music in order to produce a simulated radio broadcast that can be aired over the school's public-address system.

TV News Production: Students become newscasters, develop a script, and complete a live broadcast with a broadcast production team.

Architecture and Construction: In this module students design house plans or select from a library of previously developed plans to explore the process of contracting and constructing a house.

By 1992, technology education laboratories were in place in eight Georgia city school systems and 32 county systems (Barker 1991-92). The growth in technology education continues unabated. State education department data indicate a solid commitment to providing experiences to wider ranges of students (Georgia Department of Education 1993). Such schools also demonstrate their determination to help both college-bound and non-college-bound students to become more technologically literate.

Summary

Georgia has "turned the corner" in the transition from industrial arts to technology education. A number of school programs have completed the conversion, and new programs continue to emerge as funding becomes available.

The Explorations in Technology curriculum has created a new image for technology education in Georgia and in this region of the United States. Many states are interested in the Georgia curriculum, as evidenced by officials from at least eight other states visiting the technology laboratories in outfitted secondary schools to see how effective the classes are before starting their own programs (Barker 1992). The new focus on technology through redesigned curricula and facilities helps students prepare for what they eventually will face when they enter the workforce.

Technology education goes beyond tracking at the secondary level. It is a concrete concept that is working. It also is a program that offers a viable alternative to traditional tracking practices because technology education has value for all students. Educators must prepare every child to be technologically literate. The present and future economic health of our nation depends on having a workforce that is excited by, comprehends, and is able to take advantage of technology.

References

Alexander, N.C. "Some Aspects of My Philosophy of Industrial Arts." *Alpha Pi Journal* 1, no. 1 (1970): 5-7.

Alexander, N.C. *Technology Teacher Education B.S., M.Ed., and Ed.S. Programs*. Statesboro: Georgia Southern University, Department of Student Development Programs, 1991.

Bachler, M. "Training Begins at Middle School." *Commerce Georgia News*, 18 February 1992, p. 5.

Barker, R. *Technology Education Programs: Middle School Explorations in Technology Sites, 1991-92*. Atlanta: Georgia Department of Education, Office of Instructional Programs, 1991-1992.

Barker, R. "Georgia Takes Leading Roles in New Technology Centers." *Coastal Closeup*, 12 February 1992, pp. 1, 16.

Barker, R. "Roundtable Update by State." Roundtable presentation at the Southeastern Technology Education Conference, Blacksburg, Va., October 1993.

Dewey, J. *Democracy and Education: An Introduction to the Philosophy of Education*. 1916. Reprint. New York: Free Press, 1966.

Dyrenfurth, M.J., and Kozals, M.R., eds. *Technology Literacy*. 40th Yearbook of the Council on Technology Teacher Education. Peoria, Ill.: Macmillan/McGraw-Hill, 1991.

Georgia Department of Education, Office of Instructional Programs. *Industrial Arts/Technology Education: A Curriculum Guide on Exploring Technology in the Middle School*. Atlanta, 1988.

Georgia Department of Education, Office of Instructional Programs. *Explorations in Technology: Middle School Industrial Arts/Technology Education Program*. Atlanta, 1989-1990.

Georgia Department of Education, Office of Instructional Programs. *Directory: Explorations in Technology Teachers*. Atlanta, 1993.

Olson, D.W. *Technol-o-gee: Interpreter of Technology for the American School*. Raleigh: North Carolina State University, School of Education, 1973.

Parnell, D. *The Neglected Majority*. Washington, D.C.: Community College Press, 1985.

Snyder, J., and Hales, J. *Jackson's Mill Industrial Arts Curriculum Project*. Charleston: West Virginia Department of Education, 1981.

TRACKING AND RESEARCH-BASED DECISIONS: A GEORGIA SCHOOL SYSTEM'S DILEMMA*

BY JANE A. PAGE AND FRED M. PAGE, JR.

In her article, "Can Tracking Research Inform Practice? Technical, Normative, and Political Considerations," Jeannie Oakes challenges researchers and practitioners to engage in a process of inquiry based on new school norms: participation, communication, community, reflection, experimentation, risk-taking, and trust. Case studies that examine the technical, normative, and political aspects of detracking efforts can be useful as educators attempt to gain insight into this process (Oakes 1992).

The case study described in this chapter used this framework to examine an early effort by one Georgia school system to move "beyond tracking." The purpose of this case study was to analyze the procedures administrators used and the problems they encountered as they attempted to make research-based decisions about reforming methods of grouping students for instruction.

Methods

The methods used in this study were ethnographic and qualitative. The researchers used the conceptual schema for conducting ethno-

*This chapter is an adapted version of an article that appeared in the *International Journal of Educational Reform* 2, no. 4 (1993): 407-17. Copyright 1993 by Technomic Publishing, Lancaster, Pa. Adapted by permission.

graphic research described by Wiersma (1986). The relationships of perspectives, cultures, and the organization are identified in the schema. The direction of the research moves from the perspectives to define the cultures, which, in turn, describe the organization or some part of it.

Data sources included newspaper articles, interviews, minutes of school board and study committee meetings, audiotapes and videotapes of board meetings and news programs, and research articles and papers used as documentation by various groups. The data were gathered through April 1993 from student cultures, parent cultures (both pro-tracking and anti-tracking), teacher cultures, central office staff, and school board members. Input was analyzed in terms of its relationship to the three dimensions of change in Oakes' model: technical, norma-tive, and political. Efforts were made to ascertain immediate and long-range effects of the input offered by various groups.

History of Tracking and Untracking in Bulloch County

Until the early 1970s, all elementary schools in the Bulloch County (Georgia) School System maintained heterogeneously grouped classes. During the 1971-72 school year, the Statesboro-area schools in Bulloch County (Statesboro is the county seat) were reorganized to comply with a court order issued by Judge Alexander Lawrence on 1 July 1971 (*United States* v. *Board of Education, Bulloch County, Georgia, et al.*). This reorganization resulted in the integration of schools that formerly were segregated by race. During that academic year, a decision was made by school officials to begin a modified form of ability grouping. This modified grouping arrangement gradually evolved into strict grouping practices that separated students into three or more levels based on test scores and teacher recommendations (Moller 1993).

During the 1991-92 school year, Bulloch County curriculum directors initiated a comprehensive study of the possibility of organizing ele-mentary students in the Statesboro schools into classes that used some arrangement other than strict achievement grouping. The study to ex-amine the possibility of moving away from tracking was a result of several factors including: 1) suggestions and recommendations of accreditation reports by the Southern Association of Colleges and Schools, 2) sum-mary report of teacher recommendations from a January 1989 inservice day on "Meeting the Needs of At-Risk Students," 3) a report of areas of concern listed by some Sallie Zetterower teachers identifying them-selves as "Committee of Concerned Educators Against Homogeneous Grouping at Sallie Zetterower Primary School," and 4) an investigation by the Office of Civil Rights (McNair 1993).

The Bulloch County School Board (BCSB) meeting held on 9 July 1991 included a discussion of grouping procedures and class sizes that the study groups recommended for the 1991-92 school year. A motion was made and approved to adopt a heterogeneous-cluster grouping procedure, which was to become effective at Sallie Zetterower and Mattie Lively Elementary Schools (grades K-2) for the 1991-92 school year and at Julia P. Bryant Elementary School (grades 3-5) for the 1992-93 school year. Although all BCSB meetings are open to the public, there were no newspaper reporters at this meeting; thus the decision received little publicity.

When the school year began, parents realized that the format was very different from that in operation in past years. A group of 14 couples formed the "Citizens for Better Education" and began an active effort to challenge the board on its decision. The group circulated petitions, organized meetings, and hired lawyers to represent it (Milner 1991).

At a meeting on October 8, the lawyers, as well as groups of parents and educators supporting the "Citizens for Better Education," presented information and research evidence to support its claims for traditional tracking. This was followed by a presentation of information and research by parents, educators, and others supporting the board's decision (Howell 1991*b*).

At a meeting on October 22, the school board chairperson announced the formation of a committee to study changes made at Mattie Lively and Sallie Zetterower Elementary Schools and to make recommendations for implementing changes at Julia P. Bryant Elementary School. The committee included teachers for and against the board's decision to move away from tracking. After several months of study, including surveys of teachers in Bulloch County Schools, the committee recommended that the primary schools maintain their new arrangements and that Julia P. Bryant Elementary School make the change to heterogeneous grouping during the 1992-93 year (McNair 1993).

On 13 May 1992, a representative of the Office of Civil Rights (OCR) met with principals, central office personnel, the superintendent, the BCSB attorney, and the chairperson and vice-chairperson of the board of education. The representative indicated that OCR would be conducting another on-site investigation during the 1992-93 year. Dr. William H. "Billy" Bice, BCSB superintendent, explained this process and the preliminary findings in a news release dated 13 May 1992:

> Regarding the initial data analysis, it looks as though racially identifiable groups existed in all six schools studied during the ini-

tial review in January 1991. Some of these groups have been eliminated as a result of the recent change in grouping practices at Mattie Lively and Sallie Zetterower. The local district will conduct an in-depth review of the data from the other four schools and recommend appropriate adjustments to the Board of Education. Throughout this process administrators and teachers will be involved in developing these recommendations and the Board of Education will continue to communicate proposed changes to its constituents.

The Bulloch County School System is committed to resolving these issues. Failure to do so would result in loss of federal funds. In addition, the school system is still under a 1971 court order which required OCR to forward their findings and recommendations to the Justice Department for appropriate action. Finally, the local Board simply must adhere to the law.

In an effort to follow guidelines presented by OCR, changes and modifications were made at all the identified schools. In October 1992, the Office of Civil Rights requested demographic data from Bulloch County Schools on every class in the system. OCR planned to use this information to take into account adjustments that had taken place since its last visit (Natson 1992).

As a direct response to parents, BCSB currently is monitoring the changes. The central office also established an Enrichment Committee made up of lead teachers from the involved schools. Their task is to determine what can be done to assure parents of "able" students that their children are served well. Additionally, at the recommendation of the central office staff, the board employed the Center for Rural Health and Research to conduct an independent study of the changes, using test scores and other information (McNair 1993).

Research Used in Making Decisions

Central office staff members conducted a literature review during the 1990-91 school year. A summary of this review was compiled in a background paper titled "Classroom Assignment by Ability" (Bulloch County School System 1991). One section of this review related to research on the achievement of students in heterogeneous and homogeneous groups. The review included a discussion of Kulik and Kulik's (1984) meta-analysis of elementary studies. Slavin's (1987) best-evidence synthesis also was considered. In interpreting the research, central office personnel reported:

258

In some ways, the research evidence runs counter to what one might reasonably expect. That is to say, reducing the range of ability should presumably make teaching easier and should in fact maximize learning by increasing the direct instruction students receive. In truth, however, the question is more complex. (Bulloch County School System 1991, p. 3)

The staff also reviewed research related to social implications of grouping. The report concludes:

Finally, social consequences have often motivated such groups as the National Education Association and the National Governors' Association to oppose ability grouping. . . . Perhaps more importantly the fact remains that this practice is, from an achievement standpoint, not justifiable. If one major goal of schooling is to enhance student achievement, placing them into classrooms based on ability groups will not accomplish it. (Bulloch County School System 1991, p. 4)

As the controversy in the community expanded, central office personnel and BCSB members received a multitude of research documents exploring the pros and cons of heterogeneous and homogeneous grouping. Proponents of homogeneous grouping sent research articles by Kulik and Kulik, Rogers, and Gamoran and Berends, as well as opinion papers by a number of individuals and groups. Proponents of heterogeneous grouping sent research articles by Oakes, Slavin, and George, among others, as well as a number of position papers by education organizations and opinion papers and essays by educators, sociologists, and psychologists.

Much of the research and other formal input provided by the tracking proponents emphasized the traditional norms centered on individualism and achievement. Serving the needs of high-ability and gifted children was the central focus for much of the research. Research cited by the proponents of heterogeneous grouping focused on self-esteem, cooperation, and democratic values, as well as achievement. The technologies emphasized in the pro-tracking research were those that advocated meeting needs through stratification. The technologies emphasized in the anti-tracking research proposed meeting needs through cooperation.

Many of the articles submitted by pro-tracking individuals encouraged use of political tactics for maintaining tracking in the schools. There were political overtones in some of the articles presented by anti-tracking groups as well. Both groups were encouraged by some well-known proponents to organize themselves and become actively involved in the change process.

Perspectives Provided by Various Groups

Students. Input was not provided directly to the board by students. However, their views were made known through testimony from parents, educators, and researchers. A systematic study of the students' perspectives was undertaken by administrators of Marvin Pittman Laboratory School at Georgia Southern University. This school is a part of the Bulloch County School System. However, Marvin Pittman groups by achievement only at the eighth-grade level. The researchers surveyed eighth-grade students who were being grouped homogeneously for the first time.

Most of the students' comments were related to the normative dimensions of change discussed by Oakes, especially with regard to their conceptions of ability. Results indicated that students placed in higher levels were more satisfied with homogeneous grouping: "You are all working with people that are on your level. No one gets slowed down or pulled back by others." Students placed in lower levels were significantly less satisfied: "People brag about their group level. People make fun of you. I feel awkward." Another revealing finding indicated that students placed in upper levels felt that their teachers expected them to work hard. Those placed in lower levels were significantly less likely to respond in this manner.

The technical dimensions of curriculum and instruction also were addressed. Students at all levels considered homogeneous grouping more appropriate for math and some types of science. Students at all levels considered homogeneous grouping much less appropriate for English, history, physical education, and electives.

The political dimensions of change addressed by the students related to their relationships within the school. When asked about advantages of mixed grouping, an upper-level student responded, "You can learn from the people around you. The slower students can have people as role models and the brighter kids get more social interaction with all types of learners." When asked about homogeneous grouping, many responded with comments about relationships, such as, "You don't get to see all your friends" (Lanier, Mandes, and Tremble 1992, p. 5).

Teachers Against Tracking. Teachers against tracking provided formal and informal input to the central office and to the board through letters and reports. Additionally, they sent copies of research articles and

260

provided information orally and in writing at board meetings and at the meetings of the Elementary Study Group.

Much of the research and other input was related to normative dimensions of change. The following comments from letters, reports, and oral input emphasize normative aspects:

> As we begin a new school year we tend to reflect over the past year with mixed emotions — and begin this year with deep concern about those students who are at risk and about the path they are taking throughout our Bulloch County school system. It is with extreme frustration and concern that we now address this issue. Frustration, because we know next year the same educational situation awaits us with the same set of problems: students who have special behavior and/or learning problems grouped together feeding on each other's lowered self concepts and inappropriate behaviors. This type of situation creates frustration not only for the teacher but also for the students. . . . Are we casting "at-risk" students aside at the very beginning of their school careers because we think they are doomed to failure anyway? (Committee of Concerned Educators Against Homogeneous Grouping at Sallie Zetterower Primary School 1990)

> When low achievers are grouped together it affects not only their self-concept, but limits their experience. High achievers, when strictly grouped together, get an elitist view of the world, thinking they are the smartest, and often rest on their laurels. . . . By grouping standards (used in Bulloch County), Einstein, Edison, and Helen Keller would have been in the low group. (Sheppard 1991)

> I personally don't feel we should label five-, six-, seven-, and eight-year-old children and say, "Hey, you are below average, or you are an above-average child," because their learning has just gotten started. They are just beginning. The label sticks with them and stays with future teachers and also the parents. . . . We are now seeing children work together [in heterogeneously grouped classes] in ways they never have before. (Freeman 1991)

Teachers against tracking also provided input related to the technological dimensions of change. As identified by Oakes, the technological dimensions revolve around the areas of curriculum, instruction, meeting special needs, and assessment. The following quotations from letters, reports, and oral presentations by teachers are representative of this input:

> Schools are for children — not teachers or administrators. There is no literature that I know of that says students do better on

standardized tests if they are grouped. Therefore, why do we do it? The argument that in a heterogeneous classroom the teacher spends all her time with remedial students is not really valid. How about the teacher who has a class full of low achievers? How can she ever meet the needs of these students? (Sheppard 1991)

These students ("at-risk") have special needs that should be addressed in special ways. When they look to their peers for role models in a homogeneous class, they are not to be found. . . . Time, hands-on experiences, heterogeneous grouping of classes, and more parent involvement and communication are needed so these children can develop at their own pace and be able to make their own worthwhile contribution to society at the end of their educational careers. (Committee of Concerned Educators 1990)

Oakes maintains that tracking is sustained by the political interests of constituents. One of the areas of concern under this dimension is the redistribution of power. Comments from a black Statesboro High School teacher are representative of the viewpoints of teachers against tracking:

No matter how you slice it, people, grouping is wrong. We've had twenty years of grouping and we're more segregated now than ever before. How many of you have walked in a classroom at Statesboro High School? That's where you will see the real results of grouping. Most of these students were tracked long before they reached high school. They were tracked from the eighth day of kindergarten. That's when the teacher decided who would be successful and who would not, from the *eighth day of kindergarten*! You say grouping is good because it has always been done or has been done for twenty years. Well, let me tell you, slavery was practiced for three hundred years. It was no more right the last day than it was the first day. . . . Teachers and students know the implications of this system. It segregates, it destroys, we have no cooperation within the system or in society. I have felt the rejection that these students in low levels are feeling each and every day. I requested the higher-level classes several times. I would like to say, I was passed over several times. I watched as white teachers new and old entered the system and were selected over me. I was told that the white community may not accept me. I guess they won't because I don't look like an upper-level student. (Lee 1991)

Teachers for Tracking. Teachers for tracking formally presented information to the central office and to the board at the meeting on October 8 and by writing a report to the subcommittee studying grouping in the elementary schools during the 1991-92 school year. Two teachers also contributed input informally by providing information anonymously to a newspaper reporter who visited with them at the offices of the lawyers representing the Citizens for Better Education.

Oakes indicates that reformers must examine norms that dictate that the best way to accommodate differences among students is to sort them into separate classes. A part of this normative dimension concerns one's perception of intelligence. The following comments from teachers who support tracking reflect norms that view intelligence as static; competition and individualism are emphasized as well:

> There's such a wide range of achievement and ability, it almost feels like nobody's needs are being met. (an unnamed teacher, quoted in Howell 1991*a*, p. A1)

> The demands of slower students, academically and behaviorally, severely limit what the teacher can do for others in the class. (Julia P. Bryant Study Group 1992, p. 4)

> I think that children of all ability levels will suffer. There will be no way possible to challenge the brighter student while giving extra instruction to the slow child. I feel that the self-esteem of the students will be hurt because they will have to be compared to the brighter student. (Julia P. Bryant Study Group 1992, pp. 4-5)

> I am especially concerned about the very slow students in this situation. They have so few skills that they may become discouraged and be a worse discipline problem because their inadequacies will show up more with fellow classmates. (Julia P. Bryant Study Group 1992, p. 5)

> They ("low achievers") would never get to be "the best" of the group. (Julia P. Bryant Study Group 1992, p. 3)

> In my teaching experience there have been many things I have been able to do for students. . . . But there are some things I have not been able to do. I have not been able to change a child's potential. I have not been able to change his socioeconomic level. I have not been able to change his home life. I have not been able to change the lack of parental support in some cases. I have not been able to change the lack of priority placed on education in some homes. I have not been able to change the fact that some children are not read to at home. Our children's education should not be held hostage to the social ills of this world and educators should address education with the reality that learning habits, motivation, self-determination, and ambition are learned very early at home and are primary to any child's achievement. (Smith 1991)

Oakes defines the technology of tracking as "curricular differentiation and curricular accommodation — a division of knowledge and teaching strategies into programs or classes for students perceived to be at different levels" (Oakes 1992, p. 17). Teachers in favor of tracking presented arguments that reflect this dimension:

> I don't feel this is fair to the low children. . . . They need small classes and the Chapter 1 allotment of time. We cannot give them this quality time when mixed in with all the different ability groups. (Julia P. Bryant Study Group 1992, p. 5)

> I taught in a school system where heterogeneous grouping was implemented during 1985-1989. We changed classes for reading and math into homogeneous groups. The changing of classes created a lot of confusion and behavior problems. Also, there was a great deal of frustration among the students during social studies and science where we changed back to heterogeneous grouping. I tried to teach at a level so that all students had a good understanding of the subject and enjoyed it. I found this extremely hard to do in a classroom of twenty-five to thirty students. Those students on a higher ability level were often bored and those students on a lower ability level were frustrated. It seemed to work better for those students at an average ability level. I often had several lessons going on at one time, which was hard to implement and caused confusion in the classroom. (Julia P. Bryant Study Group 1992, p. 6)

> We who have been in education for many years know that fads come and go. We hear about magnet schools and schools of choice. I've been through open classrooms, teaching the whole child, values education, teaching-centers approach to learning, Q.B.E. [Quality Basic Education], and many other bandwagons. Now it is a bandwagon in our country to nongroup. I have a suggestion. Allow parents and teachers to choose between grouping and nongrouping. Group at Sallie Zetterower and nongroup at Mattie Lively, or vice-versa. Set up a control group. Let parents register their child for the situation they want. Let teachers choose. We can see how it works before going on to Julia P. with something unproven in our community. (Smith 1991)

Comments related to the political dimension of tracking were not prevalent among teachers in favor of tracking. However, many of the concerns expressed about the behavior of "at-risk" students seemed to indicate that teachers were in favor of isolating students from each other. The following recommendation was identified by a teacher at Julia P. Bryant School:

The middle school building at Brooklet [a community nine miles from Statesboro] should be reopened and turned into an alternative school so we can send the worst behavior problem students there. This would help reduce class size plus help eliminate part of the discipline problem. If these two things would be done it would allow us more uninterrupted teaching time and a better environment for learning. (Julia P. Bryant Study Group 1992, p. 6)

Parents Against Tracking. Parents against tracking did not formally organize themselves, as did the parents for tracking. However, as momentum in the community began to build through efforts by the Citizens for Better Education, parents favoring the board's decision began to provide input. They did this by speaking at the October 8th board meeting and at meetings held during the 1991-92 school year that were organized by the board to allow parental input for the committees studying grouping. The comments seem to reflect political and technical dimensions of change. The following comments were made by the father of children who had previously been placed in "high" groups:

I've got twin daughters in kindergarten, plus one in second grade and one in high school. I grew up in a school that wasn't grouped. The reason it wasn't grouped was we only had one first grade, we had one kindergarten, we had one second grade. And I learned to deal with people the way they were. . . . I heard statistics a while ago that were listed about test scores, the difference between Dublin [Georgia] after and before they had grouping. . . so I pulled out this little sheet that I had gotten at this meeting the other day and I looked at it. I said, Mattie Lively has had grouping. . . . The 1987 second grade test scores were 69th percentile. It was 59th percentile in 1988. Does that make grouping bad? The next year it was 55th percentile. Man, it's gone down a lot. The next year it went back to 73rd percentile. What's that got to do with grouping? I don't think it has anything to do with grouping or not grouping. (Nebel 1991)

Willie Smith assumed a leadership role among parents of African-American children by listening to them in church meetings and other places and then expressing their concerns. The following comments were delivered by Smith (1992) at a meeting held at the board office to obtain parental input for the Committee to Study Grouping in the Elementary Schools on 16 April 1992. The comments were in reaction to the report previously delivered to the Study Committee by Julia P. Bryant teachers and administrators:

The subcommittee report that was provided by Julia P. Bryant administrators and some teachers emphasizes the need for teachers to be "sold on what they are doing" to be effective. This would certainly be wonderful. However, we wonder if some changes in our nation would have ever taken place if we waited till all individuals involved were in agreement. Should we have waited for slave owners to agree to do away with slavery? Should the courts have waited for educators in the South to agree to do away with segregation? Should we wait for all teachers in the system to agree with the board before we take progressive steps to serve all of the children in our county with a quality education? I'm afraid that we may be waiting for another 20 years. Sometimes individuals must move ahead before they think they are ready. Perhaps, after these teachers have taught mixed groups for a few years, they will have the same enthusiasm for working with all children as others throughout the county do now. My wife and I are very thankful that our child is attending a school that is not tracked [Marvin Pittman Laboratory School]. However, we must look beyond our own children if we want the best for our community. We encourage the board to carry out their original decision to abolish tracking in the elementary schools.

Parents for Tracking. Parents for the continuation of tracking were very vocal. They provided their input through letters, petitions, comments at board meetings, and through formal reports using legal assistance. These individuals tended to focus on the political and technical dimensions of change. Representative comments are included:

> It was refreshing to read this morning's headline, "Angry Parents Vow to Fight School Board Decision." Finally parents get involved and stand together. . . . The people of Bulloch County voted for the current members of the board of education. . . . They were not put there to be a set of dictators ruling the Bulloch County Schools. . . . The current school board can be voted out come election day and a new set of members be voted in, a new set of rules be made. It is just that simple. (Russell 1991)

> We have had achievement grouping in our school for more than twenty years. Our board members' children were educated this way. We know it works. . . . There have always been children who are more motivated to learn than others and some who learn quicker. We believe children should be in groups of similar achievement skills. . . . There is no reasonable explanation to change a system that is proven and works well for all children. (Riggs 1991)

> One of the reasons given to support this grouping policy was the research of Dr. Robert Slavin of Johns Hopkins University. I don't know that anyone in Bulloch County ever heard of Dr.

Slavin until about two or three weeks ago. I don't even know if any members of the Board knew who Dr. Slavin was when they voted on this originally in July. . . . Slavin did not say that they learned more in a heterogeneous situation; he simply said that they didn't learn any less. Who disputes Dr. Slavin's contention? Dr. Kulik at the University of Michigan did some research in this same field. The difference was that Dr. Kulik used children in real classrooms instead of lab students. . . . Let's look at research from someone we know. We have five schools which are not grouped and two schools that are grouped in Bulloch County. The results in Bulloch County were 68.8 at the two schools that were grouped and 64.5 at the ungrouped schools. . . . The bottom line is that I don't know why the change was made. (Francisco 1991)

I think it's sad that the Board of Education and Jane Page made the controversial issue of heterogeneously grouping into a racial issue. . . . We are not and never have been racist. . . . My daughter has at least two friends of a different color. I'm not going to tell her she can't play with them any more. (Deal 1991)

Other Educators and Community Members. As the controversy expanded, other members of the community became involved. These included educators from Georgia Southern University, ministers, and journalists.

As professional educators and community leaders presented information to the community and to the board, emphasis was placed on democratic practices in schools, meeting the needs of all students, and providing opportunities for all to succeed. These comments tend to be related to the normative dimensions of change:

For the 11 years that I have worked with the young people in the Statesboro area through the Georgia Southern University Upward Bound Project, I have been amazed and at times ashamed of our acceptance of ability grouping as a necessary and valid way of educating our students. I have always considered this practice as a thinly veiled way of perpetuating de-facto segregation since many of the students relegated to the "slow" groups have been mainly African-American males. In my opinion the ultimate damage of this practice has been to the self-esteem and spirit of the students who have been classified as low achievers and slow learners. (Gunter 1991)

The board of education and the professional staff of the Bulloch County Schools deserve the support of citizens in the county for making the correct and courageous decision to mix students of varying academic abilities together. Remember that all students have areas of strength, varying interests, and different cultural backgrounds to bring to the classroom. Some differences are useful and help students to benefit from one another's experience. Little is learned by interacting only with those exactly like ourselves. (Miller 1991)

I urge the people of this community to break down these self-serving barriers which separate us. Let us become the progressive community that we portray ourselves to be. Our children and young people in Statesboro have a lot of battles to fight: alcohol and drugs, severe family problems, economic woes, and, of course, peer pressure. School — at least school — should be a wonderful place for them to grow, develop, and learn, not a place for them to be tracked into a lifetime of failure. I urge parents to look beyond your own children and your own circle that you have there and try to support what has been shown to be best for all the children in Bulloch County. And, when you do what is best for all, in the long run, I think you'll find — I know you'll find — that you'll be doing what is best for your own child. (Page 1991)

As one who has always had a keen interest in the education of our children here in Bulloch, first as president of several PTAs and PTOs and as a member of the board of education, it has always been my contention that homogeneous grouping of children is a direct contradiction of what true learning is all about. True learning comes from interacting with those whose thoughts, ideas, culture, etc., are different from what we deem as truth. (W.A. Smith 1991)

Proponents of the board's decision to move to heterogeneous grouping generally perceived ability within a framework that was much broader than the test-score concept. Additionally, professional educators concluded that the misuse of scores to support any side was alarming. The following remarks were made in a school board meeting to counter references to test scores made by a member of the group that was trying to persuade the board to reverse its decision to untrack (see the Francisco quotation above):

Opponents of the board's decision have attempted to present evidence, also. I would like to talk to you about some of that information. First of all, they presented some test-score information to you. . . . What they used is the Iowa Test of Basic Skills in second grade. . . . They averaged last year's test scores at Mattie Lively and Sallie Zetterower. Then they averaged the percentile test scores of the other schools in Bulloch County. First of all, may I say, that any competent researcher or statistician knows that you don't average percentile scores. . . . They claimed that there was a

4.3 difference. . . because of the fact that Sallie Zetterower and Mattie Lively had achievement grouping. That was the difference. I would like to ask these people, why is there a 6-point difference between Mattie Lively and Sallie Zetterower? Is that due to achievement grouping? Both are achievement grouped. What can you say? There are many, many contributing variables. In fact, you can't look at research like this. This really bothers me that you haven't been given the whole truth about this. . . and it's not fair. . . and someone needs to tell you. (Page 1991)

Input by educators and others in the community also was related to the political dimensions of change. Of special concern were the legal issues related to the practices in the Statesboro schools:

I would hope that we would be looking beyond what is legal and look instead to what is educationally sound, and ethically and morally right! But since the legal issue has come up, let me address it. I'm not a lawyer, but I've done my homework, as I'm sure Ms. Bradley and Mr. Roach [attorneys for Citizens for Better Education] have done. And they know that, although some practices of achievement grouping have been upheld in some courts, others have been ruled against in others, especially when the judge determines that the practice discriminates against minorities, and especially when the judge determines that the practice works in effect to resegregate the schools. It breaks my heart, but it's true that the African-American children in Statesboro schools are being discriminated against with this tracking procedure. If you don't believe it, visit a high-ability class and a low-ability class at Julia P. Bryant. You will see that a very high, disproportionate number of minority children have been tracked into the low levels. The tracking procedures that we have been using in Statesboro can cause us to be in real legal trouble. The school board knows this, the NAACP knows it, the Office of Civil Rights knows it, I know it, and, if you study the issue, you, too, will know it. And you will agree that we need to continue to move away from this practice. (Page 1991)

We also know that, while the OCR may be slow and deliberate in making a decision, once the decision has been made, they expect school systems to comply immediately, even if it's in mid-year. Certainly, we would not want our teachers and students to have to make major changes in the middle of the year. It has also recently come to my attention that we are still under a 1971 court order. We recommend that the board ask the central office staff to draw up a plan for appropriate changes at Julia P. Bryant to be presented at the next board meeting. (Bonds 1992)

269

Larry Anderson, editor of the *Statesboro Herald*, wrote an editorial related to the controversy after the October 8th board meeting. The excerpt below relates to the board's role in making decisions.

> The Bulloch County Board of Education decision to end grouping in early grades was a sound one. It was based on the advice of the professional administrative staff and is backed by the bulk of current educational research. When lay people serve on boards, they have to rely on the professionals they hire. The Bulloch County Board of Education is made up of intelligent people, but their specialty is not education. They simply oversee the operation of the school system and set policy. The public wouldn't be happy with the Board for long if all the decisions were made on the basis of whim or personal opinion. (Anderson 1992, p. A6)

Reflections of a Board Member

When asked to reflect on the process of change and the influence that research provided for decision making, Janna Taulbee, vice-chairperson of the board, provided the following analysis:

> The initial decision was based on recommendations from the central office. I believe they were responding to the teachers. They also were more aware of the seriousness of the OCR investigation than we probably were. After the controversy arose though, board members were concerned about the decision and the central office had Ishmael Childs come talk to us.

Taulbee observed that the board became aware of the severity of the problem on 31 October 1991 at a retreat for board members. At that retreat, Ishmael Childs, liaison person between the Georgia Department of Education and the Office of Civil Rights, spoke to the board. At this retreat meeting, Childs discussed the "plus or minus 20% rule." This "rule" was defined by Ishmael Childs (1993) as a guide that OCR uses as a red flag to determine possible discrimination problems in the grouping of students. In a school system with 42% minority, any class that had 20% over this (62% in this example) or 20% under this (22% in this example) would draw OCR's attention. OCR would then investigate further to see if a pattern of discrimination existed. Taulbee indicated, although it was not verbalized, that board members could clearly see that changes would have to be made:

> After that, we knew that we had to make the change. The decision was how to change it so that it was acceptable to the community and to the OCR. We also knew that we had to look at possible

compromises. . . . We were hoping that we could get the jump. We were hoping that we could get the changes made before the Office of Civil Rights took further action.

Taulbee de-emphasized the role of research in the board's initial decision-making process. "We knew that anyone could use research to show what they wanted to, so it was not really a factor." However, as the controversy evolved, the research became an important ally in supporting the board's decision and in providing board members with a rationale for their decisions regarding the implementation of the changes.

When asked about the purpose of the subcommittee to study grouping, which she co-chaired, Taulbee indicated that board members felt that this additional study time would give people a chance to realize that something had to change. She stated that they knew which school would be the "holdout" and that the study group would provide a chance for its faculty and administration to "work through the process."

A problem resulted when pro-tracking teachers and administrators from this school on the subcommittee held firmly to the concept of ability grouping and did not submit acceptable alternatives. Part of the difficulty with the study group was the publicity it received. "We ended up having lots of people observing, including newspaper reporters. And sometimes, if people say things and it's quoted, then they don't want to back down from it." Near the end of the process, Taulbee changed strategies by having the committees meet in small groups in which the pro-tracking teachers and administrators were separated and mixed with other teachers and administrators. The small-group discussions were not easily heard by observers, and the process worked to strengthen the focus on recommending *how* changes should be made, rather than *whether* they should be made.

Conclusion

The controversy that occurred in Bulloch County during the 1991-92 school year is not unlike situations taking place all across the United States as school systems undertake reform efforts that include changes in grouping patterns. The situation in Bulloch County was complicated by an apparent lack of communication among the various cultures as the changes were made. And, when communication did occur, individuals accepted only ideas that fit their current beliefs related to the normative, technological, and political dimensions of education. The community as a whole and, to some extent, educators, administrators, and board members have not made the paradigm shift needed for successful change.

In her book, *Crossing the Tracks*, Anne Wheelock provides examples of schools and systems that successfully moved forward with un-tracking efforts. She indicates that grouping changes cannot be made in isolation if schools want to achieve their goal of providing the best education possible for all students:

> These grouping changes are made in tandem with shifts in curriculum, teaching approaches, and assessment strategies designed to enhance learning for more diverse groups of students. These schools also adopt routines and structures redesigned to extend expectations for success to all students and to foster a strong sense of the school as a community of learners. Moving into uncharted territory, untracking schools create new conditions for learning and teaching and, in the process, redefine their own character in relation to a true commitment to discover and nurture the genius in all their students. (p. 7)

Paul George, in *How to Untrack Your School*, suggests that an initial problem for systems such as Bulloch County relates to the failure of the system to build a "common vision" for inclusive schools:

> Educators must envision the inclusive school, one in which all students are deemed worthy and capable of learning everything the school has to teach and in which all students feel like important parts of the group. The vision emerges from studying what research and experience tell us about ability grouping and articulating a convincing case for diversity. (pp. v-vi)

The Bulloch County Board of Education made the decision to change grouping strategies based on the recommendations of the central office administration. This recommendation was based on research. However, the underlying concern during much of the research and deliberation was the apprehension emerging from the investigation by the Office of Civil Rights. Just as changes were made in the early 1970s to respond to pressure from the courts, changes are being made 20 years later because of pressure from another federal agency. Thus an important question may be, How long will it last? In the 1970s classes were initially fully integrated. When the monitoring of classes by the courts ended, the classes, once again, became racially identifiable through the practice of achievement grouping. What will happen when the OCR investigation has been completed? If changes are not made in the basic normative, technical, and political dimensions, the new grouping arrangements may be doomed to failure.

Oakes (1992) presents several recommendations that may prevent this negative outcome in Bulloch County and similar systems. She identifies, respectively, normative, technical, and political considerations:

> Efforts to change tracking. . . require a critical and unsettling rethinking of the most common and fundamental educational beliefs and values. . . . Such rethinking may result in a shift away from the dominant norms of competition and individualism toward more democratic norms of support and community. (p. 19)

> It [detracking] will require sustained inquiry into new strategies for organizing schools and classrooms; new curricular designs, pedagogy, and assessment; and new means for distributing school resources. It will also require well-grounded guidance about how schools gain the capacity to develop, adapt, and implement the array of new techniques in ways appropriate to their particular context. (p. 18)

> Implementing tracking reforms will require that competing interest groups — such as advocates for the gifted, for the disadvantaged, and for minorities — create a collective advocacy for schools that serve all children well. (p. 19)

Five major implications for decision makers in school systems are evident:

1. Communication with all cultures related to possible changes is vitally important. It is critical that this communication include listening as well as effective sharing.
2. Decision makers should be advised early in the process of OCR guidelines that may affect grouping procedures.
3. Changes in grouping procedures necessitate changes in pedagogical procedures. Teachers need substantial assistance in making these changes.
4. Continual assessment utilizing varying evaluation techniques is necessary to validate changes and provide appropriate data for making necessary modifications.
5. Throughout the change process, the control focus should remain on the students themselves.

As we attempt to make a difference in the lives of children, it will be increasingly important to study the cultures affecting their education. Simple community surveys will not provide the in-depth understanding needed by researchers and professional educators to begin to ameliorate the problems. Instead, longitudinal case studies that follow the changes through planning to implementation and evaluation will be needed. This study is an initial attempt to fulfill this need.

References

Anderson, L. "BOE Makes Sound Decision on Grouping." Editorial. *Statesboro Herald*, 13 October 1992, p. A6.

Bice, W.H. News release. Statesboro, Ga.: Bulloch County School System, 13 May 1992.

Bonds, C. Speaker, Bulloch County School Board meeting. Audiocassette. Statesboro: Georgia Southern University, 13 May 1992.

Bulloch County School System. "Classroom Assignment by Ability." Manuscript. 1991.

Childs, I. Personal communication. 6 April 1993.

Committee of Concerned Educators Against Homogeneous Grouping at Sallie Zetterower Primary School. "Report to the Committee for At-Risk Students." Manuscript. 1990.

Deal, C. "In Support of Tracking." Letter to the editor. *Statesboro Herald*, 13 October 1991, p. A6.

Francisco, W.H. Speaker, Bulloch County School Board meeting. Videotape. Statesboro, Ga.: Northland Cable News, 8 October 1991.

Freeman, S.S. Speaker, Bulloch County School Board meeting. Videotape. Statesboro, Ga.: Northland Cable News, 8 October 1991.

George, P.S. *How to Untrack Your School*. Alexandria, Va.: Association for Supervision and Curriculum Development, 1992.

Gunter, R. "Grouping Is Just Another Kind of Jim Crow Law." Letter to the editor. *Statesboro Herald*, 20 October 1991, p. A6.

Howell, E. "Mixed Classes Taxing on Teachers." *Statesboro Herald*, 5 October 1991, pp. A1, A4. a

Howell, E. "BOE Hears Both Sides Argue Grouping: Board Meeting Largest Ever." *Statesboro Herald*, 9 October 1991, pp. A1, A4. b

Julia P. Bryant Study Group. "Julia P. Bryant Report." Manuscript. 1992.

Kulik, C.L., and Kulik, J.A. "Effects of Ability Grouping on Elementary School Principals: A Meta-Analysis." Paper presented at the annual meeting of the American Psychological Association, Toronto, August 1984.

Lanier, J.B.; Mandes, C.P.; and Tremble, J. "Achievement Grouping: Perceptions of Middle-Grades Students." Paper presented at Phi Delta Kappa Leadership Skill Institute, Savannah, Ga., November 1992.

Lee, D. Speaker, Bulloch County School Board meeting. Videotape. Statesboro, Ga.: Northland Cable News, 8 October 1991.

McNair, N. Personal communication, 23 March 1993.

Miller, J. "Board's Grouping Decision Will Help All Local Students." Letter to the editor. *Statesboro Herald*, 21 September 1991, p. A4.

Milner, L. "Group Urged to Fight for Achievement Groupings." *Savannah Morning News*, 30 September 1991, p. C1.

Moller, C. Personal communication. 31 March 1993.

Natson, E. Personal communication. 6 April 1992.

Nebel, R. Speaker, Bulloch County School Board meeting. Videotape. Statesboro, Ga.: Northland Cable News, 8 October 1991.

Oakes, J. "Can Tracking Research Inform Practice? Technical, Normative, and Political Considerations." *Educational Researcher* 21, no. 4 (1992): 12-21.

Page, J.A. Speaker, Bulloch County School Board meeting. Videotape. Statesboro, Ga.: Northland Cable News, 8 October 1991.

Riggs, J. "Reader Disputes Grouping Research." Letter to the editor. *Statesboro Herald*, 24 September 1991, p. A6.

Russell, B.A. "School Board Wrong to Eliminate Grouping." Letter to the editor. *Statesboro Herald*, 17 September 1991, p. A6.

Sheppard, K. "Grouping Fosters Elitist View for High Achievers." Letter to the editor. *Statesboro Herald*, 6 October 1991, p. A6.

Slavin, R.E. "Ability Grouping and Student Achievement in Elementary Schools: A Best-Evidence Synthesis." *Review of Educational Research* 57 (1987): 293-336.

Smith, M.S. Speaker, Bulloch County School Board meeting. Videotape. Statesboro, Ga.: Northland Cable News, 8 October 1991.

Smith, W. "Report to the Committee to Study Grouping in the Elementary Schools." Manuscript. 1992.

Smith, W.A., Sr. "Grouping's Facade to Maintain Segregation." Letter to the editor. *Statesboro Herald*, 6 October 1991, p. A6.

Taulbee, J. Personal communication. 5 April 1993.

United States v. Board of Education of Bulloch County, Georgia, et al., No. 462 Civ. (S. D. Ga., 1 July 1972).

Wheelock, A. *Crossing the Tracks: How "Untracking" Can Save America's Schools.* New York: New Press, 1992.

Wiersma, W. *Research Methods in Education: An Introduction.* 4th ed. Boston: Allyn and Bacon, 1986.

A CALL TO ACTION:
THE TIME HAS COME
TO MOVE BEYOND TRACKING

BY HARBISON POOL AND JANE A. PAGE

This book was intended to be an informational, honest treatment of its subject: understanding the nuances of tracking, nontracking, and untracking and what educators can do to maximize the likelihood for success when they decide — or are required — to untrack. We realize that many readers of this work — be they scholars, practitioners, students, or others — will pick and choose from among the chapters according to their particular interests or research needs. Even the reader who reads from beginning to end will not find all authors of exactly one mind.

However, we imagine that most readers will have discerned an overall message, which is that there are many benefits to inclusiveness. Traditional elementary, middle, and high schools in urban, rural, and suburban settings, serving a variety of socioeconomic groups and racial mixes, can succeed when untracked. Moreover, drawbacks can be overcome. This is not just theory or platitude. Thriving untracked schools of every stripe exist throughout the United States. Help and support are available to those who decide to take the plunge — to move, as it were, beyond tracking. This book endeavors to be one such source of assistance.

Examining the Pros and Cons

The weight of professional, social, and political argument and the preponderance of research data seem to be on the side of moving beyond tracking in U.S. schools. To do so is to assert America's egalitarian principles. However, many teachers and administrators in tracked schools are comfortable with and strongly defend the status quo, even when it flies in the face of overwhelming evidence of more effective alternatives.

For one thing, they "just *know*" that when you separate students by ability, it is easier to teach them; *and*, these educators are convinced, their students will learn more, too. To address the second point first, Good and Brophy (1987), in a careful and evenhanded analysis of six credible reviews of research on tracking or between-class ability grouping published since 1970, indicate that when all factors are taken into account, all "findings can be interpreted as consistent with the conclusion that homogeneous grouping does not improve student achievement" (p. 406). A subsequent research synthesis (Slavin 1988) agrees. Indeed, many schools that have made the deliberate decision to untrack find the positive counterpart: students at all levels experience cognitive growth at the same time that the school environment is improving, students' attitudes toward a diverse set of peers are much more understanding and tolerant, and discipline problems diminish (Wheelock 1992).

What about the "easier to teach" argument? Some advocates of untracking concede that heterogeneous classrooms may make greater demands on teachers. One might ask, though, by comparison with what? Who ever said that any kind of high-quality education would be easy? If it is tougher, is it worth the added effort? O'Neil (1993) relates the experience of a recently untracked high school, as seen through the eyes of its principal, Pam Fisher:

> Students' grades reflect "tremendous gains in academic achievement and commitment." The whole environment of the school has changed, she says; students are more "academically focused."
>
> Teaching in an untracked school is more difficult, Fisher admits. "My teachers are exhausted," she reports, but "they love it." They like the challenge, and they like being on teams. And when they see students of limited ability rising to the challenge in mixed-ability classes, "that's really exciting." (pp. 7-8)

Once the Decision Is Made

When parents and educators want to help their traditionally organized schools move beyond tracking, they can take a number of positive steps:

1. Hire — or groom — a well-informed, progressive, conscientious, dedicated, and courageous principal to facilitate their school's campaign for better education.
2. Involve all professionals and lay citizens who are willing or can be persuaded to participate, drawing on their ideas in the development of a truly inclusive school.
3. Read the relevant literature on tracking, grouping, and related concepts.
4. Write a philosophy or mission statement that sets forth an unwavering determination to meet all students' needs.
5. Begin the *initial* thrust toward an exemplary school.
6. Develop locally appropriate versions of nontracking-compatible administrative and supervisory approaches, organizational structures, curricula, and instructional methodologies, for example:
   a. site-based leadership that recognizes the individual school as the primary locus for meaningful change;
   b. teacher and student empowerment;
   c. situational leadership styles;
   d. teachers in mentor-protégé partnerships and peer-coaching relationships;
   e. team planning and teaching;
   f. nongraded or multigrade environments;
   g. thematic, problem-solving, real-world, enriched, interdisciplinary subject matter;
   h. continuous progress; and
   i. cooperative learning.
7. Plan for the short term and the long term, thinking ahead but keeping options open.
8. Take risks and be willing to accept negative consequences on the occasions when innovations fail to pay off.
9. Be somewhat impatient and never procrastinate (champions of a five-year untracking plan might push to see their design enacted in half that time).
10. View setbacks and mistakes as opportunities for refinement and exploration of alternatives, not as excuses for throwing in the towel.
11. Build a location-appropriate inclusive school on a solid foundation, earnestly and expeditiously, but prudently, being sure one brick is firmly in place before laying the next one ("all deliberate speed" does not mean overnight).
12. Get started by setting in motion a location-appropriate plan.

A Call to Action

We believe that each community's unique ideal-school blueprint should contain a built-in dynamic. There is a natural, constant effort to achieve the perfect inclusive school; of course, we never quite get there. Even if we did, the triumph would be short-lived, indeed momentary, because times change, needs evolve, new ideas come along, and student-teacher combinations shift. This it-can-never-be-exactly-right phenomenon is just one more reason to avoid further delay.

Reputable research is one-sided in the direction of untracking, and all sorts of schools have created their own successful inclusive models. Most child advocates who become informed want their traditional schools to untrack. With the heavy artillery virtually all on their side, proponents of inclusive schools are almost certain to prevail in any pitched battle. But there is reason in most cases to accommodate reluctant parents with other options. Most will have their children participate in inclusive schools and classes when they see how much better off they will be. Our experience and research in Ohio, New Jersey, Montana, and Georgia lend credibility to this expectation.

Thus it should be with positive anticipation and enthusiasm that educators stride forth to join the untracking crusade or, to employ a term Rogers (1993) used in a related context, "the inclusion revolution." As we see it, the potential is great, the need is urgent, and there is no time like the present.

References

Good, T.L., and Brophy, J.E. *Looking in Classrooms*. 4th ed. New York: Harper & Row, 1987.

O'Neil, J. "Can Separate Be Equal? Educators Debate Merits, Pitfalls of Tracking." *ASCD Curriculum Update* (June 1993): 1-3, 7-8.

Rogers, J. *The Inclusion Revolution*. CEDR Research Bulletin No. 11. Bloomington, Ind.: Phi Delta Kappa, May 1993.

Slavin, R.E. "Synthesis of Research on Grouping in Elementary and Secondary Schools." *Educational Leadership* 45, no. 1 (1988): 67-77.

Wheelock, A. *Crossing the Tracks: How "Untracking" Can Save America's Schools*. New York: New Press, 1992.

ABOUT THE AUTHORS

N. Creighton Alexander, associate professor of technology education at Georgia Southern University, was hired in 1990 to convert GSU's industrial arts program to technology education. Previously, Alexander operated his own construction company in Birmingham, Alabama. He has been a teacher and administrator in higher education and at the secondary level in Alabama and North Carolina. He is the author of several articles.

Michael G. Allen is associate professor of middle grades and secondary education at Georgia Southern University. Allen has taught social studies at the middle school level in Vermont and California and in teacher education programs in Vermont, Maine, and North Carolina. He was the director of curriculum for a large school district in Vermont. He has published articles, reviews, and monographs in the fields of middle school education, social studies, and special education. Allen is the co-author of the textbook, *Middle Grades Social Studies*, recently published by Allyn and Bacon. He also served as the director of publications for the New England League of Middle Schools.

Suzanne E. Aubin is the Reading Department chairperson and a reading specialist at Patapsco Middle School for the Howard County Public Schools in Ellicott City, Maryland. Aubin has written curriculum software and been an administrative assistant for ERIC-Higher Education at George Washington University.

James J. Barta, assistant professor of early childhood education and reading, has taught in Alaska, Colorado, Georgia, and Oregon. He also has worked with children in Norway and England. Barta has written for several professional publications, including a recent article in *Cooperative Learning* on the use of "scaffolding" to extend children's learning.

Dorothy A. Battle, associate professor of educational psychology at Georgia Southern University, received the Virginia Tech Phi Delta Kappa Innovative Teacher Award in 1989. She has taught sixth-graders and elementary and middle-level gifted children. Her current research includes case studies of gifted adolescent females in rural settings and of African-American teachers in southeast Georgia.

Barbara G. Blackwell is associate professor and coordinator of educational leadership for graduate programs in Administration and Supervision at Augusta College in Augusta, Georgia. Blackwell taught in the public schools in Baltimore, Chicago, and Hartford. She also has served as the principal of elementary and magnet schools in Bloomfield, Connecticut, and Alexandria, Virginia, and as the assistant superintendent in Bloomfield. She teaches chess to young children and is the executive director of an education consulting firm.

Jomills Henry Braddock, II is professor and department chair of sociology at the University of Miami in Coral Gables, Florida. Previously the director of the Center for Research on Effective Schooling for Disadvantaged Students at Johns Hopkins University, Braddock has broad research interests and has published on such topics as social justice/inequality and school organization in the *Phi Delta Kappan, Journal of Social Issues, Equity and Choice, Encyclopedia of Sociology, Encyclopedia of Education,* and *Review of Research in Education.*

Cherry C. Brewton, assistant professor of early childhood education at Georgia Southern University, gives frequent workshops in science education and cooperative learning. Brewton, a former laboratory school demonstration teacher, recently defended her doctoral dissertation at the University of South Carolina. She has published a chapter in a book on at-risk students and has given addresses at several professional conferences.

Kathleen Cruikshank is assistant professor in the Department of Curriculum and Instruction at Indiana University. Her main research interests are the history of curriculum thought and interdisciplinary curriculum theory and planning. She recently completed her Ph.D. in Curriculum and Instruction at the University of Wisconsin-Madison.

Bryan Deever is assistant professor of educational foundations and Curriculum at Georgia Southern University. Deever is a student of power and has written in the fields of critical pedagogy and curriculum history. He is published in *Contemporary Education, Teacher Education Quarterly, Journal of Education, Journal of Curriculum Studies,* and *Urban Review.*

Thomas O. Erb, professor of curriculum and instruction at the University of Kansas, is the editor of the *Middle School Journal.* He has served as a middle grades teacher in both the United States and Angola. Until recently, Erb was chair of the National Middle School Association's Professional Preparation and Certification Committee. He also has edited the *Kansas Middle School Journal*. Erb's research and writing focus primarily on interdisciplinary teaming and curriculum integration. His publications include a co-authored book, a chapter on "Teamwork in Middle-Level Education," and a monograph titled *Encouraging Gifted Performance in Middle Schools*.

Paul S. George, professor of education at the University of Florida, has been referred to as "the foremost expert on middle schools in the country" by the American Association of School Administrators. George has published five books and some 125 book chapters, monographs, journal articles, and multimedia materials. His textbooks are used in many universities and school districts. He has consulted broadly and lectured to audiences now numbering more than 75,000 people at professional conferences, workshops, and meetings, including guest lectures at 25 universities in the United States, Canada, France, and Japan.

Stephen O. Gibson is the principal of Patapsco Middle School of the Howard County Schools in Ellicott City, Maryland. He also has taught at Johns Hopkins University and George Washington University. An award-winning teacher and administrator, Gibson has made numerous presentations before state and national forums, including the last four annual conferences of the National Middle School Association.

Bryan W. Griffin is assistant professor of educational research at Georgia Southern University. His research interests include multilevel modeling, survey research, and structural-equation modeling. Griffin has presented on these topics at various conferences, including the American Educational Research Association annual meetings.

Howard D. Hill is director of chapter programs for Phi Delta Kappa International in Bloomington, Indiana. He also serves as an education consultant and as adjunct professor of Afro-American Studies at Indiana University. Hill has published monographs and articles on effective strategies for teaching minority students, the multicultural curriculum, and empowering students for success. He has delivered papers at the annual conferences of several national and international professional associations.

John J. Hobe is assistant professor of education at Armstrong State College in Savannah, Georgia. Formerly a teacher at the elementary and middle school levels in Ohio and California, Hobe has worked for some years as a consultant and staff member with the Exemplary Center for Reading Instruction, a project of the National Diffusion

Network, U.S. Department of Education. One of his current research interests and much of his writing concerns student syntax acquisition.

Stephen J. Jenkins, associate professor of educational research at Georgia Southern University, previously taught at Eastern Illinois University and the University of Nevada-Reno. He has a long list of publications in a number of major journals in the fields of personality and education research.

Charlotte A. Jones is principal of Metter Primary School in Metter, Georgia. Previously, Jones served as assistant principal and taught at the elementary level for a number of years. She has served on the State Special Instructional Assistance Task Force, presented at many conferences about Metter Primary's innovative program, and during 1991-92 was a representative to Educational Leadership Georgia, a program for the advanced training of selected administrators and supervisors.

Malcolm Katz, professor emeritus of educational leadership at Georgia Southern University, is a teacher, researcher, and writer in the fields of leadership theory and practice. Katz also served as a school superintendent and as deputy state superintendent in Michigan. His current research interests, which focus on the matching of superintendents' and school boards' leadership styles, have led to several articles and a number of addresses, including three national conferences of the American Association of School Administrators.

Nancy B. Norton is assistant superintendent of the Candler County School System in Georgia. Norton is a former teacher of social studies, remedial reading, and fourth grade and previously has served as a building-level administrator. She is a frequent presenter on restructuring schools and has published in the area of the change from traditional report cards to portfolios. Norton recently earned her doctorate from the University of Georgia. She is the recipient of the Georgia Association of Educators 1994 Outstanding Educator Award.

Jeannie Oakes is professor of education at the University of California at Los Angeles and a consultant at the Rand Corporation. Her research and writing on the impact of government and district-level policies on curriculum, teaching, and the schooling opportunities of minority and disadvantaged students have been cited widely in the popular press and in scholarly and professional journals. One of her books, *Keeping Track: How Schools Structure Inequality*, was named one of the 10 "must-read books for 1985" by the National School Boards

Association. The Educational Press Association of America awarded Oakes a 1986 Distinguished Achievement Award for a series of articles in the *Phi Delta Kappan*.

Fred M. Page, Jr. is professor of middle grades and secondary education and coordinator of laboratory experiences at Georgia Southern University. His research interests include middle-grades teachers, the student-teaching triad, methods of supervision, and teachers' views of the profession and have led to numerous professional publications and presentations.

Jane A. Page is professor and department chair of educational foundations and curriculum at Georgia Southern University. Her current research specializations are the decline in the number of African-American teachers, teachers' perceptions, and heterogeneous versus homogeneous grouping. Page is a regular contributor to national professional meetings and periodicals.

Harbison Pool is professor of educational leadership at Georgia Southern University. He has been a public school teacher and an administrator at the site and central office levels in Massachusetts, California, Ohio, New Jersey, and Maryland. He also has served in professorial and administrative capacities at Oberlin College, the University of Pennsylvania, and the University of Montana. Pool's current research and writing interests include the reform of public education, collegial leadership and integrated supervision, reordering instructional priorities, holistic curriculum and discipline, and school public relations.

Dan W. Rea is associate professor of educational psychology at Georgia Southern University. His research and publications currently center on motivational strategies that distinguish successful from unsuccessful students and how effective teachers promote classroom motivation. Rea conducts numerous preservice and inservice workshops on the classroom applications of learning styles, motivational strategies for teachers, and other current topics.

Sally M. Reis is associate professor of educational psychology at the University of Connecticut, where she also serves as principal investigator of the National Research Center on the Gifted and Talented. Reis is the coordinator of Confratute, the summer institute at University of Connecticut. She has conducted workshops in school districts across the country on the design of enrichment programs based on the Enrichment Triad Model and the Revolving Door Identification Model. Reis has written or co-authored several books and articles and serves on the editorial board of *Gifted Child Quarterly* and on the board of the National Association for Gifted Children.

Daphrene Kathryn Sheppard currently is teaching secondary English and middle-grades Spanish in Hico, Texas. Previously she served as a demonstration school teacher at Marvin Pittman Laboratory School at Georgia Southern University, where she taught middle-grades language arts, Spanish, and problem solving. Sheppard has written about middle-level education and language arts and has presented at professional meetings. She is on the NCATE Board of Examiners and is a member of the National Resolutions Committee for the National Middle Schools Association.

Robert E. Slavin is director of the Elementary School Program at the Center for Research on Effective Schooling for Disadvantaged Students at Johns Hopkins University. He has authored or co-authored more than 140 articles and 14 books, including *Educational Psychology: Theory Into Practice, School and Classroom Organization, Effective Programs for Students at Risk, Cooperative Learning: Theory, Research, and Practice,* and *Preventing Early School Failure.* He received the American Educational Research Association's Raymond B. Cattell Early Career Award for Programmatic Research in 1986 and the Palmer O. Johnson Award for the best article in an AERA journal in 1988.

Edward B. Strauser is associate professor of education at Armstrong State College. Strauser worked for several years as a middle school teacher and a school psychologist. He has presented throughout the United States and Canada on the issues of dropout prevention and at-risk adolescents. Strauser also served in a community school where the emphasis was on elementary intervention for at-risk students.

Robert W. Warkentin is assistant professor of educational psychology at Georgia Southern University. Warkentin's research interests include investigating the relationship among course features, students' self-directed study activities, and achievement. He has presented at a number of professional and scholarly conferences, including the annual meeting of the American Educational Research Association.

Anne Wheelock is an education writer and researcher. As a policy analyst for education and children's policy issues at the Massachusetts Advocacy Center, she prepared many reports on practices to benefit vulnerable students in public schools, with a particular focus on dropout prevention and middle school reform. Wheelock also is the author of *Crossing the Tracks: How "Untracking" Can Save America's Schools*. This book, published in 1992 by New Press, is considered one of the seminal works on the principal subject covered by *Beyond Tracking*.